CW01596989

Psychology AS

The Teacher's Companion

Sara Berman
•
Cara Flanagan
•
Adrian Frost

Text © 2004 Sara Berman, Cara Flanagan and Adrian Frost

Original illustrations © Nelson Thornes Ltd 2004

The right of Sara Berman, Cara Flanagan and Adrian Frost to be identified as author of this work has been asserted by him/her in accordance with the Copyright, Designs and Patents Act 1988.

All rights reserved. The copyright holders authorise ONLY users of Psychology AS: The Teacher's Companion to make photocopies for their own or their students' immediate use within the teaching context. No other rights are granted without permission in writing from the publishers or under licence from the Copyright Licensing Agency Limited. Further details of such licences (for reprographic reproduction) may be obtained from the Copyright Licensing Agency Limited, of 90 Tottenham Court Road, London W1T 4LP.

Copy by any other means or for any other purpose is strictly prohibited without prior written consent from the copyright holders. Application for such permission should be addressed to the publishers.

Any person who commits any unauthorised act in relation to this publication may be liable to criminal prosecution and civil claims for damages.

Published in 2004 by:
Nelson Thornes Ltd
Delta Place
27 Bath Road
CHELTENHAM
GL53 7TH
United Kingdom

05 06 07 08 / 10 9 8 7 6 5 4 3

A catalogue record for this book is available from the British Library

ISBN 0 7487 8077 7

Page make-up by GreenGate Publishing Services, Tonbridge

Printed and bound in Great Britain by Antony Rowe

Contents

Dedication

To my clever, attractive wife (AF)
and our smart, dashing husbands with resources (SB and CF)

Acknowledgements

Sara, Cara and Adrian would like to thank all the other people who have contributed to the production of this 'Companion'. Nigel Harriss can be blamed for the front cover and the design of the book - though we thought his ideas were great. James Rabson has overseen the production, a tricky task of bringing together all the loose ends, responding to the authors' picky requests and never complaining (to us at least). And last, but not least, Rick Jackman, our publisher, who facilitates the work of great writers such as us! We are grateful to him for all the kind words of encouragement and gentle guidance.

Illustration credits

The authors and publisher would like to thank the following for permission to reproduce copyright material:

Bettmann/CORBIS (images on Handouts 88L and 105); Getty Images (images on Handouts 60 and 88R); PICIMPACT/CORBIS (image on Handout 35).

Images on Handouts 36 and 37 adapted from Bransford and Johnson (1972) Contextual prerequisites for understanding: Some investigations of comprehension and recall. *Journal of Verbal Learning and Verbal Behavior*, 11, 717–726.

Images on Handout 39 adapted from Bartlett, F.C. (1932) *Remembering*. Cambridge: Cambridge University Press.

'Blacky the Dog' on page 89 was adapted from an original drawing by Gerald Blum.

Every effort has been made to contact copyright holders, and we apologise if any have been overlooked. Should copyright have been unwittingly infringed in this book, the owners should contact the publishers, who will make corrections at reprint.

Introduction

Between the three of us we have taught for over 50 years, yet we go on finding new ways of teaching psychology and also go on discovering that the things that we thought were going well were actually complete fiascos! The skill of teaching remains a work in progress.

We have also got nearly 40 years examining experience between us (though Adrian is only 34 years old) and part of this involves running teacher courses. We often speak to teachers who belong to a department of one – and they are often new to psychology as well. We have been in similar positions ourselves and it was with such people in mind that we have written this pack. We have tried to be the other person in your team, the person you would go to for advice and suggestions. In addition this book has given each of us the opportunity to share ideas with each other and, like us, other 'old hands' might benefit in the same way.

Given the nature of our approach we have found ourselves writing in the first person. 'I' may refer to Sara, Cara or Adrian or all three of us. We have entered your workplace as the Teacher's Companion; please don't resist the temptation to let us know how any of the activities have gone! We can be contacted by e-mail at cara.flanagan@btopenworld.com.

Pippen

Lucky

Bagpuss

Sara, Cara and Adrian are senior examiners for a major awarding body. Sara is Head of Psychology at Claires Court School in Maidenhead, Cara is a freelance academic author and Adrian is Head of the School of Mathematics and Science at City of Bristol College.

What you get

The written materials start with a Table of Contents which will show you where to find everything. This is organised according to the sections of the Specification, subdivided into topics. In each topic we have provided one or more of the following.

- **A 'starter' activity** (indicated by). This is a short activity that might be done at the start of the lesson, which assumes no (student) knowledge about the topic. In some cases our suggestion is so brief that it is only given in the Table of Contents and requires no further explanation, therefore there is no page reference.
- **A 'longer' activity** (indicated by). Such activities assume that you have introduced the topic to your students and aims to provide material/ideas to help students process the material. These 'longer' activities may be research activities, discussions, quizzes and so on. Some of them are 'generic', that is they have been placed in a particular topic but could be used when delivering many other topics. In many cases there are handouts for particular activities. The page number for these is given next to the handout symbol in the Table of Contents. We haven't offered any timings for the activities because this is so difficult to calculate.
- **Links to resources:** possible videos that you might use, useful websites (bearing in mind that unfortunately these come and go but were there at the time of writing), and materials on the CD that accompanies this pack (PowerPoint/OHTs, illustrations, journal articles, newspaper clippings, and so on).
- **Links to research methods:** in *Psychology AS: The Complete Companion* the research methods module was covered throughout the book rather than as a stand-alone chapter. The Table of Contents shows when particular topics were covered in the book. To help you cover research methods in this way we have provided a photocopiable Research Methods Student Booklet to record the necessary information as you go along (see pages R1–R19).

The pack itself is divided into three sections.

Section 1: General Topics

This covers topics such as how to teach students to make effective notes, how to conduct a discussion, how to make your marking easier, how to use videos and how to construct your own website. Full details of the general topics are given in the Table of Contents.

Section 2: Lesson Notes

Notes about the different activities, their rationale and how you might organize them. Links are given to handouts.

Section 3: Handouts

Ready-to-run material.

The accompanying fully photocopiable **CD-ROM** contains:

- all the materials in the pack in PDF format;
- all the handouts in Word format;
- PowerPoint presentations for key definitions, Star Studies and explanations;
- resources such as original journal articles and newspaper clippings, plus mcqs and summaries from *The Complete Companion*;
- notes on coursework, including detailed instructions on writing the report and marked student examples;
- exam questions, including a mock exam and mark scheme, and student answers to exam questions with examiner's comments;
- illustrations from *The Complete Companion* and other sources.

Materials on the CD are distinguished by the symbol in the Table of Contents.

CD-ROM installation

Minimum system requirements

- Windows 98/NT/2000/XP
- Pentium 400 MHz processor
- 128 MB RAM
- 16× speed CD-ROM
- 800 × 600 screen resolution
- Explorer 5.0+ or Netscape 6.2+
- Adobe Reader (this can be downloaded free from www.adobe.com)

Standalone installation

1 The Psychology AS disk should auto-run when you insert it in your CD-ROM drive. If your auto-run is disabled, double-click on the 'Setup.exe' file listed in the contents of the CD-ROM.

2 Once you are sure you have exited all Windows programs, click 'Next' to continue.

3 Read the licence agreement and click 'I accept the terms of the licence agreement', and then 'Next' to continue.

4 If you wish to change the destination folder for the installation, click 'Change'. Click 'Next' to continue.

5 Click 'Install' to begin installation.

6 Click 'Finish' to complete this part of the installation.

7 Follow the instructions to install the Flash Player on your machine.

Network installation

1 Install the program, at your server, following steps 1–6 above. Ensure that you install the program to a shared folder accessible by all workstations.

2 Create a shortcut to the above URL on the desktop of each workstation. To create a shortcut, navigate to the area on the server where you installed the program, open the 'index.html' file, click on the icon in the address bar next to the URL and drag it to the desktop.

Alternatively, the program may be launched from a workstation without a shortcut by opening the browser and typing the following URL:

http:\\<path to installation folder on server>
\Nelson Thornes\Psychology AS\index.html

Launching

Double-click on the 'Psychology AS' icon that was placed on the desktop during installation, or the shortcut that has been created on the desktop of a workstation.

AQA 'A' Specification changes for teaching
from September 2005 (first exam January 2006)

The major changes, which affect teaching, are identified below.

APFCC studies

Cognitive psychology: Reduced to four studies: a study of the nature of STM, the nature of LTM, reconstructive memory, the role of leading questions.

Developmental psychology: Reduced to three studies: APFCC: a study of individual differences in attachment, of cross-cultural differences in attachment, into the effects of privation.

Individual differences: Reduced to two studies: a study into biological explanations of eating disorders, into psychological explanations of eating disorders.

Cognitive psychology: Human memory	
Research into the nature and structure of memory, including encoding, capacity and duration of short-term memory (STM) and long-term memory (LTM) *Changed to:* The nature and structure of short-term memory (STM) and long-term memory (LTM) (e.g. encoding, capacity and duration).	Means that no questions specifically asked on encoding, capacity and duration.
Loftus' research (e.g. role of leading questions) *Changed to:* Memory research into eyewitness testimony (e.g. Loftus), including the role of leading questions.	Means that questions can be asked on the role of leading questions but not specifically on Loftus' research.
Developmental psychology: Attachments in development	
Bowlby's maternal deprivation hypothesis. Research into the effects of deprivation/separation (e.g. Robertson & Robertson, Bowlby). *Changed to:* Bowlby's maternal deprivation hypothesis, including evidence on which it is based.	Means questions only set on Maternal Deprivation Hypothesis but not on deprivation/separation.
Added: ... including the extent to which the effects of privation can be reversed.	Means that a question can be set on this topic.
Physiological psychology: Stress	
Removed: The role played by culture.	Means that questions no longer set on the role of culture in stress.
Removed: The role of 'control' in relation to stress.	Means that questions no longer set on the role of 'control in relation to stress.
Individual differences: Defining abnormality	
Limitations associated with these attempts to define psychological abnormality (including cultural relativism). *Changed to:* Limitations associated with these attempts to define psychological abnormality (e.g. cultural relativism).	Means that questions no longer set on cultural relativism (but this can still be used as a limitation of each definition).
Removed: Treatment of abnormality	Means that questions only set on assumptions made by models in relation to the *causes* of abnormality.
Explanations of these disorders in terms of biological and psychological models of abnormality, *Changed to:* Explanations of eating disorders in terms of biological and psychological models of abnormality.	Can teach anorexia and bulimia together if wished. Except must know separate clinical characteristics.
Social psychology: Social influence	
Issues of experimental and ecological validity associated with such research. *Changed to:* Issues of internal and external validity associated with such research.	Means that questions no longer set on experimental and ecological validity; will be set on internal and external validity.
Explanations of psychological processes involved in obedience, the reasons why people obey and how people might resist obedience. *Changed to:* Explanations of why people obey and how people might resist obedience.	Means that questions no longer asked about 'psychological processes'.
Research methods	
'Null hypothesis' and 'frequency polygons' removed. *Terms added:* extraneous variables, opportunity and volunteer sampling.	Means that these terms must be covered
Analysis of qualitative data derived from naturalistic observations, questionnaire surveys and interviews. *Changed to:* The nature of qualitative data including strengths and weaknesses.	Means that qualitative *analysis* does not have to be studied but candidates do need to know strengths and weaknesses of qualitative data.

Table of Contents

Key to Table of Contents

Indicates the activity is something you might use to start a lesson or as a short 5-minute activity, assuming no knowledge about the topic.

Indicates that this is a longer activity, assuming some knowledge about the topic.

Handout which can be found in Section 3 of the pack.

Videos listed in 'resources': the sources for these videos are given on page 31 of the General Topics (Section 1).

Illustrations: the page numbers refer to the location of these illustrations in *The Complete Companion*. All illustrations listed are available on the CD, arranged by topic.

Material on CD

Table of Contents

General Topics

Table of Contents

STM and LTM

Cognitive Psychology

Table of Contents

Forgetting

Cognitive Psychology

Table of Contents

Table of Contents

The development and variety of attachments

Developmental Psychology

Table of Contents

Deprivation and privation

Developmental Psychology

Table of Contents

Table of Contents

Stress as a bodily response

Physiological Psychology

Table of Contents

Sources of stress

Physiological Psychology

Table of Contents

Critical issue: Stress management

Physiological Psychology

Table of Contents

Defining psychological abnormality

Individual Differences

Table of Contents

Biological and psychological models of abnormality

Individual Differences

Table of Contents

Conformity and minority influence

Social Psychology

Table of Contents

Obedience to authority — **Social Psychology**

Critical issue: Ethics in psychological research

Social Psychology

Table of Contents

Research Methods

Student booklet		Page no.	Resources	Debriefing
	Student booklet One way to deliver the research methods part of the specification is to introduce the various concepts throughout the AS course. This is the way the material has been covered in *The Complete Companion*. In order to do this effectively it is desirable for students to keep a note book of all the terms and concepts that have been covered. This can then be referred to at other times and used for revision. The booklet provides spaces for students to record the following information: Key concepts These are concepts identified in the specification, which means that questions may be asked in the exam that specifically use these terms. Other terms Research concepts not identified in the specification, but that are likely to be useful when answering questions. Question bank The Question Bank (adapted from *The Complete Companion*) allows students (or teachers) to create their own questions to test research methods knowledge. There are descriptions of studies and graphs, and questions that can be used with these.	R1–R19	**Illustrations** • Examples of positive, negative and zero correlation (p.81) • Examples of questions to use in a questionnaire (p.107) • Examples of correlation coefficients (p.105) • Examples of histogram and bar chart (p.197) **PowerPoint** Definitions of terms in Research Methods **Journal article** Orne (1962) **Web** http://www.mcli.dist.maricopa.edu/proj/res_meth/index.html (interactive research methods site)	

Endmatter	Crossword	110–112	

1 General Topics

TOP TEN MISTAKES WE MADE AT THE START

My top ten irrational beliefs as a Psychology teacher

by Adrian Frost

Given that I spend most of my time in lessons talking about my family and spouting stream-of-consciousness material, the line between lesson and therapy session does tend to blur (though I seldom get the unconditional positive regard I am due). Indeed, from a more cognitive approach, the last decade or so can be viewed as a process of identifying and removing some distinctly irrational beliefs. I present these, in no particular order, in case they may illuminate the way for any fellow sufferers.

1 'The textbook is a good guide concerning what needs to be covered.'

This is not true. You do not have to cover everything that is in any textbook – *whoever* wrote it. They are a resource. Dip in. Take stuff. Shut them again. Don't let them guide you any further. If they've got eight sides on the peripheral nervous system, that's their problem.

2 'There is no one out there who can help me.'

There sure is. Everyone at the Board is very nice. The AQA staff training days (see AQA website) are useful. Plus you've got a coursework adviser allocated to your region. Then there's the Association for the Teaching of Psychology, plus plenty of useful sites on the web.

3 'It's probably best to give out copies of the Specification at the end of the course.'

The Specification is the bottom line. It should drive the whole thing from the start. Learn how it works and exactly what it demands of you. Then teach this to your students. There are a very precise set of rules and regulations. Which, if you learn them, will guide you to success. (This is a long-winded way of saying 'become an examiner' – provided you have an understanding and supportive partner and a restricted social life).

4 'It came up last year, so it won't be on this year's paper.'

Hmmmm ... anyone remember that time on the old syllabus in the mid 1990s when 'Forgetting' seemed to come up about four times in a row?

5 'They'll never ask a question on that ...'

Oh yes they will. If it's on the Specification, it's as likely to come up as anything else is. (This includes 'culture and stress' and 'the cognitive model of abnormality' on Unit 2.)

6 'They usually set 18-mark questions on the critical issues parts of the Specification.'

They never promised that ...

7 'I'll just write 'Class Discussion – 20 minutes' on my lesson plan ...'

Discussion is a rare and beautiful thing. It might happen, it might not. If it does, you are unlikely to restrict it to 20 minutes, but if it doesn't, no force known to man will force 20 teenagers to discuss something they don't want to. The most energetic class discussion I ever had was 'Would my psychology teacher win a fight with a panda?', so you can't predict these things. Always have something more structured in reserve, just in case.

AS PSYCHOLOGY: THE TEACHER'S COMPANION Published by Nelson Thornes Ltd. © 2004 Sara Berman, Cara Flanagan and Adrian Frost

8 'My students don't understand. They must do more background reading.'

Which will give them more not to understand. The AQA A Specification is very clear. It lays out very clear topics – about which students will only have to write, at most, a longish paragraph. The whole thing can be condensed into about 40 sides of notes (see *The Mini Companion* published by Nelson Thornes). Section by section, as per the Specification, get that clear in their heads. Then use background reading to build on it when they've got the skills and confidence that they need.

9 'The more discussion points the better!'

To a certain extent true – so only 'sort of' irrational. But beware of the 'shopping list' that able, well-prepared candidates can often present. They have so many points to make, that they don't have the time to do anything with any of them – thus their discussion is only ever 'limited'. As a general rule, 'go deep' on three or four points, rather than going for breadth. This means you need to extend your able candidates by teaching them to do more with the material that they have got, rather than giving them more material.

10 'If I am working, they are learning.'

No, if *they* are working, they are learning. Look at your lessons – who is working harder? You or them?

Mistakes I have made

by Sara Berman

I started teaching A Level Psychology towards the end of the twentieth century when (almost) the only resource was Gross (first edition). Over the years I have made some serious mistakes; in fact I am still amazed that some of my first cohorts of students managed to pass the exam at all. When I think back to some of the strategies I adopted, or exercises I asked my students to try, I cringe with embarrassment. So, in no particular order, here is a list of my top ten mistakes.

1 'If it's in the textbook then that's all they need to know.'

This is most definitely not true. Textbooks, both then and now, cover much more than AS students need to know, many topics are covered in much more detail than is necessary. (No matter how interesting it is, there just isn't enough time and the students get overloaded.)

So ... don't be ruled by the textbook.

2 'If it's not in the textbook then I don't need to cover it.'

Sadly, another myth. Textbooks are written for a variety of audiences and different authors have different interests. Some topics are less accessible and some get left out due to available space. Whatever the reason, textbooks should not be considered as the definitive list of what to teach. This leads me onto my next point.

So ... don't be ruled by the textbook.

3 'If I give my students the Specification it will put them off or scare them.'

The Specification (or syllabus as it used to be called) is not just a guideline, but also a document that should be read from cover to cover in great detail. It is possibly the most important document on your list of reading and every word should be read carefully. All students should have their own copy and should understand that this is what they need to know; the excuse 'but it's not in my textbook' just won't work. Students need to be very familiar with the Specification and they way it is phrased (see my next point).

So ... give all students their own copy of the Specification.

4 'Question setters can write what they like.'

Another mistake. Question setters have to follow the Specification closely. If it's on the Specification they can ask a question on it, but if it's not on the Specification they can't.

So ... know what's on the Specification.

5 'Group work is fun.'

Well it might be fun for the students but I have found that in the past it was a nightmare. The students didn't learn much, a lot of time was wasted and in the end I was left to fill in all the gaps – so it would have been easier to do it myself in the first place. Now, whenever I get the class working in small groups I make sure that each group has to present something to the whole class and that all students will be given an assignment (essay, test, etc.) that can only be completed once all the groups have contributed.

AS PSYCHOLOGY: THE TEACHER'S COMPANION Published by Nelson Thornes Ltd. © 2004 Sara Berman, Cara Flanagan and Adrian Frost

So …plan group work very carefully; the AS year is a very short one.

6 'Role-play is a useful way of learning.'

In all the years I have been teaching, role-play worked well, once! Perhaps I was unlucky with all my other students, or perhaps there was 'teacher bias' involved; I am not very comfortable with role-play myself. After several years of trying to get my students to role-play a range of topics, I don't even try anymore. (But I do know of some teachers who use this technique successfully.)

So … role-play – but know your students well.

7 'Knowledge is more important than skills.'

I have learned the hard way that students need both knowledge and skills in order to do well in an exam. These skills need to be practised during the year; they cannot be tacked on at the end of the year just before the exam. Students need to understand the difference between A01 and A02 and they need to be given time to develop these skills, especially A02.

So … skills need practicing.

8 'Writing lots of essays at home is the best way to prepare for the exam.'

While this might have been partially relevant for the old A Level, it is definitely not true for the AS exam. Students need to know exactly how to present their material in order to get the best marks. For the AS student this includes writing short answers (e.g. 6 marks) under timed conditions, knowing how to tackle an 'apfcc' question (aims, procedures, findings, conclusions, criticisms), as well as how to write a balanced answer to the part (c) questions.

So … exam skills need practicing.

9 'When in doubt show a video.'

With the old A level this was less of a mistake than with the new AS Specification. In the past I had two years to get through all the material and there was plenty of time for the occasional 'not quite relevant' video. Anyway the students always appreciated them. But the new AS is much more constrained by time, so videos must be highly pertinent and add to the topic in a substantial way. I now use videos selectively, often only showing a short clip if I feel it will enhance a point. (The students still appreciate them, possibly even more than in previous years!)

So … use videos selectively and not as a way of passing the time.

10 'But I'm all on my own.'

When I started teaching I was the only psychologist in my college and, apart from some friendly sociologists, I didn't know where to go for help. So I simply muddled on, hoping that somehow it would all be OK. It is very different now, there are several organisations that offer help and advice to teachers. The Board is very approachable and if they can't help they can put you in touch with someone who can. The ATP is also a valuable source of support and has many local groups that meet regularly over the year.

So … investigate who's out there and talk to them.

CONTENT: WHAT TO TEACH AND WHEN

How to work out what to teach

This section is designed to guide you in terms of how much to teach for each section. It's meant to help you establish a baseline. There will be sections where you'll go further, wider and deeper, because, hopefully, there's more to studying Psychology than preparing to pass exams, but adherence to these guidelines will at least put you in a position where you can feel reassured that you've got it covered.

To this end, we need to look at a few key questions.

Do I really need to teach all of that material on physiology in the textbook?

In a word – no.

Many textbooks are very comprehensive in many areas ... perhaps *too* comprehensive (even those specifically written for this specification) and can induce real anxiety in the most experienced teachers. The rule is **do not use textbooks as your guide concerning how much to teach**.

Prune the material. Cast a critical eye over each section. Could a student be realistically expected to cram that amount of material into an answer under exam conditions? If not, prune it.

Areas ripe for pruning often include the following.

- The body's response to stress. Exactly how much detail on the endocrine system or the ANS do they really need? This area seems uniformly over-covered in textbooks.
- Obedience studies. Many students know far too much on procedure here. Students always seem to know the exact wording of Milgram's newspaper ad. If they get halfway down a side of A4 before they get to '... and then the other one pulled a piece of paper out of the hat and said ...' they probably know too much detail!

When it says 'research', how many theories/pieces of research do they need to know?

In a nutshell, I (AF) would say two in detail, plus *the findings and conclusions and criticisms* of one or two others.

Let's justify this by looking at how the material could come upon an exam paper, using obedience research as an example.

Let us say that the candidate knows Milgram's research in some detail, plus has a reasonable grasp of Hoffling's research with nurses and a slightly less detailed idea of Meeus and Raajmakers' findings.

The Milgram research could be used in a specific aims/procedures/findings/conclusions/evaluation question. This format only requires in-depth knowledge of a single study (but keep this in context, it's still only 3 marks for procedures).

A slightly more general (but still legitimate) question could be the request to outline 'findings' from obedience research. This could include the work of Hofling, as well as that of Milgram; or the answer could just stick to Milgram's work, if the student knew the material in enough depth; or add in Meeus and Raajmakers' findings as well. The broad brush or the in-depth approach will work just as well and both could attract full marks. Either way, it is doubtful that more than three studies would be required.

Even if the more demanding 18-mark question is devoted to obedience studies, there are still only six marks available for description of those studies – so two may well suffice.

In this case, Milgram may well serve as A01 material, and the other studies could be used to highlight A02 points such as ecological validity or ethics.

The question setter can only ask for 'two or more' studies, theories, etc. They are not permitted to ask for three or four or whatever. This means that in most cases **two of anything is enough**.

The only exception I have seen to this rule is when 2-mark single point responses are required e.g. 'Three characteristics of AN' or 'Three differences between STM and LTM'.

The other area where it doesn't quite apply could be the longer 18-mark questions. These won't insist on more than two of anything, but two might be a bit limiting, so we may have to modify the rule to: **two in-depth, plus brief knowledge of a couple of others for A02 if required**. (In the case of research studies, this 'brief knowledge' would probably mean findings and conclusions, rather than procedures.)

How much should I teach on each theory or piece of research?

This is best answered by the posing of another question: 'How much do they need to know?'

Let the exam questions be your guide. Consider in what form the material is likely to arise.

For example, if you find yourself spending a whole lesson providing students with a densely packed A4 side of description of Milgram's obedience research, ask yourself: what will happen to this in an exam? What's the worst question that they could be asked?

The worst question in this case is probably 'Outline and evaluate one study of obedience' (18 marks).

AS PSYCHOLOGY: THE TEACHER'S COMPANION Published by Nelson Thornes Ltd. © 2004 Sara Berman, Cara Flanagan and Adrian Frost

So what's the maximum we'd need in terms of A01 material required?

Answer – 6 marks worth.

Indeed, on this Specification, you will never need more than 6 marks of A01 material for any given topic, for a single question. Even if a whole 18-mark question is solely devoted to the topic, it still only requires 6 marks of A01 material.

So what does 6 marks of A01 material look like?

With my students, I use the rough formula:

6 marks = 6 minutes = 6 inches

So there you have it – the most you have to know – six inches worth.

(But we have to remember that that there is a 'law of diminishing returns' with most material i.e. it shrinks as it moves from your notes, to theirs, to the exam!)

What to do after the AS exam

Many teachers decide to use the time after the AS exams to complete the coursework component of the A2 course (Unit 6) or to make a start on the A2 units.

- You can combine both by choosing a piece of coursework for your class which also introduces a new topic area.
- Or you can offer your students a selection of activities that you have used as research activities through the AS year, such as an experiment on memory.

Bear the following in mind:

1 Marks are only awarded for the report, not the time spent designing and conducting it.

2 Designing research is difficult (base your study on an already established design.)

3 Why re-invent the wheel? Use existing questionnaires and other materials.

4 The scientific process – *consider the background literature FIRST*! The hypothesis should be generated from previous research. Do not begin with a hypothesis and wonder what research could be used.

5 Keep it simple. Simple projects are more likely to get full marks. This is because simple projects produce simple data which can easily be analysed and discussed.

6 Consider ethical issues – consult your coursework adviser. The Board now suggests that no children under 16 years are used in coursework unless parental consent is gained.

7 You want your students to get full marks. The coursework is worth 15 per cent of the final A level mark.

8 Coursework is fun. Some students give it as a reason for choosing Psychology.

How much help do I give my students?

Design decisions are awarded marks in A1 and A2 of the mark scheme, 6 marks out of a total 60 marks.

There are three routes.

1 Teacher selects the topic and conducts the study in class. Students use *pooled data* and lose all 6 marks (from A1 and A2).

2 Teacher assists students with the design and students collect the data on own and/or with three other friends. Lose 3 marks (from A1).

3 Student designs the study entirely on own (can adapt a previous study) and work on own. Student loses no marks for A1 but may lose marks for a poor design (A2).

You could make a coursework file for your students. Present them with a folder of all they need, which might contain the following.

- Details of background literature for *one study*: two or three directly relevant studies. Summaries or original articles to help them in designing their study and writing the introduction. Photocopies of original articles can be obtained by giving a full reference to your local library who will obtain them through inter-library loan. It pays to let students see how research articles are written.

AS PSYCHOLOGY: THE TEACHER'S COMPANION Published by Nelson Thornes Ltd. © 2004 Sara Berman, Cara Flanagan and Adrian Frost

- Or you could present a choice of studies and the background material for each. Move on to offering a choice when you feel confident.
- A checklist of design decisions to be made (there is a checklist in the AQA Specification support document on the website:

  www.aqa.org.uk/qual/gceasa/psyA_teach.html

  You could also adapt our coursework notes on the CD.
- The coursework marksheme (there is an abbreviated version on the CD).
- Template project brief (from AQA website).
- Template for writing report (create one on Word for them to use).
- Exemplar project brief with notes about filling this in (see exemplars on CD).
- Exemplar report with notes highlighting where mistakes are made (see exemplars on CD).

Some coursework ideas

- **Relationships**

  Dunbar (1995) found that 'lonely hearts' advertisements supported this: women seek resources and offer attractiveness whereas the reverse is true for males. There were differences related to age and also heterosexual versus homosexual couples. Students should collect advertisements from magazines/newspapers and devise a system to categorise criteria used in advertisements (this is a kind of observational study – content analysis).

  Murstein (1972) investigated the matching hypothesis by asking judges to rate the photographs of couples to see if they were similar in attractiveness. An example of a related piece of coursework is shown in the coursework materials on the CD. Participants are asked to rate the female photographs on a scale of 1 to 10, and do the same for the male photographs. For each couple the average ratings are then correlated.

- **Pro-and anti-social behaviour**

  Cunningham (1979) considered whether people are more willing to help on a sunny day (weather and helping). Participants were stopped in the street on a sunny or cloudy day and asked if they would be prepared to answer a long questionnaire. The dependent variable was whether they said yes or no. Could be linked to mood and negative state relief model (which predicts that people help to avoid their own distress.

- **Memory and cognitive psychology**

  Craik and Tulving (1975) levels of processing. This is described on page 46 of the Lesson Notes.

  Stroop effect (**Stroop** 1935). Participants are asked to read lists of colour words which are either written in the right colour (e.g. RED written in red) or conflicting colour (e.g. RED written in blue). It takes longer to read conflicting list.

- **Conformity**

  This is a partial replication of **Jenness** (1932). Two groups are tested individually. Each participant is asked to estimate how many beans there are in a jar (or smarties or pasta shells). They must record their estimate on a sheet which happens to show the estimates previously given by four other people. These answers are, of course, fake. One group has high estimates on their answer sheets, the other group has low estimates. The aim is to see if previous estimates affect participants' behaviour. There is an example of this study in the coursework materials on the CD.

References

Cunningham, M.R. (1979) Weather, mood and helping behaviour: Quasi-experiments with the sunshine Samaritan. *Journal of Personality and Social Psychology*, **37**, 1947–56.

Craik, F.I.M. and Tulving, E. (1975) Depth of processing and the retention of words in episodic memory. *Journal of Experimental Psychology*, **104**, 268–294.

Dunbar, R. (1995) Are you lonesome tonight? *New Scientist*, 11 February, 26–31.

Jenness, A. (1932) The role of discussion in changing opinion regarding matter of fact. *Journal of Abnormal and Social Psychology*, **27**, 279–296

Murstein, B.I. (1972).Physical attractiveness and marital choice. *Journal of Personality and Social Psychology*, **22**, 8–12.

Stroop, J.R. (1935) Studies of interference in serial verbal reactions. *Journal of Experimental Psychology*, **18**, 643–62.

AS PSYCHOLOGY: THE TEACHER'S COMPANION Published by Nelson Thornes Ltd. © 2004 Sara Berman, Cara Flanagan and Adrian Frost

SKILLS

Making notes

Since very few students are taught how to make notes, I (SB) spend the very first lesson teaching them how to do it. This has the advantages of (i) making sure that they have some idea of how to make notes from a variety of sources, (ii) introducing them to some psychology, (iii) being able to set them some meaningful homework after the first lesson and (iv) stressing the importance of keeping up-to-date and accurate notes in some form of file. I also warn them that at half term I shall be looking at their notes.

Start by giving them a short article to read. Many of the chapters in Banyard and Grayson's (1996) book (*Introducing Psychological Research* published by Macmillan) will do, but any interesting topic that is only a page or two long can be used. I have one on learned helplessness that I am currently using. Without any introduction I ask them to read the article and make notes. No help is offered at this stage. I watch carefully to see how many launch straight into the task without skimming through first, giving them about five minutes, then stop them. Reassure them that I don't expect them to have finished. Ask who skimmed through first and if some did ask why. If no-one did then explain why it is so important to read the article through quickly before starting – to decide what is and what is not relevant. Although some students might point out that they don't really know what is important.

I then ask them what is the purpose of notes and why they are important. We have a short discussion and then I tell them that I am going to give them a talk/lecture on making notes. I start by pointing out that I said 'making' and not 'taking'; that this is an active process that they have to work on. I then cover the following points and they have to make notes.

- Source. Teacher talking, video, books, etc. Advantages and disadvantages of each.
- Purpose. To retain information, help learn, etc. and ultimately pass exams.
- Format. Never in whole sentence, abbreviations, headings, subheadings, different colours, bullet points, etc. Use A4 pad, file them – after each lesson? After each week? End of topic? Discuss the strengths and limitations of each approach.

I then get them to make notes again on the first article and then to compare with each other, look at different layouts, content (i.e. what one student thinks is important information another doesn't. This is always a useful point because I can then explain why it is so difficult to 'borrow' somconc else's notes.)

If there is time I also prepare my own notes on the article and show them how I've done it.

Finally I give them another article and for homework ask them to make notes. This allows me to see if they have understood the whole purpose of notes (i.e. you don't copy out chunks of text) and it allows them to do something manageable. I do warn them about their files and that I will be looking at them in six weeks/half term or so. Students who have come straight from GCSE where teachers often dictate everything find the transition from that method to AS – or rather to the way I choose to deliver – daunting. They want to be reassured that what they are writing is 'correct'. But it is worth spending time on this exercise. It makes them much more independent, better at listening to what I am saying and then writing things down and better at making notes from text books.

The art of précis

I've chosen to illustrate this using Selye's General Adaptation Syndrome because this is an area of the Specification that students seldom approach in a concise way.

Students often feel less than comfortable with the physiological terminology, but knowing that a simple 'Outline the GAS' question could come up, conscientious candidates will usually be able to produce a rote learnt description of the GAS, similar in quality to that produced in the first box on **Handout 1** – which, of course, they will be well rewarded for, if the question does indeed surface on the paper.

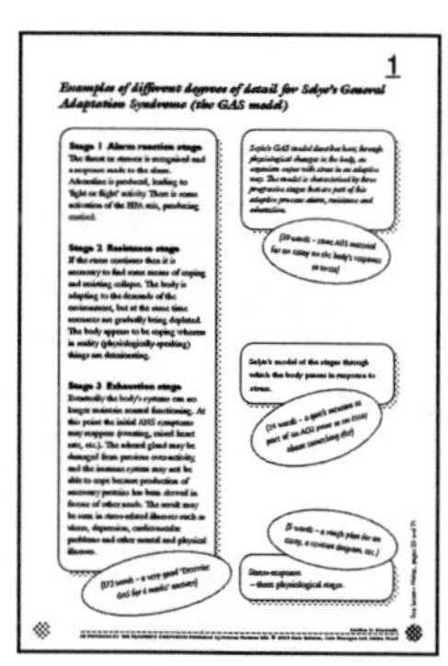

AS PSYCHOLOGY: THE TEACHER'S COMPANION Published by Nelson Thornes Ltd. © 2004 Sara Berman, Cara Flanagan and Adrian Frost

That said, this approach can lead to difficulties when they have to deploy such knowledge elsewhere. For example, the GAS could have a perfectly valid role to play in any '18-marker' that involves any kind of link between stress and the body, but such essays will seldom require a full description of each of the three stages. However, that is often what they give. The letters 'GAS' seem to act as a trigger, with candidates thinking 'I've revised it – so you're gonna read it' (a similar thing seems to happen in response to the words 'id', ''ego' and 'superego').

These exercises are about helping students to be able to offer a clear and, most importantly, concise description of an area of research, leaving time to move onto more fruitful discussion. The added benefit is that, in identifying such key points, students should process the material more deeply and understand it better.

The material in **Handout 1** shows how a description of the GAS may be compressed for various purposes. This can be achieved in several ways.

1 Give students worksheets with boxes of varying sizes upon them, and ask them to summarise specified material (perhaps from a textbook) in each box – filling each box, but not going outside the allocated space. This can help with note-taking activities, as it prevents the 'taking notes, by presenting a copy of what was on the page' approach. They are forced by the restriction of the box to précis it – but it also prevents them from writing too little.

2 Ask students to summarise material using a set number of words. These numbers can be chosen entirely at random; indeed the colleague who suggested this to me just uses the first numbers that come into her head. It takes real thought to get the General Adaptation Syndrome into a paragraph of, say, 47 words. In my experience, students can get quite competitive about this, if it becomes a race to see who can do so first. It sometimes pays to start off with quite high numbers, so that a range of relevant ideas are included and then demand that the material is whittled down to gradually smaller and smaller summaries, until only the very key words are left. (Once you get down to single figures, you'll probably have to abandon grammar, sentences, etc.)

3 It's interesting to get into the habit of asking students to summarise material into just three key words (e.g. here's an easy one: Freud = sex + unconscious + childhood). It really focuses them on 'key' issues, and really helps when they come to producing their own revision material, as they are able to 'see' the key issues so much more clearly.

NB: similar material is available on page 47 of the Lesson Notes, under the 'Levels of Processing Approach'.

Promoting discussion: Build a bridge

This is a difficult activity to use, as it needs a confident class with whom the teacher has a good rapport, but if built into the routine of a class it can be really useful.

It is designed to encourage students' evaluative skills.

One of the problems with evaluation is that students will often try to approach it in the same way as they approach the AO1 skills – i.e. they will try to rote learn a relevant range of 'AO2 Points', which can then be reproduced alongside AO1 content.

There is of course a place for this approach – students feel reassured that they have 'official' evaluative points as validated by their teacher, but this emphasis can lead to several problems. Not only will students find themselves with pre-learnt points that may not necessarily fit the question that is set, but, once such points have been covered, the student has no further avenues to explore. This can lead to the phenomena, familiar to many exam invigilators, of students running out of steam and staring blankly ahead for the last 15 minutes of an exam.

Most importantly, AO2 is meant to be about more than rote-learnt material. This activity is designed to get students actively thinking.

1 **Identify some kind of line or route around the class**. (This is easier if you arrange your class in a semicircle.)

2 **Identify a body of AO1 content.** (For example, biological explanations of eating disorders.)

3 **Give students some time, individually or in pairs, to develop evaluative discussion points for the identified material.** (Five minutes should do.)

AS PSYCHOLOGY: THE TEACHER'S COMPANION Published by Nelson Thornes Ltd. © 2004 Sara Berman, Cara Flanagan and Adrian Frost

4 **Identify a starting point for the 'bridge'.** (It's important that this varies each time, as the students near the start of the bridge will be able to use the familiar 'easy' points, whereas those near the end have to think that much harder!)

5 **Start the 'bridge'.** Work along the route from the beginning to the end. Each pair or individual student has in turn to add an appropriate evaluative point as a 'block' in the 'bridge'. If at any point students are unable to contribute a relevant evaluative point, then the bridge has 'collapsed'.

6 **Stop and discuss or note down points as the activity progresses.** (There's nothing to stop teacher/other students interjecting and elaborating at any point.)

At the end you should have generated a range of useful material. This activity, at least for the first couple of uses, will need some kickstarting. A list of standard A02 prompts might be useful here. There are many versions of these. Mine are given on **Handout 2**.

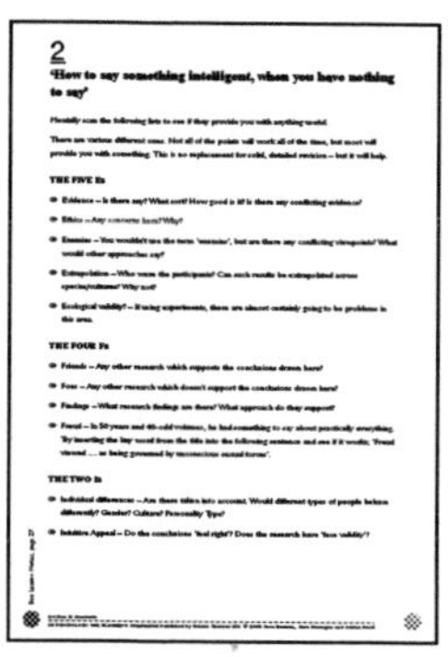
2
'How to say something intelligent, when you have nothing to say'

Obviously this activity needs some careful handling, especially with regard to the pressure that is put upon the weaker or less confident students, or those towards the end of the 'bridge'. Some students will get quite competitive – genuinely pleased when they are able to scrape together further comment, or open up a new avenue for discussion. There will also be groans when a cherished point is made by someone earlier on in the line – leading to a frantic scramble for a new point, before their place is reached.

The problem of course, is how to handle points when the bridge does collapse, as students have no points to make (the awful 'tumbleweed moment'). This can be handled in various ways; students can 'phone a friend', or be prompted in a particular direction. Careful decisions about where to start the bridge can often alleviate particular trouble spots.

If this is done regularly, students will rapidly develop real skill and confidence in producing evaluative material. They will also gain confidence and start to view their own critical viewpoint as a valid addition to their rote-learned points.

In some cases, I (AF) have used this activity to generate several sides of worthwhile evaluative material and students are surprised that they have, amongst themselves, developed an 'essays-worth' of A02 material without any direct teacher or textbook input.

See also **Handout 105** 'The Donny and Marie approach: Debate justifying Milgram' for further ideas on promoting a discussion (pages 106–108 of the Lesson Notes).

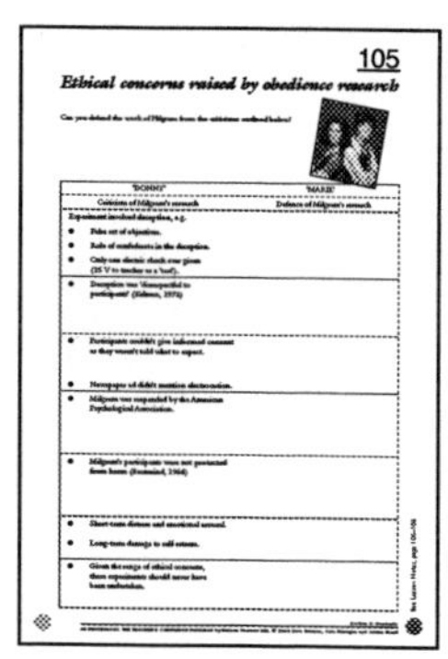
105
Ethical concerns raised by obedience research

MARKING AND HOW TO AVOID IT

Ideas and instructions to help your students do your marking for you

There can be no other job where a fully-grown adult still gets that sinking, Sunday evening, 'I've not done my homework' feeling. Often all it takes are the opening bars of the theme to the *Antiques Roadshow* to evoke that weekly ritual of gloom as 25 unmarked 'Explanations of Anorexia' essays beckon from the briefcase.

AS PSYCHOLOGY: THE TEACHER'S COMPANION Published by Nelson Thornes Ltd. © 2004 Sara Berman, Cara Flanagan and Adrian Frost

Marking presents the teacher with a thorny dilemma. No one likes it, but the more feedback the student gets the better. Solutions such as setting less work or giving less feedback only detract from the usefulness of the task in the first place, so it's difficult not to get dragged down by the burden of unmarked work. This results in most teachers having a pile of unmarked essays somewhere, quietly nagging away at their conscience like Poe's beating heart.

There are some solutions, though.

1 Give oral feedback

Students are surprisingly predictable in terms of the mistakes they make. In any given set of essays there will probably be half a dozen 'needs to relate to the questions/comments', nine or ten 'needs to include more discussion material' and a handful of 'only give evaluation where it is required' comments.

Lots of time can be taken up by writing the same feedback over and over again on different essays. I got so exasperated by this that I once wrote on the bottom of a student essay: 'Your mate Dave has made the same mistake as you here. Please see feedback on his essay'.

One way around this is to keep a scrap of paper by your side as you are marking. Note down common mistakes or other general points that need to be made, but don't give much feedback for each essay (or give brief feedback such as 'problem with structure – see lesson feedback').

Then, when the work is returned, go through the list with the class and get *them* to write the points at the foot of the work.

'Levels of Processing' Theory even lets you do this with a clear conscience as the very act of writing forces the student to pay attention to points which, let's face it, they may not otherwise read with any real degree of attentiveness.

Even the students who didn't make the mistakes in question may well benefit from discussion of the mistakes that they *didn't* make, as it helps them understand why they got an A-Grade. This activity also provides an opportunity for positive reinforcement and encouragement and a chance to reflect on current progress. (I – AF – often used to make one class feedback point one something like 'My teacher slept soundly last night, secure in the knowledge that his pass rate will be OK').

2 Get your students to do your marking

Not easy. Most students grew up on playground rhymes such as the following;

God made the bees
Bees make the honey
We do the work
Teachers get the money.

It will not be easy to get them to do your marking but, joking aside, there is real educational merit in students marking their own or other people's work, if it can be used to provide them with a real understanding of how exam marks are gained or lost.

I've often found that students feel very uncomfortable about marking each other's work, but their (understandable) reluctance can be addressed if the following are the case.

1 Students get to choose who marks their work ('A special magic marking friend').
2 The marking task is well structured (see below).
3 They are not asked to actually give a mark or grade – just comments.
4 The activity is a regular part of what goes on in class.
5 The quality of their feedback is commented on by the teacher.
6 All judgments made are checked/validated by the teacher in some way.
7 The whole thing is quite light-hearted (i.e. they get to write 'Pathetic – See me' and other teacherisms at the bottom of the work).

Quite understandably, most students dislike marking because they don't know how to. There is, after all, no real reason why they should. But they are happier to mark if the task is clear. For example, students could be asked to identify and highlight one or two of the following.

1 Appropriate use of technical terminology.
2 Sentences that link essay material to the question.
3 Aims/procedures/findings/conclusions.
4 Evidence of background reading.
5 A01/A02 material.

As student confidence increases, mark schemes can be introduced. Perhaps not the whole thing, but a

AS PSYCHOLOGY: THE TEACHER'S COMPANION Published by Nelson Thornes Ltd. © 2004 Sara Berman, Cara Flanagan and Adrian Frost

simple distinction, for example, between 'detailed', 'less detailed' and 'lacking detail'. Generally the depth and quality of what the students are being asked to provide in terms of feedback can be gradually increased. Different skills can be introduced essay by essay – 'commentary' one week, 'analysis' the next and so on.

This tasks works better if a structured feedback sheet is provided for the student. It can contain questions such as: 'Often students find it difficult to focus solely upon *findings* for this question. Has this happened in this essay?' or 'Has the 'Executive Monkey' material been related to the workplace?'

This needn't be a big deal. You could just write three or four such questions on the Board and ask each marker to answer them at the foot of the piece of work. (Or you could provide a structured feedback sheet – more on this later).

The important final stage is that you 'officially' mark the work, but you may well find that students have already identified and highlighted a good number of the points that you would have made. You're still reading it and giving a mark, but as time goes on you may find that you only have to write 'agreed' next to comments that a student has already written, and that cuts down on red pen time for you.

If consistent attention is paid to this activity it will reap real reward. You will find that the depth of analysis and understanding that students are able to bring to each other's work (and by implication their own) will steadily increase. In fact, this can really take off in certain groups. As a small group of students go through a real process of examining, comparing and evaluating each other's work, such an activity can become the foundation for a real support network based on friendly competition.

Of course, the converse is true and there will be groups who fail to engage with this activity at all, but you may find that what started out as a scheme, in part, to reduce the amount of time you spent writing repetitive feedback, fosters a genuine sense of understanding and ownership amongst many of your students.

I always know that this is starting to work when I start to get students questioning the validity of the marks I'm giving or the legitimacy of the questions that I set. At that point they are probably ready to move on!

3 Use rubber stamps or stick-in labels

As emotionally literate types, well aware of the need for unconditional positive regard, we need to find a way to let students down firmly, but gently. This is where my big, black 'Darth Vader' stamp comes in. This is used in extreme cases of lack of revision – for work where a U grade and a 'Mark of Vader' are all that is required to make the point. Two or three such 'trips to the dark side' and students know that their work is starting to cause real concern.

I did once hope to reduce my marking down to two rubber stamps, a good and a bad one, but students are seldom satisfied with such a basic level of feedback. However, an only slightly more elaborate scheme can be usefully employed if you develop stick-in feedback labels. These are especially good for areas such as short answer research methods tests. Here you really have only perhaps one or two messages that you may want to convey, perhaps 'do more revision', 'seek help' or plain old 'well done'.

Slightly more feedback along these lines can be provided using Simpsons 'stick-ins' like the ones shown below. If you are a techno-literate type, you may even be able to print these straight on to sheets of sticky address labels, with the addition of illustrations.

Examples of quick 'stick-in' feedback for tests

DOH!

Clearly some areas that still need work.

Please do the following:

- Re-examine your revision strategy.
- Discuss areas that you are concerned about with me.
- Make a learning support appointment.

A 'Marginal' Performance!

- Not bad, but still some areas to look at. You should now do the following:
- Check through the spec to ensure that you understand every key term.
- See me if there are any areas you're still not sure on.
- Practise using more past papers.

AS PSYCHOLOGY: THE TEACHER'S COMPANION Published by Nelson Thornes Ltd. © 2004 Sara Berman, Cara Flanagan and Adrian Frost

Excellent Smithers!

A superb understanding of the relevant concepts!

- Just need to go over the spec to make sure that there aren't any areas that you've missed out and that your revision notes are complete.
- Don't forget to check back over the odd mistake that you did make!

4 Use a pre-printed feedback sheet

Vocational courses are traditionally much better at using this type of thing, but feedback sheets can be very useful for AS Level.

Two examples are given in this pack. The first is specific to a particular essay (see **Handout 3**) and the second is more generic in its approach (see **Handout 4**). They can be a lot of hassle to produce, but once in place, they reap real reward in several ways. For example, they cut down on your need to write repetitive feedback comments and can structure students' attempts to mark each other's work.

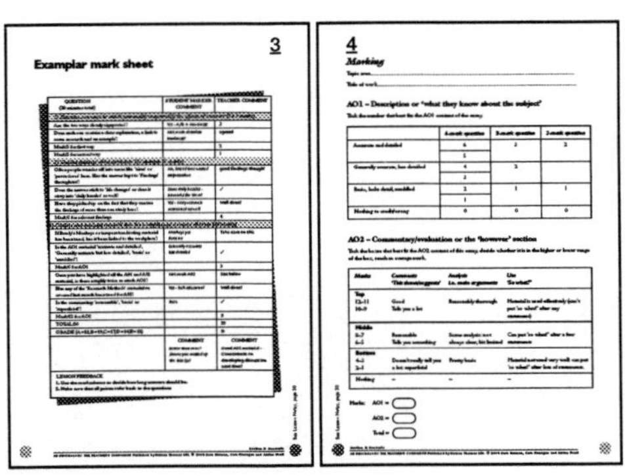

Once you have got a couple in place, you can just adapt them for further assignments.

The essay-specific example draws together many of the ideas already mentioned. As you can see, the bulk of the comments come from the student marker, with the teacher only having to provide the marks and the odd comment such as 'agreed' or 'well done'.

Despite the lack of teacher comment, students have been required to consider a range of issues relating to exam technique such as:

- the need to focus upon the demands of the question
- the usefulness of examples in elaborating material
- the need to focus on AO2 in part (c)
- the use of Research Methods material as AO2 evaluation
- the terminology employed by mark schemes.

This process is finished off as the work is returned, when the student summarises lesson feedback in the box provided.

These issues have been raised in an active, engaging manner, rather than conveyed through a scrawl of red ink at the bottom of a page. Hopefully this means that students will develop a genuine understanding of where marks are won or lost in their own work. At the same time, you've expended less red ink, which is where we came in.

5 Practice marking

If you would like to give your students practice in marking exam answers we have provided some students' answers to questions, along with examiner's comments. These can be found on the CD.

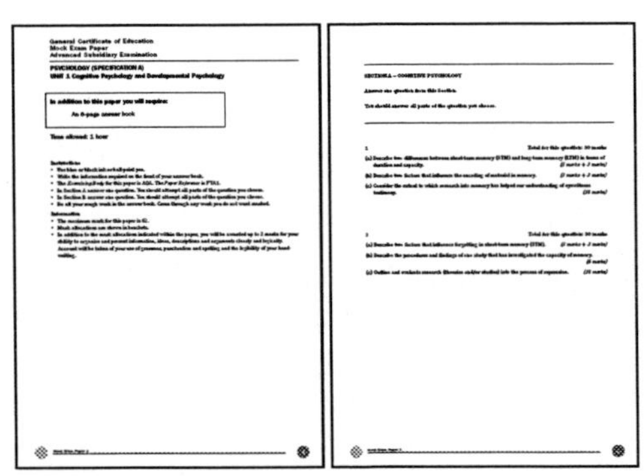

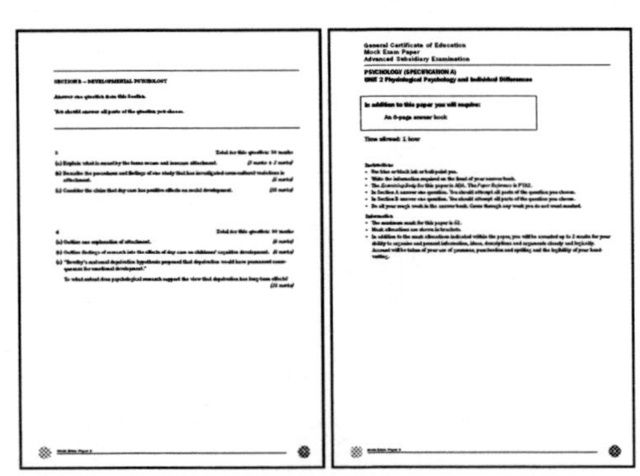

AS PSYCHOLOGY: THE TEACHER'S COMPANION Published by Nelson Thornes Ltd. © 2004 Sara Berman, Cara Flanagan and Adrian Frost

RESOURCES

Videos and how to watch them

Students are always asking, 'Can we watch a video?' and while I (SB) often do have a video that is linked to the topic we are studying, the big decision is: will it be worth taking the time to show it, given how much material we have to get through in such a short timescale? After several false starts, I now have a selection of videos that I can use at various stages throughout the course. But I have learnt the hard way that these videos must be *used* effectively if they are to benefit the students.

When to use

- At the start of a topic, to introduce it, to set the scene.
- At the end of a topic, to summarise the main theories/studies/concepts.
- During the topic if it highlights a specific issue or helps to answer a specific question.

How to use

- Be prepared to use only a small part of a video, sometimes only five to ten minutes is enough. For example in '*Five steps to Tyranny*' (first shown 14 Feb 2001) there is a small section showing Milgram's classic obedience study and then a modern experiment. A confederate on a train asks for someone's seat, even though there are plenty of spare seats. Fifty per cent of the passengers gave up their seats and when a man in a uniform accompanied the confederate this rose to 100 per cent. This clip only lasts a few minutes but is enough to interest the students and to illustrate the point well.
- Every video should have some sort of worksheet to go with it. This could take the form of a list of questions that must be filled in after the video is watched; questions that can be completed during the watching, etc. It is important that this worksheet can be kept along with the students' own notes and can be used for revision. It is important that students can reference the video too (e.g. title, psychologists (if relevant), programme, date.)

An example of a worksheet like this can be found on page 195 (eating disorders).

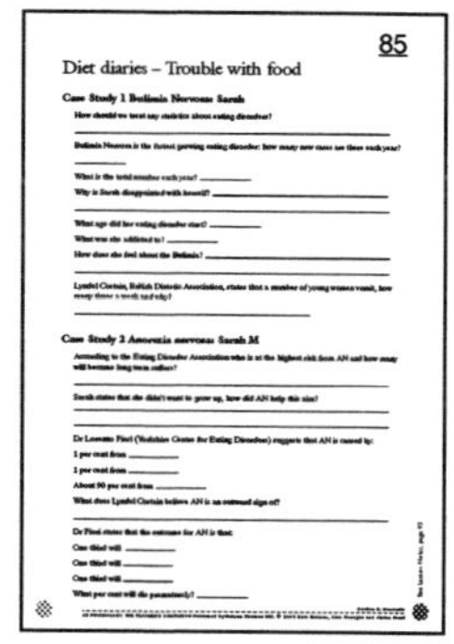
85

Diet diaries – Trouble with food

Case Study 1 Bulimia Nervosa: Sarah

Case Study 2 Anorexia nervosa: Sarah M

Where to find them

ATP (Association for Teachers of Psychology) (www. TheATP.org). Publications with links to video titles and worksheets.

Concord videos (http://www.concordvideo.co.uk/cp1home.html). Videos for sale or hire, including the films by the Robertsons and Bowlby of children separated from parents.

Halovine videos (www.halovine.com) have a set of videos on each of the five critical issues. Each video lasts 30 minutes. For example, the video on eating disorders uses some real case studies of teenagers and attempts to explain the causes of their disorder using a range of models. The girls are shown discussing their own illnesses in a residential clinic. I found this useful as a summary of the main theories, but it might also work well as an introduction to the topic.

Horizon (homepage www.bbc.co.uk/science/horizon/). Search the archive for interesting programmes back to 1996. Can borrow video tapes from their library. Some programmes have accompanying notes of transcript in full. For recent programmes the transcript is available online.

Open University (http://www.ouw.co.uk/index.shtm). Buy OU resources online, but expensive.

Richmond College (www.rutc.ac.uk). They record from television (great for all those programmes that you meant to video but managed to miss). They also have a huge list of programmes recorded as long ago as 1989.

AS PSYCHOLOGY: THE TEACHER'S COMPANION Published by Nelson Thornes Ltd. © 2004 Sara Berman, Cara Flanagan and Adrian Frost

RITE (Resources in Training and Education) Cross Tree, Walton-in-Gordano, Clevedon, Somerset, BS21 7AW. Wide range of videos covering many topics, e.g. memory, abnormality, conformity and obedience. Each one lasts 30 minutes and are probably best used to illustrate key points rather than watch all the way through in one go.

Uniview (www.uniview.co.uk) Worldwide Ltd, PO Box 20, Hoylake, Wirral, CH48 7HY. Have some excellent videos. For example *The Quiet Rage* (the Stanford Prison Study); a 50-minute video made in the 1990s by Philip Zimbardo using archive material of tapes made during the experiment as well as some interesting footage of the debriefing sessions. The video also includes some post-experimental interviews with both prisoners and guards. It is a little slow in parts and probably best shown in small sections. It is very good not just for conformity and obedience but also for stimulating a discussion on ethics and research methods. Some students find it hard to believe that 'regular' undergraduates could behave in this way!

Uniview also have a video of Milgram's Obedience Study filmed in 1963 in the laboratory at Yale.

Build your own website

Maybe I'm (AF) preaching to the converted, but then again, I'm not sure that there's that many of us A-Level psychology teachers out there on the web.

Here's a selection of those who are:

http://www.garysturt.free-online.co.uk/
http://www.holah.co.uk/

Unfortunately, both of these sites are geared towards 'rival' exam board Specifications.

This section isn't intended to explain in detail how to build your own psychology website (though it will give you some pointers), and it certainly won't add much to the knowledge of those who may already be approaching 'webmaster' status. What it will do, I hope, is encourage those who have never even thought of starting up a site to consider giving it a go, by explaining just how easy it is.

Indeed, if you can do basic stuff like move Word files around, rename them, send them as email attachments etc. then you could have a fully functioning, rather neat looking and, most importantly, totally free, website up and running in under two hours. All this without absolutely any knowledge of meta-tags, HTML, Java or other such nonsense.

Why bother setting up your own website?

1 Many schools and colleges have their own websites or intranets, but these can often be rather bland, corporate, centrally managed affairs. Having your own site gives you the opportunity to gear it to your own teaching and be flexible, creative, spontaneous, etc.

2 You can use it as a 'one-stop shop' for all of your students' needs, but it will help you as well. For example, if you're fed up with photocopying past papers, why not link straight to the AQA website at:

   http://www.aqa.org.uk/qual/gceasa/psyA_assess.html

   and let students download their own?

3 It becomes a handy place to store all of your notes and teaching materials. The major reason I set one up was to get rid of all those irritating requests from students for copies of the notes from last February, as they were 'away'. If they want it, it's on the site.

4 It helps students who are absent stay in touch and it helps students in other classes gain access to a wider range of material.

5 You can also have a bit of fun with it – why not link to the 'Make Your Own Mr Men Site' if it cheers things up a bit?
   (It's http://www.mrmen.com/makemrmen.htm if you're interested ...)

Where does the content come from? – I haven't got time to produce all that!

I use mine to store all of the teaching notes that I was producing anyway. This is why I ended up using web pages to link to Word files, rather than creating content on the web pages themselves. Just as I used to save anything I produced to disc, I now upload it to the site as well, but it doesn't have to contain material generated by you.

You could use it to store and share work that your students do. If each contributes one piece of homework per term in the form of a Word document, and each one is uploaded to your site, it will soon become a large resource to be shared amongst all of your students (and the rest of the world!).

AS PSYCHOLOGY: THE TEACHER'S COMPANION Published by Nelson Thornes Ltd. © 2004 Sara Berman, Cara Flanagan and Adrian Frost

How to get started

All you'll need is an email address, a couple of Word documents and perhaps a picture (JPG file) to load onto your site and a hour or two of peace.

Your first task is to find a web host. If you try typing 'free website' into a search engine like Google, you'll get a good idea of the sheer number of people are out there who want you to have a free website – normally so they can plaster it with pop-up advertising, but that's the price you pay. Some internet service provides (such as btopenworld and blueyonder) provide web pages for free but may offer less help on constructing the site.

They all vary in a multitude of ways, but you've two main questions at this point: 'Is it free?' and 'Is it easy?'. There'll be plenty of the former, but less of the latter. Everyone wants to host your website, but not everyone will be that helpful in terms of helping you build it. Many will assume that you have access to, and can use, software for creating web pages. (If this is the case for you, I'm guessing that you've stopped reading by now anyway ...).

Best bet is to sign up for one or two and see how you get on. I'm not pushing any particular company here, but I used geocities on www.yahoo.com. They provide you with a piece of software called Pagebuilder, which is a piece of cake to use. For example, you don't have to convert any of your Word documents to HTML before you upload them to the site. The minor drawback is that you have to spend five minutes downloading Pagebuilder every time you want to use it.

It pays at this point to do just a bit of messing around. Stick some text on a web page, with a pretty picture if you like. Then upload some Word documents and link them to the page. Then provide some links to some other useful websites. Add in a guestbook for visitor comments. Tweak the background and font colours until you get something suitably pleasing and there you go!

All of the above is dead easy. They even provide little templates and 'wizards' if you want to use them. (I'm not sure I'd recommend the templates though. It's probably best to start from scratch, rather than try to adapt something called 'Pictures of My Pets'). As you close down Pagebuilder, it publishes your site on the web and you are officially a webmaster!

There are other web providers of course. You might like to look at www.schoolzonekit.ik.org/ which is particularly designed for teachers, or have a go with http://www.freeservers.com/

My colleague Peter Rouncefield has constructed an excellent Sociology site using www.homestead.com. If you go to the FERL site at http://ferl.becta.org.uk and put 'Rouncefield' into the search box, you should be able to find a comprehensive article he's written about website development. The FERL site acts as a gateway to all sorts of useful advice and resources in this area.

Another useful source of advice is www.webmonkey.com

I've tried not to give comprehensive lists of sites here, as there is a mountain of material out there and it can all give you too much to consider. I definitely come from the 'Don't read the instructions, just mess about with it and see what works' school of thought.

That said – here are a few lessons it took me a while to learn on Pagebuilder:

- if you are uploading Word files – give them names that don't include any spaces;
- whatever your homepage is going to be, make sure its name ends with index.html;
- forget about scanned stuff.

A word of warning

It'll vary from institution to institution, but many schools and colleges regard anything that you produce for use in lessons as 'belonging' to them. Attitudes may vary with regard to how happy your managers are to see your teaching materials on the web. In some ways it's a shame, and I think goes against what the web and the teaching profession are supposed to be about, but some will be concerned.

Many 'official' institution websites jealously guard their teaching material behind password-protected barriers. (I always find it mildly annoying to find my site being linked to by a college site that I can't access in return, because I've not got a password). The case with regard to your students' work is probably less clear-cut, but either way, probably best to cover yourself by checking first.

 © 2004 Sara Berman, Cara Flanagan and Adrian Frost

Might also be best to put a disclaimer on your site, disassociating yourself from your employer. With luck, your institution will probably be pleased to see you working so hard on behalf of the students and give you loads of encouragement!

Now for those with no IT skill/interest/inclination at all.

How to build a website in two hours with not much input from you

1 Take list of 'Star Studies' for the AQA A Specification (i.e. the ones that might come up in an aims/procedures/findings/conclusions question) and divide amongst students. (This list is given on **Handout 5**.)

2 Ask each to produce an A4 summary Word document, giving details of their allocated study.

3 Use threats/bribes to persuade malleable and IT literate student (there's always one) to become webmaster and build free website. It will only take them an hour. They might even be able to get IT key skills evidence in this way, if your gratitude isn't enough.

4 Ask students to email copies of Word documents to you or webmaster and upload to site.

5 Bask in glow of admiration as you share excellent revision resource with the rest of the online world.

Once you've got it up and running

There are of course, a multitude of things that you can now do with your site. At the start it will consist mostly of links to Word documents. You might want to look at developing more content on the web pages themselves.

As it gets bigger you will also have to think about site structure and navigation – i.e. how will visitors find their way around your site? There are plenty of people out there happy to give you a free site search facility. Indeed practically anything you want for your website can be found by typing its name plus 'free' into a search engine.

The next step – interactivity

This is the Holy Grail of educational websites. Interactivity is the key to a good educational website. It is certainly my aim over the next few months to put something more than 'notes' online. There are plenty of sites out there which will help you develop online, multiple-choice quizzes and suchlike. The most famous is probably Hot Potatoes at http://web.uvic.ca/hrd/halfbaked/, but you could try the following as well.

http://www.luziusschneider.com/QuizHome.htm
http://www.questionmarker.com/home.htm
http://www.topshareware.com/WebQuiz-download-261.htm

A final word

All of this will take time and 'messing about' to achieve and you might decide not to bother, but, once you get started, I bet you won't. Instead, you may find yourself obsessively scouring the internet for animated images, constantly checking your site statistics and taking offence when the BBC decline to list your 'baby' in their education section.

Before long, your site could be a graphics-heavy, difficult to navigate ego-trip with a guest book full of pointless trivia that serves partly to indulge your own childish pre-occupations with the film Star Wars or whatever …. A Scottish educational site referred to mine as 'not for everybody', but I'm trying not to take it personally – check it out on www.geocities.com/psychade2002

Good luck with your site if you decide to go for it. Why not send me your URL when you are up and running?

AS PSYCHOLOGY: THE TEACHER'S COMPANION Published by Nelson Thornes Ltd. © 2004 Sara Berman, Cara Flanagan and Adrian Frost

TEMPLATES

One of the things that students have real problems with when taking notes is knowing when to stop (as well as ensuring that they have enough). The use of a simple template, such as those included in this pack, help students to break material down into manageable chunks. If used regularly these can really help with students' note-taking and précis skills. It also helps them focus their material on the demands of the exam questions. They can be used eventually for revision. Filled in examples can be found in *The Mini Companion* (published by Nelson Thornes).

Certainly as a teacher I (AF) always use something like this when preparing lessons to make sure I have a sense of the size and shape of the knowledge I'm going to teach.

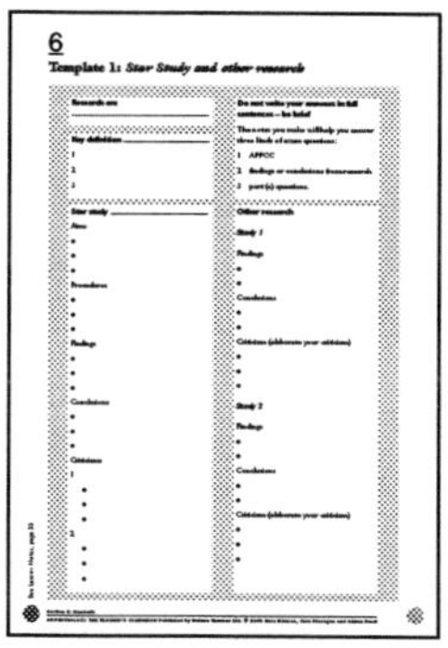

Students need
3 marks-worth of
APFCC

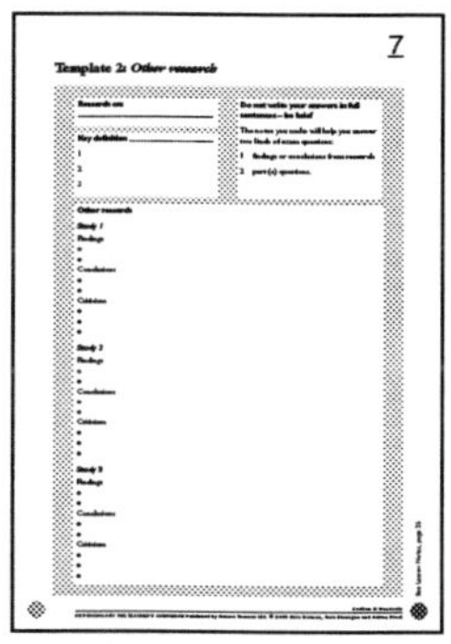

Students need
3 marks-worth of FCC

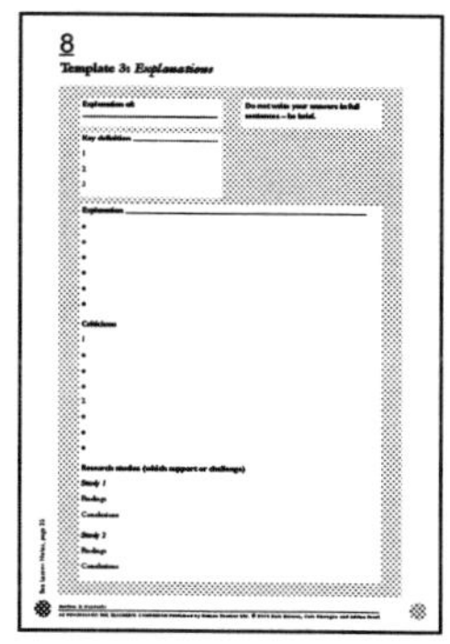

Students need
6 marks-worth for
theories plus 3 marks-
worth of criticisms

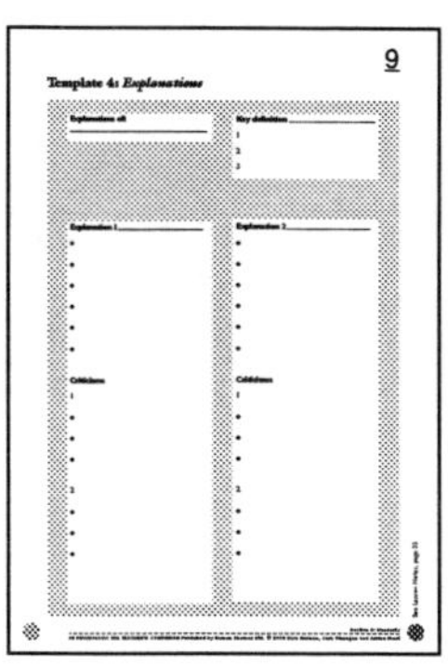

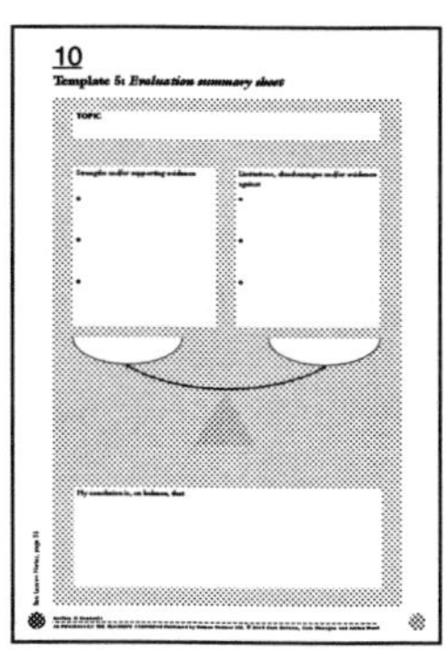

AS PSYCHOLOGY: THE TEACHER'S COMPANION Published by Nelson Thornes Ltd. © 2004 Sara Berman, Cara Flanagan and Adrian Frost

WEBSITES

Here are some general websites that may be useful.

http://www9.biostr.washington.edu/cgi-bin/DA/imageform
Images of the brain and nervous system – 3-D computer graphic reconstructions are best. Paste into your own presentations.

http://www.mhhe.com/socscience/ intro/ibank/set3.htm
(Introductory Psychology Image Bank: illustrations of lots of Psychological concepts, to liven up your PowerPoint displays/OHTs.)

http://www.s-cool.co.uk/topic_index.asp?subject_id=14
(Loads of excellent revision notes and summaries, as well as test questions with answers.)

http://epsych.msstate.edu/index.html#
(Operant conditioning, interactive site: click on the 'Adaptive Mind' for operant conditioning. You get to condition a strange little furry creature by switching coloured lights on and off.)

http://psychology.about.com/
(Site with lots of psychology-related information.)

http://www.holah.karoo.net/about.htm
(Interactive site for OCR AS students)

http://teachpsych.org
(American society for teaching psychology.)

http://www.secondaryschoolsonline.co.uk/clubs_list.asp?groupid=1471&unionid=35

http://www.secondaryschoolsonline.co.uk/club_downloads.asp?unionid=35&clubid=4579
(Herschel school website with essays and worksheets, references to relevant New Scientist articles, etc.)

AS PSYCHOLOGY: THE TEACHER'S COMPANION Published by Nelson Thornes Ltd. © 2004 Sara Berman, Cara Flanagan and Adrian Frost

2 Lesson Notes

MODULE: **Cognitive Psychology**
SECTION: **Short-term and long-term memory**
TOPIC: **The nature and structure of memory: Duration in STM**

Research activity: Peterson and Peterson (1959)

Peterson, L.R. and Peterson, M.J. (1959) Short-term retention of individual verbal items. *Journal of Experimental Psychology*, 58, 193–8

A replication of this key study is likely to help students recall the details in an exam, and to be able to outline and elaborate valid criticisms of the method (especially useful for part (c) questions).

You could conduct this as a single or even double blind exercise before learning about the research of the Petersons. Students to work in pairs. One student is the experimenter and the other is the participant.

Note that a summary of this study is on the CD as a Star Study PowerPoint.

Equipment needed

A stopwatch.

Optional: a metronome to act as pacemaker.

Standardised procedures

Use table from original experiment. (See **Handout 12**). This has a list of nonsense trigrams, and a set of three digit numbers, and retention intervals of 3, 6, 9, 12, 15, or 18 seconds. In the original experiment each participant was tested eight times at each of the recall intervals. The table has a column ('Recall') to record the results.

1 Experimenter says trigram outloud, followed by a three-digit number. Experimenter starts timing seconds.

2 Participant counts backwards until told to stop (depending on the retention interval).

3 Participant recalls trigram, experimenter records whether this is right or wrong.

Handouts 11 and 12

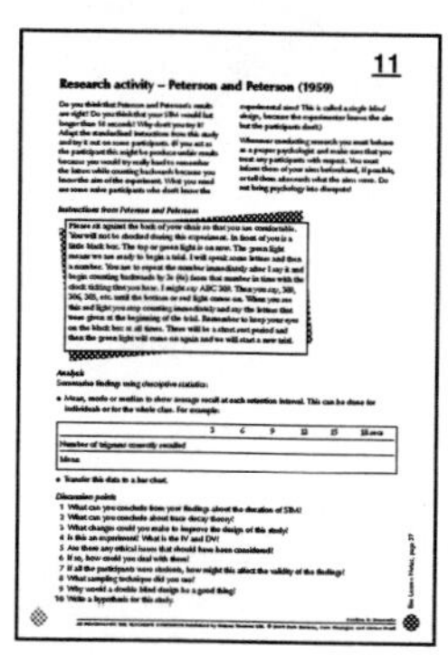

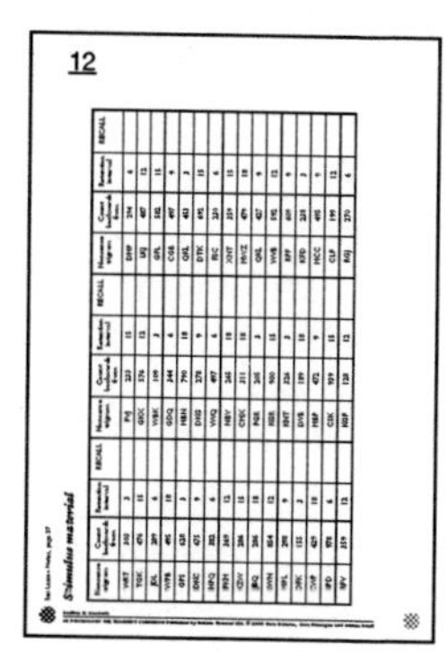

AS PSYCHOLOGY: THE TEACHER'S COMPANION Published by Nelson Thornes Ltd. © 2004 Sara Berman, Cara Flanagan and Adrian Frost

MODULE: **Cognitive Psychology**
SECTION: **Short-term and long-term memory**
TOPIC: **The nature and structure of memory: Duration in STM**

The three point rule for criticising studies and theories

Students are required to offer evaluation (or criticisms) at all times – when answering questions on star studies (such as 'Describe the findings of *one* study of short-term memory and give *one* criticism of this study. [3 marks + 3 marks]'), or when answering 18-mark questions (such as 'Briefly outline research on short-term memory and consider the strengths and limitations of such research' or 'Outline and evaluate the multi-store model of memory').

Students lose marks, when giving criticisms, because they fail to *explain* their criticism. They often say 'It was artificial' or 'It was well controlled'. What they need is to be able to provide three points:

1 **State your criticism**. [Peterson and Peterson's study was artificial.]

2 **Justify this criticism**. [It was artificial because they used trigrams to test memory which are not like the real-life memory tasks.]

3 **Explain why this is a strength or limitation**. [This means you can't generalise the findings to real life.]

Try the three point rule with these other criticisms of Peterson and Peterson's study. (Remember that criticisms can be positive as well as negative.)

- They used students as participants.
- It was a valuable study.
- Trigrams have no meaning.

MODULE: **Cognitive Psychology**
SECTION: **Short-term and long-term memory**
TOPIC: **The nature and structure of memory: Duration in LTM**

Your earliest memory

Discussion: What is your earliest memory? How can you prove it really is *yours*?

Read about ideas for discussion in the General Notes on page 26.

Research activity: Bahrick *et al.* (1975)

Bahrick, H.P., Bahrick, P.O., and Wittinger, R.P. (1975) Fifty years of memory for names and faces: A cross-sectional approach. *Journal of Experimental Psychology: General*, 104, 54–75.

Replication of Bahrick *et al.*'s original study may only be possible in a school setting where many of the students were at primary school together or can access friends from primary school. (Note that there is a summary of this study on the CD as a Star Study PowerPoint.)

Ask students to bring in photographs from primary school. They might well have group photographs and can test each other with these.

Students should be encouraged to write **standardised procedures** for the study. These would include:

- arranging to show these photographs to appropriate individuals;
- asking each participant to name as many individuals as possible (standardised instructions);
- producing findings – scoring the answers given by each participant and expressing this as a percentage of possible correct answers.

Findings

These can be compared with findings from Bahrick *et al.*, using graphical techniques (see Star Study in *The Complete Companion*).

AS PSYCHOLOGY: THE TEACHER'S COMPANION Published by Nelson Thornes Ltd. © 2004 Sara Berman, Cara Flanagan and Adrian Frost

MODULE: **Cognitive Psychology**
SECTION: **Short-term and long-term memory**

TOPIC: The nature and structure of memory: Duration in LTM

Spot the mistakes: Revision exercise for Bahrick *et al.* (1975)

Handouts 13 and 14

Handout 13 requires students to correct mistakes in an outline of Bahrick *et al.*'s classic study.

A correct version os supplied on **Handout 14**.

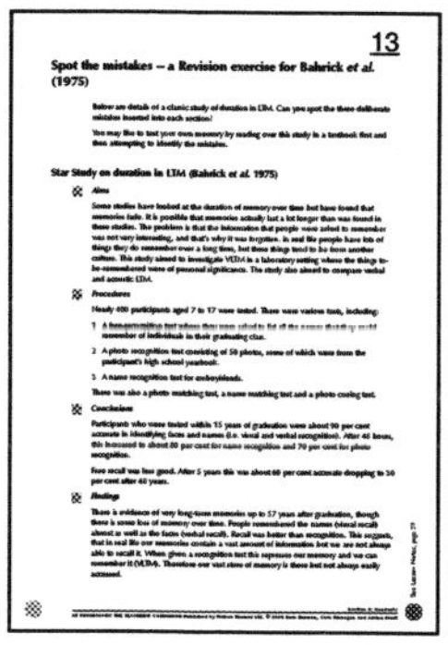
13

Spot the mistakes – a Revision exercise for Bahrick et al. (1975)

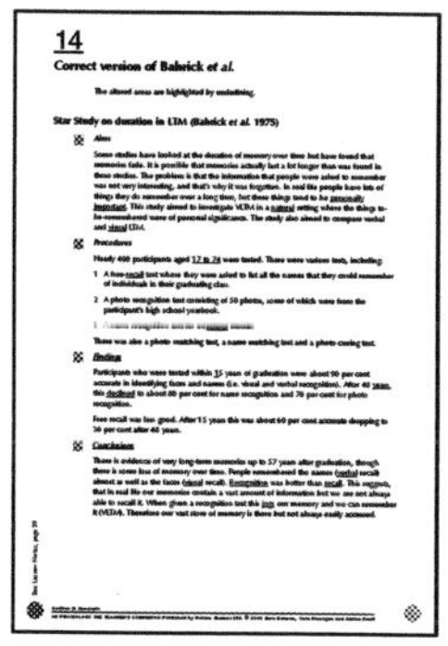
14

Correct version of Bahrick et al.

MODULE: **Cognitive Psychology**
SECTION: **Short-term and long-term memory**

TOPIC: The nature and structure of memory: Capacity

Chunking

There are many different ways of illustrating chunking, two possibilities are suggested here.

On OHT/PowerPoint show a list of letters for a few seconds, remove and ask the students to write down as many as possible. Ask the class how many they each remembered. Then show them that by chunking they could remember many more. The actual letters will depend on the type of students, etc.

For example:

CBBCMPBAIBMUPSDHLTNTUCASEU

OR: CBBC MP BA IBM UPS DHL TNT UCAS EU

Another way to illustrate chunking is to show the following, briefly, and again ask students to recall the letters in the correct order:

A	O	O	E	H
M	O	P	H	T
O	C	S	T	O
O	Y	S	L	R
T	N	K	I	B

The trick to this one is to start at the bottom left-hand corner and read up each column (i.e. 'Too many cooks spoil the broth'). Any saying like this will work; use whatever you think will be familiar to the students.

AS PSYCHOLOGY: THE TEACHER'S COMPANION Published by Nelson Thornes Ltd. © 2004 Sara Berman, Cara Flanagan and Adrian Frost

MODULE: **Cognitive Psychology**
SECTION: **Short-term and long-term memory**
TOPIC: **The nature and structure of memory: Capacity**

Research activity: Immediate memory span

A partial replication of Howard (1983) experiment on immediate memory span. (Howard D.V. 1983 *Cognitive Psychology*. New York: Macmillan.)

Procedures

Divide class into pairs, one being the experimenter the other the participant. The 'experimenter' reads the items in the top line of each set (see **Handout 15**) at an even rate, such as 1 per second. The participant repeats them back in exactly the same order. If they are correct the experimenter reads the next line and continues until the participant makes a mistake. The maximum number of items the participant can repeat accurately is their immediate memory span. This procedure is repeated for each of the three sets.

It is very important that the experimenter reads the material out in a standard and regular manner. It is too easy if the experimenter (usually unintentionally) reads the numbers out by chunking them, rather like a phone number!

Then the students can switch roles.

Discussion points

- Which set is easier to recall and why? Usually numbers. Why? Because this is one of the few instances where we do have some practice, i.e. recalling phone numbers. Though maybe with students' reliance on their mobile phones this is not the case anymore. Although if you count all the separate letters most information is recalled in the last set.
- Do participants use any strategy to help them recall information?
- Is there a repeated measures design bias? Since the student who goes second will have a much better idea of what is going on and will be more familiar with the information. Though I have to say that in fact this doesn't usually make any difference.

Handout 15

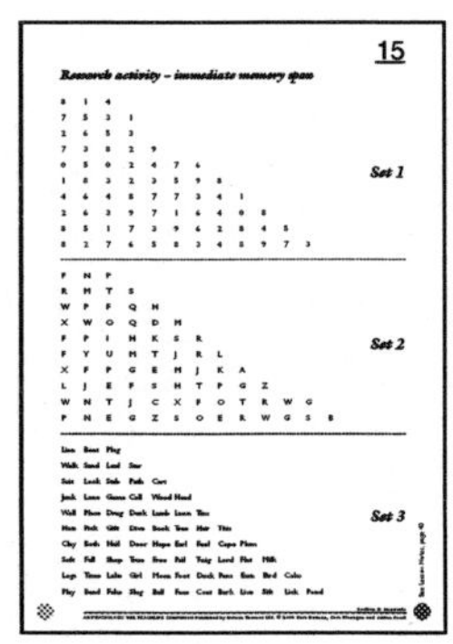
15

Set 1

Set 2

Set 3

MODULE: **Cognitive Psychology**
SECTION: **Short-term and long-term memory**
TOPIC: **The nature and structure of memory: Encoding**

Discussion of encoding

Ask students how you do up shoe laces (enactive memory), how you get from A to B (visual memory), how you remember the fourth line of a song (acoustic memory), and so on.

AS PSYCHOLOGY: THE TEACHER'S COMPANION Published by Nelson Thornes Ltd. © 2004 Sara Berman, Cara Flanagan and Adrian Frost

Research activity: Baddeley (1966)

Baddeley, A.D. (1966) The influence of acoustic and semantic similarity on long term memory for word sequences. *Quarterly Journal of Experimental Psychology*, 18, 302–9.

Taking part in this replication should make the concepts of 'acoustic similarity' and 'semantic similarity' clearer.

Experiment testing STM

Read out instructions: I will read a list of words and then show you the same words in a different order, asking you to try to recall the correct order for this list. I will then repeat this with other word lists.

Step 1: read word list A to class.

Step 2: display recall list A (words in jumbled order) and ask participants to place words in the correct order. Collect responses and remove recall list.

Repeat for lists B, C and D. (You can if you wish omit lists B and D.)

Score 1 point for each word recalled in the correct position. At the end each participant should have a score for each word list (i.e. 4 scores).

The reason for this method of recall is because this is the only way to ensure that acoustic confusions are detected. Participants just have to get the order right. In the original experiment participants only were in one condition – list A, B, C or D, and were shown the list 4 times, recalling the words each time. This is an independent groups design.

Experiment testing LTM

In Baddeley's experiment the same procedure was followed as above except that 20 minutes was left between viewing the list and asking for recall. This clearly is not possible within a lesson for all 4 words lists.

Repeat the method above but this time do not ask for immediate recall. Instead leave a gap of five minutes before recalling each list. In the interval participants should perform another task.

Handout 16

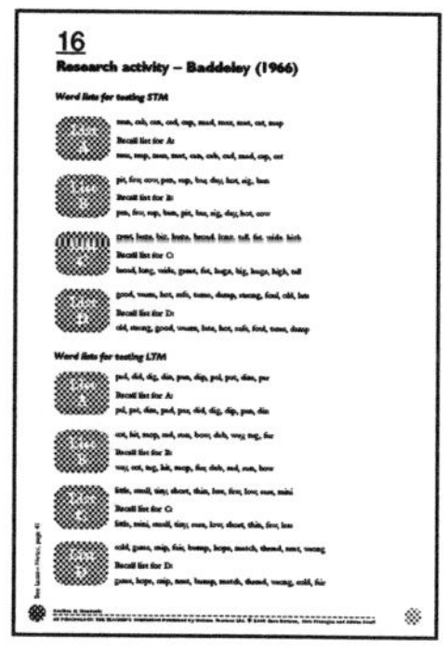
16
Research activity – Baddeley (1966)

List A acoustically similar (words all sound the similar).

List B acoustically dissimilar, similar words to list A but all sound different.

List C semantically similar (words with similar meaning).

List D semantically dissimilar, similar words like list C but all different meaning.

Lists A and B test STM.

Lists C and D test LTM.

Discussion

- How could you have designed the experiment better?
- Did participants guess what the study was about?
- Might it have helped to vary the order of presentation?
- What are the relative advantages of this repeated measures design compared with an independent measures design?
- Why was it a good idea to use lists B and D?
- What conclusions can you draw from your findings?

Research activity: Brandimote *et al.* (1992)

Brandimote, M.A., Hitch, G.J., and Bishop, D.V.M. (1992) Influence of short-term memory codes on visual processing: evidence from image transformation tasks. *Journal of Experimental Psychology: Learning, Memory and Cognition*, 18, 157–65.

Baddeley's research (1966) suggests that an acoustic code is used to store information in STM but this may be related to the kind of information used to test STM (he used word lists). If *visual* stimuli (pictures) are used Brandimote *et al.* (1992) found that participants used visual encoding in STM if they were prevented from doing any *verbal* rehearsal (they had to say 'la la la') in the retention interval before performing a *visual* recall task. Normally we 'translate' visual images into verbal codes in STM but since verbal rehearsal was prevented they did use visual codes.

Handout 17

Replication of this study requires the use of six pairs of pictures as shown on **Handout 17**.

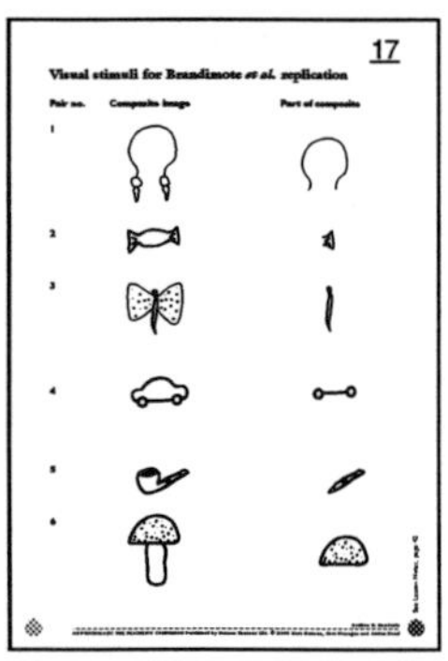

The first member of each pair is a composite picture and the second member is part of the composite. If you 'subtract' the part from the whole you get the images shown in the table at the bottom of this page.

Procedures

1 **Demonstration**: show participants composite image 1, and then remove and show them part image 1. Ask them to subtract the part from the composite in their mind. What image results?

2 **Experiment**: divide participants into two groups and test separately. Group 2 should not see the images until it is their turn.

3 Tell group 1 to study composite figures 2 to 6. They should be told that they will be tested on these later and to wait until they are confident that they have learned them all in the correct order. When they are ready, remove items 2 to 6 and show them the part objects 2 to 6. Ask them to subtract the part from the whole composite and write down the image that is left.

4 Test group 2 in the same way except they are asked to say 'la la la la …', throughout the memorisation task.

Findings

Swap answer papers and score correct answers. Total up correct answers for group 1 and for group 2. (Group 2 should do better because the verbal task prevented acoustic coding so they would use a visual code and then perform better on the subtraction task.)

Picture	Composite picture	What remains after subtraction
1	Skipping rope	Ice cream cones
2	Sweet	Fish
3	Butterfly	Bow tie
4	Car	Cloud
5	Pipe	Bowl
6	Mushroom	Vase

Discussion

- Why did group 2 do better than group 1? (If they didn't, can you explain that! Perhaps the 'la la la' task was ineffective, or participants guessed the purpose of the experiment.)
- Why did Baddeley find that participants used an acoustic code for short-term memory?
- As participants what did you think about while doing the experiment? How might this have affected the findings? Did you try to guess the purpose of the experiment?
- In the original experiment the order of images was different for each participant as a counterbalance. How would this help?
- Can these findings be applied in any way to the real world?

You could also ask questions about the design: What was the method? What was the design? What are the strengths and weaknesses of this method/design. How was sampling done? How were participants allocated to conditions?

AS PSYCHOLOGY: THE TEACHER'S COMPANION Published by Nelson Thornes Ltd. © 2004 Sara Berman, Cara Flanagan and Adrian Frost

Describing MSM

Ask the students to work in pairs. One partner has a diagram of MSM and has to describe it to the other partner who can't see it but has to draw it.

Research activity: Serial position curve

Glanzer, M., and Cunitz, A.R. (1966) Two storage mechanisms in free recall. *Journal of Verbal Learning and Verbal Behavior*, 5, 351–60.

This exercise shows the serial position effect, as proposed by Glanzer and Cunitz (1966). If the experiment works it should result in a graph with a U-shape, showing that words at the start of a list and words at the end of a list are better recalled (primacy and recency).

Handouts 18 and 19

On **Handout 18** are five lists. It would be helpful if each list could be reproduced on a separate piece of paper.

Handout 19 allows students to record their findings.

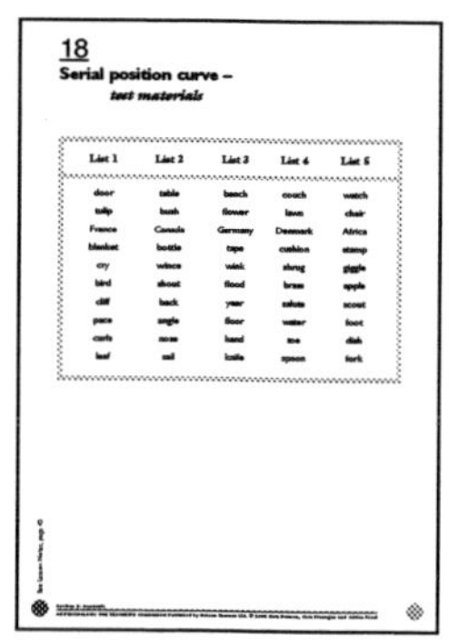
18
Serial position curve – ***test materials***

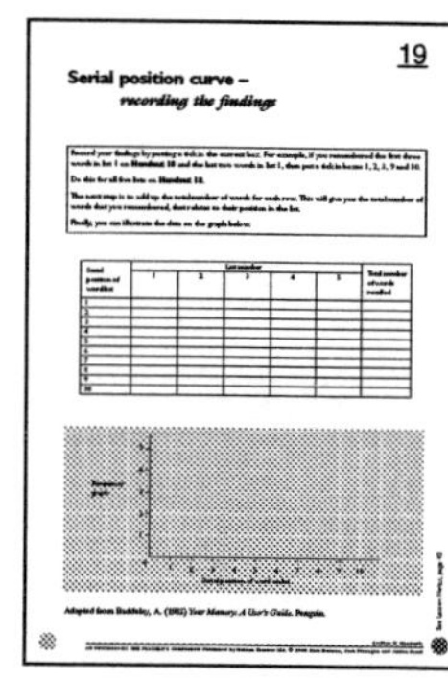
19
Serial position curve – ***recording the findings***

Procedures

Students should read through list 1 carefully (once) and then turn it over and write down as many of the words as they can remember, in any order. Then do the same with the rest of the lists.

When students have finished all five lists they can complete the table on **Handout 19**, putting a tick in the correct box. For example, if they remembered the first three words in list 1 and the last two words in list 1, then put a tick in boxes 1, 2, 3, 9 and 10. They do this for all five lists. The next step is to add up the total number of words for each row. This will give you the total number of words related to their position in the list. Finally, they may illustrate the data on the graph.

Analysis and discussion of data

Data could be collected from the whole group and recorded and/or you might discuss individual differences in findings.

Try this sum

1 Try this very simple little task (that doesn't always work!) Ask students to do some mental arithmetic e.g. add 443 + 659. Then ask them HOW they did it. Did they visualise the numbers, hear teacher's voice, what happened to the sub-totals? This should illustrate the WM model by showing them that their STM is an active store.

2 Try reading something while saying 'the the the …' silently to yourself. Does this disrupt your reading? The working memory model suggests that the phonological loop is important in reading new material. If you read something you know well, is 'the the the …' less disruptive?

Research activity: Hitch and Baddeley (1976)

Glanzer, M., and Cunitz, A.R. (1966) Two storage mechanisms in free recall. *Journal of Verbal Learning and Verbal Behavior*, 5, 351–60

Hitch, G., and Baddeley, A.D. (1976) Verbal reasoning and working memory. *Quarterly Journal of Experimental Psychology*, 28, 603–21.

Miller, G.A. (1956) The magic number seven, plus or minus two: Some limits on our capacity for processing information, *Psychological Review*, 63, 81–93.

Working memory:

- is a limited capacity system, as demonstrated by Miller (1956 – 7 ± 2) and Glanzer and Cunitz (1966 – primacy and recency effect found in free recall);
- has a separate unit for processing speech (the articulatory loop);
- is governed by a central executive that deals with tasks requiring thought, such as a sentence verification task (see next page) or generating random digits.

This means that we would expect people to cope well with a sentence verification task (see below) when simultaneously performing a short-term memory task (memorising six letters for later recall) or simultaneously performing a task involving the articulatory loop (e.g. saying 'the the the' repeatedly) because all of these tasks involve different components of the working memory system.

However, we would expect people to have greater difficulty with the sentence verification task when having to produce a random number sequence instead of saying 'the the the' because the random number generation should involve the central executive as well.

Sentence verification task

This is based on verbal reasoning tasks. There are several varieties: active affirmative (A follows B), active negative (A does not follow B), passive affirmative (A is followed by B), passive negative (A is not followed by B). All possible forms are combined to produce 32 variations which are shown on **Handout 22**.

Cont'd …

Handouts 20, 21 and 22

Make into set of cards. One set needed for every pair of students

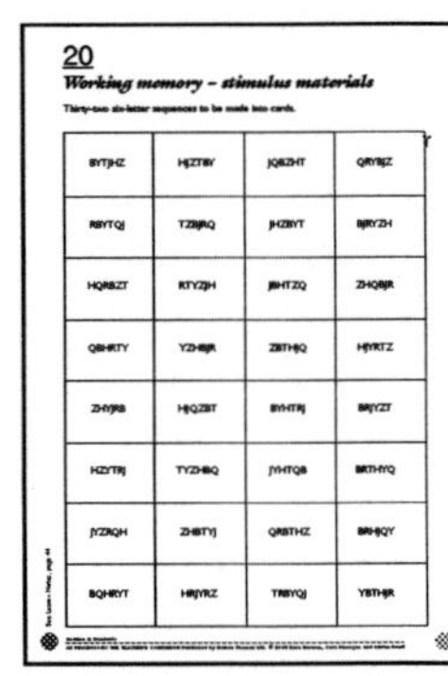

One sheet needed for every pair of students

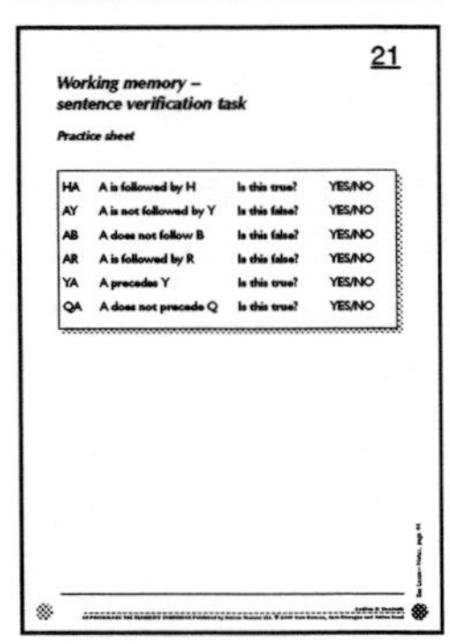

One sheet needed for every student

MODULE: **Cognitive Psychology**
SECTION: **Short-term and long-term memory**
TOPIC: The working memory model of memory

...Continued from previous page

Procedures

Thirty-two cards need to be prepared with the 32 six-letter sequences. These are given on **Handout 20**.

The group should be divided into two. Group one will say 'the the the' repeatedly when doing the sentence verification task (as given on **Handout 22**). Group 2 should say random digits while completing the other task (you need to make sure they are doing this and not just saying '2 2 2' or '1 2 3 4 5 ...').

It may be best for students to work in pairs, where person 1 times person 2, turns the cards over for person 2, monitors what they are doing and checks for accuracy. Then person 2 can do the same for person 1. One member of the pair might belong to group 1 and the other to group 2.

All participants should be told that the main task is to memorise the six letters to be able to recall them accurately *after* answering the sentence verification task.

1. All participants can start by doing the practice sheet (**Handout 21**). Use any six cards with this.
2. On each trial, the participants turn over one card showing the six letters to remember and then place it face down. They should then read the sentence verification task and circle yes or no as quickly as possible. Finally they should write the six letters in the final column. They then look at the next card, turn it face down and complete the sentence verification task and fill in the six letters in the final column. And so on. It is important that they try to be correct and that they do the recall task after the sentence verification.
3. The time taken from start to finish must be recorded.
4. The answers should be checked and the final column on **Handout 22** filled in.

Discussion

- What is the clearest way to present your findings?
- Was there a difference in the speed of the two groups?
- What can you conclude from your findings?
- How should you deal with participants who were very inaccurate? (What counts as sufficiently accurate?)
- What were your impressions of being a participant? Were there things that adversely affected your behaviour? How might these have affected the validity of the findings?
- What does 'random' mean? Which of the following is a more random sequence: '1 2 3 4 5' or '2 5 3 1 4'?

MODULE: **Cognitive Psychology**
SECTION: **Short-term and long-term memory**
TOPIC: The levels of processing model of memory

Card sorting task (adapted from Mandler, 1967)

Mandler, G. (1967) Organisation and memory. In K.W. Spence and J.T. Spence (Eds), *The Psychology of Learning and Motivation: Advances in Research and Theory*, Vol. 1. London: Academic Press.

Mandler (1967) asked participants to sort a pack of 52 cards, each with a word on it. The instructions were to sort the cards into whatever categories the participant choose. Once the first sort was completed, the cards were collected in and then handed back to the participant with the same instructions. The participants were asked to repeat the sorts until two consecutive sorts were almost the same. Then they were asked to write down as many words as they could remember. Not surprisingly they did rather well, and the more categories a participant had used the more words they recalled.

Why? Because in sorting the cards the words were processed in a meaningful way, and this caused the words to become lodged in memory. No participant tried to memorise the words, the words simply became part of that person's knowledge. This is the way we acquire most of what we know. It can be applied to the study and recall of psychology. Engage in active processing and you will remember things effortlessly.

Cont'd ...

AS PSYCHOLOGY: THE TEACHER'S COMPANION Published by Nelson Thornes Ltd. © 2004 Sara Berman, Cara Flanagan and Adrian Frost

...Continued from previous page

You could conduct a brief replication of this with your class.

- Prepare a list of 50 words (select ten categories: animals, fruit, cars, etc., and record five words for each). One example is given in the table below, and the same words are jumbled in **Handout 23**. Alternatively, you can use **Handout 30**, but the words need to be jumbled.
- Show the list to the class (e.g. on an OHT). Ask the class to organise the words into five or fewer categories. Alternatively, give half the class a slip of paper asking them to simply memorise the words and instruct the other half to categorise the words.
- Remove the list and ask all students to try to recall as many words as possible.
- Ask each student how many categories they used.
- Analyse your findings. What can you conclude?

Handout 23

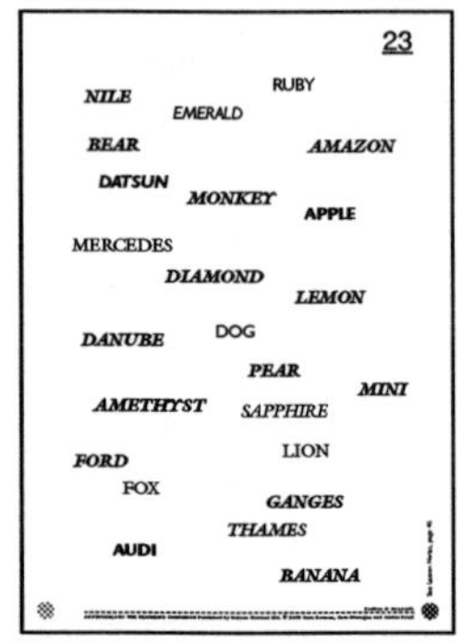
23

NILE RUBY EMERALD BEAR AMAZON DATSUN MONKEY APPLE MERCEDES DIAMOND LEMON DANUBE DOG PEAR MINI AMETHYST SAPPHIRE LION FORD FOX GANGES THAMES AUDI BANANA

Animals	**Fruit**	**Cars**	**Gemstones**	**Rivers**
Bear	Apple	Ford	Ruby	Thames
Dog	Orange	Mini	Diamond	Nile
Fox	Pear	Datsun	Emerald	Amazon
Lion	Banana	Mercedes	Amethyst	Ganges
Monkey	Lemon	Audi	Sapphire	Danube

Research activity: Craik and Tulving (1975)

Craik, F.I.M., and Tulving, E. (1975) Depth of processing and the retention of words in episodic memory. *Journal of Experimental Psychology*, 104, 268–94.

The activity described here is a replication of the study by Craik and Tulving. The original study was a repeated measures design but it could also be conducted as an independent measures study. Trying both designs will enable students to gain experience of conducting an experiment and comparing the relative advantages and disadvantages of both methods of design.

Handouts 24 and 25

Handout 24 explains how to conduct the *repeated measures design*.

Handout 25 provides a list of words to use when creating the stimulus material

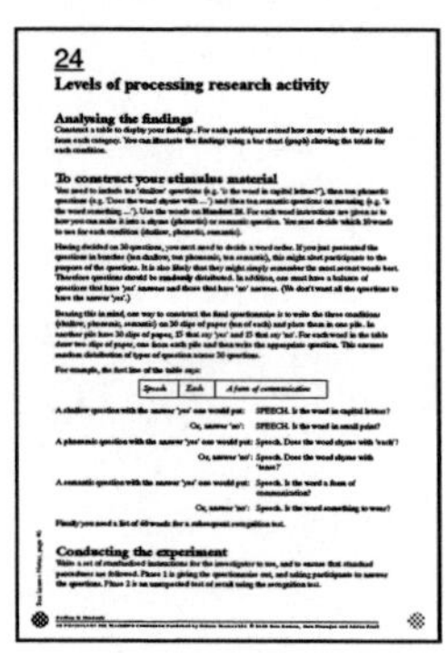
24
Levels of processing research activity
Analysing the findings
To construct your stimulus material
Conducting the experiment

25
Stimulus words for levels of processing research activity

For alternative: independent measures design

Constructing the stimulus material

Select 30 words from the table. For each word compose one stimulus list of rhyming questions only (List A) and one of semantic questions only (List B). You could again ensure that half of the questions have an answer 'yes' and half are 'no'.

Cont'd ...

AS PSYCHOLOGY: THE TEACHER'S COMPANION Published by Nelson Thornes Ltd. © 2004 Sara Berman, Cara Flanagan and Adrian Frost

...Continued from previous page

(You could have a third condition, List C which is all shallow questions.)

Conducting the experiment

Give List A to half of the participants and List B to the other participants. How do you decide which list to give to which participants? You could give List A to the first ten participants, and List B to the second ten participants. Or you can *randomly allocate* participants to conditions. You can do this by putting all 20 words (List A and List B) in a pile and shuffling them up. This random allocation ensures that there is no pattern in who becomes members of each group.

Analysing the findings

You can construct a table of findings and use graphs to illustrate these.

Using levels of processing: The three bears problem

In the AS examination candidates often have two problems: they either write too much or they write too little. Questions are worth 2, 3, 6 or 18 marks. The marks-worth indicates the amount of time that should be spent on the question – about one minute per mark – and also how much should be written. About 300 words is about right for the 18-mark question and about 100 words for six marks. This paragraph is about 100 words – just about the right length for an answer to the question 'Outline one model of memory'. Students don't have time to write much so every word they write must count.

It may help to reduce all material to three bullet points or six bullet points. Start with six bullet points. Identify 'six things that I would write about the levels of processing model'. Students might work in pairs and consult more than one book. The process of selecting their six points helps to make the information memorable because of the processing that must be done. They can then reduce the six bullet points to three bullet points (more processing and therefore greater understanding and recall). Each bullet point might be just a few words but they should be able to elaborate the point to a full sentence.

Students migth practise producing a 100 word description from their six bullet points

Being armed with six bullet points in the exam ensures that students write an answer that isn't too short or too long.

In this lesson you could ask students to prepare 3-mark and 6-mark answers for the models of memory that you have studied. An example is shown below – however, what is important is that students do this for themselves. It is the *processing* which is vital. When they have done the activity, they could compare theirs with ours. However, it is critical that students produce their own versions because it is *making* the lists that is a crucial part of this activity.

Handout 26

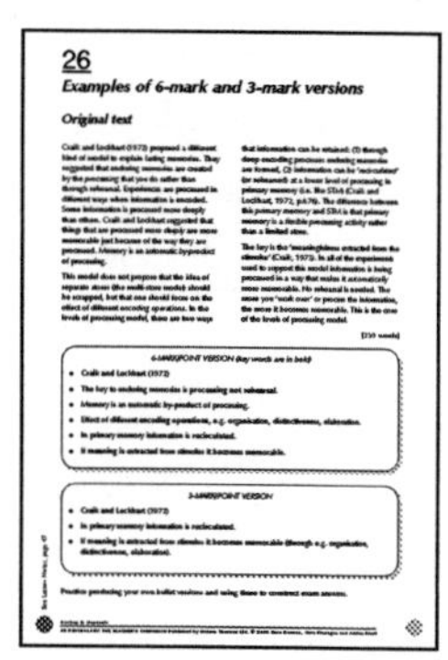
26
Examples of 6-mark and 3-mark versions
Original text

AS PSYCHOLOGY: THE TEACHER'S COMPANION Published by Nelson Thornes Ltd. © 2004 Sara Berman, Cara Flanagan and Adrian Frost

MODULE: **Cognitive Psychology**
SECTION: **Short-term and long-term memory**
TOPIC: **The levels of processing model of memory**

Experimental design exercise

This is an activity for students who have studied experimental design (which is covered on page 17 of *The Complete Companion*). **Handout 27** gives them statements that have to be placed in the appropriate spaces. You can read the correct answers out from below.

Handout 27

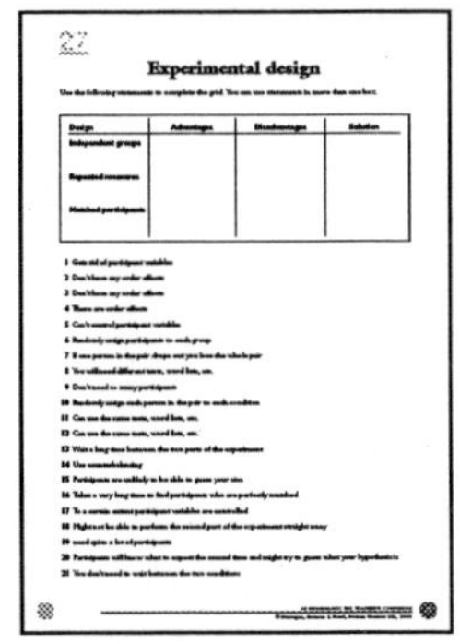
Experimental design

Answers

Design	Advantages	Disadvantages	Solution
Independent groups	2, 11, 15, 21	5, 19	6
Repeated measures	1, 9	4, 8, 18, 20	13, 14
Matched participants	3, 12, 17	7, 16	10

MODULE: **Cognitive Psychology**
SECTION: **Forgetting**
TOPIC: **Explanations of forgetting in short-term memory**

Recalling nonsense trigrams

Remind students of the work of Peterson and Peterson (see pages 4–5 in *The Complete Companion* and page 37 in the Lesson Notes). **Handouts 12** and **13** can be used.

Research activity: Waugh and Norman (1965)

Waugh, N.C. and Norman, D. (1965) Primary memory, *Psychological Review*, 72, 89–104.

This study uses a serial probe technique to test decay and displacement in STM.

Waugh and Norman (1965) used the *serial probe technique* to investigate forgetting in STM. They presented 16 numbers to participants. If the probe was early in the list, recall was poor (less than 20 per cent). If the probe came near the end of the list, recall was good (over 80 per cent). This supports displacement theory because forgetting must be due to the fact that subsequent numbers increasingly displaced earlier numbers.

Waugh and Norman did the same experiment reading digits out at different speeds: at a rate of one per second (slower) or four per second (faster). This timing affected recall. If the numbers were presented faster, recall improved – which must be because the numbers had less time to decay away. Displacement would have remained constant. This supports decay.

Cont'd ...

AS PSYCHOLOGY: THE TEACHER'S COMPANION Published by Nelson Thornes Ltd. © 2004 Sara Berman, Cara Flanagan and Adrian Frost

TOPIC: Explanations of forgetting in short-term memory

...Continued from previous page

Try it out using the numbers provided on **Handout 28**. There are 16 sets of 16 numbers, each set followed by a probe number.

Handout 28

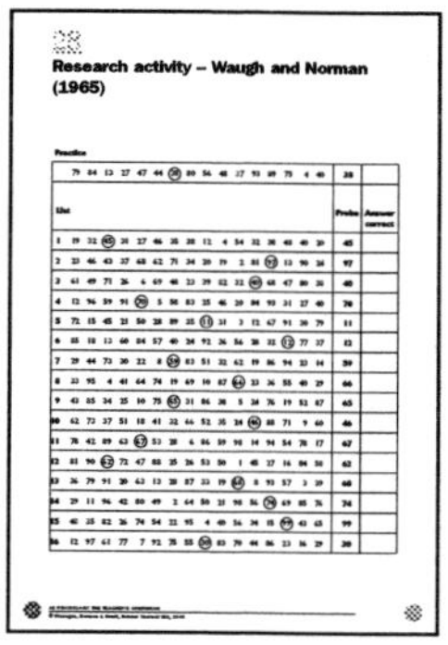
Research activity – Waugh and Norman (1965)

- Participants should be instructed that on each trial (list) they will hear 16 numbers and are required to remember these as best they can. At the end of each list of 16 numbers, one number will be read out (the 'probe') and participants must try to recall the number that came *after* this in the list.
- Read/play the practice list, and then state the probe number and record whether the participant gave the correct answer.
- Repeat this for all eight lists.

Findings

Compare performance on lists 1, 4, 5 and 7 (early probe) wiht performance on lists 2, 3, 6 and 8 (late probe). Ask students for ideas on how to present these findings.

Experiment 1: Demonstrating displacement

- Use lists 1 to 8 on **Handout 28**.
- The numbers can be read to participants or the lists may be recorded. The numbers should be read at a constant rate of one per second in a monotone voice.

Experiment 2: Demonstrating decay

- Now test all participants using the second set of numbers (lists 9 to 16). This time present the numbers at a rate of four per second (just about possible!).
- Lists 9, 11, 12 and 16 are early and 10, 13, 14 and 15 are late probes.

MODULE: **Cognitive Psychology**
SECTION: **Forgetting**

TOPIC: Explanations of forgetting in long-term memory

How to use cues to smuggle information into the exam (legitimately!)

(Note – this exercise involves memory for names of psychologists and I (AF) sometimes worry that students place too much emphasis upon this. It's the ideas that are more important, but, for the purposes of this exercise, the names become useful pegs upon which to hang such ideas.)

As we know, students tend to sit their exams in large halls far removed from their normal classroom environment. They are in a different position, in a different place and are therefore deprived of a whole range of classroom memory cues, thus preventing them from utilising any 'context-dependent' recall.

However, a former colleague of mine argued that they did still have one visual cue, in that they have *each other*. If chunks of useful information could be attached to, say, each of the lads in the back row, or everyone on the table by the door, then the presence of such students in the exam hall could trigger the retrieval of that information.

He decided to attach a psychologist of the 'useful guest appearance' variety to each student. Both of us tried this over a period of time, though it only really works if you use it consistently throughout the year.

The hard bit is generating the initial list of psychologists, so here's one I prepared earlier:

Cont'd ...

AS PSYCHOLOGY: THE TEACHER'S COMPANION Published by Nelson Thornes Ltd. © 2004 Sara Berman, Cara Flanagan and Adrian Frost

...Continued from previous page

Useful 'guest appearances' in Psychology essays

Psychologist	Key idea	Usage
Boring 1957	Experimental method is most significant method of research into human minds	Anywhere involving lab experiments
Heather 1976	Dismissed lab methods as lacking ecological validity	Anywhere involving lab experiments
Brehm 1992	Lab methods limited in terms of *range* of behaviours that can be studied	Anywhere involving lab experiments
Orne 1962	Participants' behaviour often subject to demand effects	Anywhere involving lab experiments
Hawthorne effect*	Participants' behaviour affected by knowledge that they are observed	Many kinds of study
Rosenthal 1963	Experimenter effects – experimenters find what they *expect* to find	Many kinds of study
Rosenberg 1969	Social Desirability Effect – participants give socially desirable responses to questions	Questionnaires/interviews
Gergen 1985	There are no facts, only values. Psychology reflects the values of investigators	Social psychology, stress research, abnormality
Friedman and Rosenman 1974	Individual differences need to be accounted for. It may matter if participants are type A/ non-type A	Social psychology, stress research, abnormality
Aronson 1992	Cost-benefit analysis must be done in areas of ethical concern	Social psychology, stress research, abnormality
Wilkinson 1991	Psychological theories often neglect/exclude women	Social psychology, stress research, abnormality
Rosenzweig 1992	Psychology is rooted in Western, specifically American, culture	Social psychology, stress research, abnormality

*Hawthorne is the name of an industrial plant, not a person.

The points on this list could be usefully employed to add depth to a whole range of essays. Students stuck for an A02 point should be able to deploy at least one or two for any given question. As with other such lists, they require some skill on the part of the student, in order fully to integrate the material with the question, but this comes with practice. (Even if you don't want to pursue the memory activity I'm about to outline, the list could be useful in promoting A02 discussion.)

Now to ensure that the recall of details on this list is 'triggered' by the appearance of students in the class.

As these points arise throughout the year, formally attach a particular student to each psychologist. If you can, remember to refer to the student assigned to Wilkinson, as 'Wilkinson' throughout the year. (This can be fun – I can never resist assigning 'Heather' to a male student, though you have to be careful who becomes 'Boring'.)

Whenever a relevant point is reached in the discussion, 'Wilkinson' can be asked for comment, and that student can then point out, as per the table, that gender issues may well need addressing in this context. They could then be asked to speculate as to how this might be the case.

In a similar fashion, 'Orne' can be asked to identify any particular demand effects, or 'Aronson' asked to weigh up issues of ethical concern and so on.

In my experience, if you remember to maintain this approach consistently (and that's the difficult part), students very quickly learn the relevant

Cont'd ...

...Continued from previous page

names and viewpoints and become adept at applying them to the question in hand. Some even become quite possessive of their psychological alter ego.

As they sit in the exam room, their peers should provide visual reminders of a range of useful points. This does, however, work better for the ones sitting at the back. The ones at the front can't view their classmates without being accused of cheating and may have to 'visualise' their classmates instead! This is effectively using the 'method of loci'. It is not usually a problem as, in my experience, most students will steadfastedly refuse ever to be removed from 'their' seat in the classroom, so an accurate recall of everyone in the classroom is usually possible.

There are many ways to adapt this idea For example, rather than assigning psychologists' names to students you could assign concepts such as ethical issues, internal validity, ecological validity and so on.

References

Aronson, E. (1992) *The Social Animal* (6th Edn). New York: Freeman.

Boring, E.G. (1957). *A History of Experimental Psychology* (2nd Edn). New York: Appleton-Century-Crofts.

Brehm, S.S. (1992) *Intimate Relationships* (2nd Edn). New York: McGraw-Hill.

Friedman, M., and Rosenman, R.H. (1974) *Type A Behaviour and your Heart*. New York: Knopf.

Gergen, K.J. (1985) The social constructionist movement in modern psychology. *American Psychologist*, 40, 266–75.

'Hawthorne Effect' in Roethlisburger, F.J., and Dickinson, W.J. (1939) *Management and the Worker*. Cambridge, MA: Harvard University Press.

Heather, N. (1976) *Radical Perspectives in Psychology*. London: Methuen.

Orne, M.T. (1962) On the social psychology of the psychological experiment: With particular reference to demand characteristics and their implications. *American Psychologist*, 17, 776–83.

Rosenberg, M.J. (1965). When dissonance fails: On eliminating evaluation apprehension from attitude measurement. *Journal of Personality and Social Psychology* 1, 28–42.

Rosenthal, R. (1966) *Experimenter Effects in Behavioural Research*. New York: Appleton-Century-Crofts.

Rosenzweig, M.R. (1992) Psychological science around the world. *American Psychologist*, 47, 718–22.

Wilkinson, S. (1991) Feminism and psychology: From critique to reconstruction. *Feminism and Psychology*, 1 (1), 5–18.

Research activity: Proactive and retroactive interference

Word lists are provided on **Handout 29**.

Handout 29

To demonstrate *proactive interference* you give participants (experimental group 1) a list of word pairs using list A and list B (e.g. 'cat' from list A and 'tree' from list B, the word pair is cat-tree). The participants then have to learn a second list consisting of words from list A and C (e.g. cat–stone). Finally participants are asked to recall the list C words given the list A words. How well do they do?

In order to assess recall it is necessary to use a *control group*. This is a second group of participants who are given no interference task so we are able to see how people would normally cope with this task. The control group learns another list (of completely different words, list D) and then learns A–C and recalls A–C.

Cont'd ...

AS PSYCHOLOGY: THE TEACHER'S COMPANION Published by Nelson Thornes Ltd. © 2004 Sara Berman, Cara Flanagan and Adrian Frost

...Continued from previous page

To demonstrate retroactive interference

A third group (experimental group 2)

- Learns A–B, then A–C.
- Test by giving list A words and ask to recall list B.

Retroactive interference is stronger than proactive interference. In other words participants in group 3 should do less well recalling the words from the first list (A–B) learned than group 1 does recalling words from the second list (A–C).

Discussion

- What would be the best way to present the findings?
- What can you conclude about interference from your findings?
- If there are unexpected findings, compared to those outlined above, how would you explain them?

Research activity: Tulving and Pstotka (1971)

Tulving, E. and Psotka, J. (1971) Retroactive inhibition in free recall: Inaccessibility of information available in the memory store. *Journal of Experimental Psychology*, 87, 1–8.

Tulving and Psotka found the more lists a participant learned, the worse their performance (retroactive interference) *but* if they were given cues (category names) then recall was a fairly constant 70 per cent for all lists no matter how many were learned. This shows that the memories are there and have not in fact been lost through interference. Forgetting is due to retrieval failure not disappearance of the memory.

Procedures

In the original study there were six experimental conditions:

- condition 1 (E1) called for learning one list of words;
- condition 2 (E2) for two lists;
- condition 3 (E3) for three lists and so on up to E6 for six lists.

There were six different word lists (see **Handout 30**), each with 24 words. Each list had six different categories of four words (36 categories in all). All the words from one category were presented in a block, so that it was 'obvious to all but the most uninterested' participants that there was a link between that group of words. The category names were not included in the list.

Words were presented on a TV at the rate of one word per second. The entire list was shown three times, and then participants were asked to write down all the words they could remember, guessing if they weren't sure. They were given 90 seconds for each immediate recall test which was followed by the next list. After hearing all the word lists, they were tested on free recall twice (with a ten minute gap in between doing a neutral activity to prevent rehearsal) and then last of all they were given a cued recall test and 90 seconds for each free recall test.

To conduct this study in class

Construct word lists as shown on **Handout 30**. Words should be written clearly on cards or OHTs. The categories (cues) are written on cued recall sheets.

Divide the class into groups:

Group 1 learns only the first list, group 2 should learn two lists and so on. It may be easiest to have two conditions. Group 1 learns lists 4, 5 and 6. Group 2 learns all six word lists.

After each word list is presented, test immediate recall by asking students to write down all the words they can remember. When you have shown all the word lists, ask all students to write down all the words they can remember from their word lists. Give them a short neutral activity and then test free recall again. Finally perform the cued-recall test by stating category names and asking them to recall items from that category.

Cont'd ...

AS PSYCHOLOGY: THE TEACHER'S COMPANION Published by Nelson Thornes Ltd. © 2004 Sara Berman, Cara Flanagan and Adrian Frost

...Continued from previous page

Discussion

- In the original experiment the order of words was changed for each participant. Why was this important?
- This study used an independent measures design. Could you do it with a repeated measures design? How?
- What do you do if people recall words not on the list? Or words that are almost right?

Handout 30

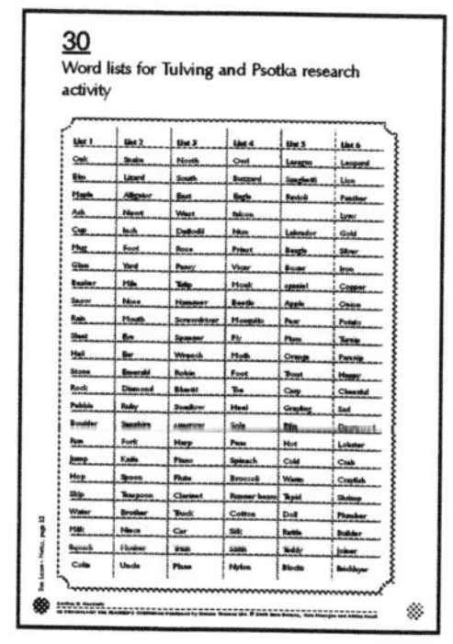
30
Word lists for Tulving and Psotka research activity

MODULE: **Cognitive Psychology**
SECTION: **Forgetting**
TOPIC: **Emotional factors in forgetting: Flashbulb memories**

Where were you when you heard about ...?

Discuss students' memories of their whereabouts when they first heard of momentous world events (e.g. the attack on the World Trade Centre, New York). Ask: Are you sure? How do you know? Discuss their personal experiences of flashbulb memories.

Research activity: Construct your own flashbulb memory questionnaire

Brown, R. and Kulik, J. (1977) Flashbulb memories. *Cognition*, 5, 73–99.

This activity may provide an opportunity to (1) think about the design of questionnaires, (2) find out more about flashbulb memories. Instead of a questionnaire your students could conduct interviews, with the intention of finding out more about interviews. Interviews can be closed, in which case the design would be the same, or they can be open, in which case students (interviewers) should be prepared to ask further questions depending on the answers that interviewees give.

Considerations for designing a questionnaire or an interview are provided on **Handouts 31** and **32**.

Note that the details of the study by Brown and Kulik are provided on the CD as a Star Study PowerPoint.

Handouts 31 and 32

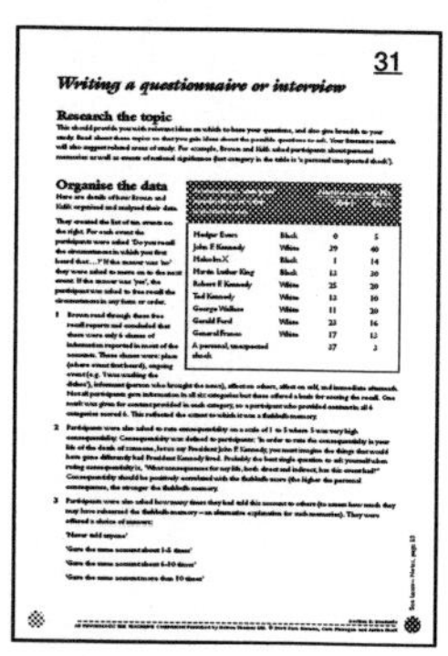
31
Writing a questionnaire or interview

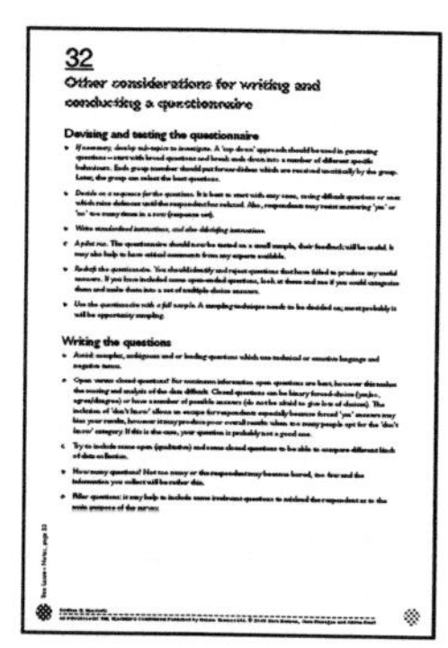
32
Other considerations for writing and conducting a questionnaire

Discussion

Afterwards, discuss how best to present findings: quantitative and qualitative findings. You can correlate strength of memory (flashbulb score) with consequentialty. Also consider what the results tell us about flashbulb memories.

AS PSYCHOLOGY: THE TEACHER'S COMPANION Published by Nelson Thornes Ltd. © 2004 Sara Berman, Cara Flanagan and Adrian Frost

Spot the mistakes in a study of repression

Williams, L.M. (1994) Recall of childhood tauma: A prospective study of women's memories of childhood abuse. *Journal of Consulting and Clinical Psychology*, 62, 1167–76.

Handout 33 contains a report of a study on repression by Williams (1994). There are three deliberate mistakes in each section.

Handout 33

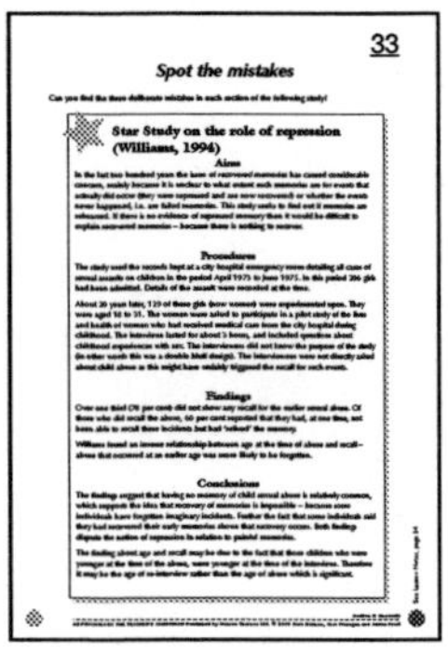

The correct version is given above, with alterations underlined.

Star Study on the role of repression (Williams 1994)

Aims

In the last few decades the issue of *recovered memories* has caused considerable concern, mainly because it is unclear to what extent such memories are for events that actually did occur (they were repressed and are now recovered) or whether the events never happened, i.e. are false memories. This study seeks to find out if memories are repressed. If there is no evidence of repressed memory then it would be difficult to explain recovered memories – because there is nothing to recover.

Procedures

The study used the records kept at a city hospital emergency room detailing all cases of sexual assaults on children in the period April 1973 to June 1975. In this period 206 girls had been admitted. Details of the assault were recorded at the time.

About 20 years later, 129 of these girls (now women) were re-interviewed. They were aged 18 to 31. The women were asked to participate in a follow-up study of the lives and health of women who had received medical care from the city hospital during childhood. The interviews lasted for about 3 hours, and included questions about childhood experiences with sex. The interviewers did not know the purpose of the study (in other words this was a double blind design). The interviewees were not directly asked about child abuse as this might have unfairly triggered the recall for such events.

Findings

Over one third (38 per cent) did not show any recall for the earlier sexual abuse. Of those who did recall the abuse, 16 per cent reported that they had, at one time, not been able to recall these incidents but had 'recovered' the memory.

Williams found an inverse relationship between age at the time of abuse and recall – abuse that occurred at an earlier age was more likely to be forgotten.

Conclusions

The findings suggest that having no memory of child sexual abuse is relatively common, which supports the idea that recovery of memories is possible – because some individuals have forgotten real incidents. Further the fact that some individuals said they had recovered their early memories shows that recovery occurs. Both findings support the notion of repression in relation to painful memories.

The finding about age and recall may be due to the fact that those children who were younger at the time of the abuse, were younger at the time of the interviews. Therefore it may be the age of re-interview rather than the age of abuse which is significant.

AS PSYCHOLOGY: THE TEACHER'S COMPANION Published by Nelson Thornes Ltd. © 2004 Sara Berman, Cara Flanagan and Adrian Frost

Research activity: Loftus and Palmer (1974)

Loftus, E.F., and Palmer, J.C. (1974) Reconstruction of automobile destruction: An example of the interaction between language and memory. *Journal of Verbal Learning and Verbal Behavior*, 13, 585–9.

This key study can be replicated using a short video clip taken from the TV, or using the photographs on the CD of a car accident. I've also seen student's coursework where photographs of footballers in collison were used – and worked.

Students should be encouraged to design this study themselves and thus learn about experimental design. The details of the Loftus and Palmer study on the CD as a Star Study PowerPoint and both studies are summarised on **Handout 34**. Questions to help guide the design process are set out on **Handout 35**.

The questions assume that students know about: research aims, hypotheses (directional, non-directional and null), experimental design (repeated and independent measures), independent and dependent variable, types of experiment, experimental control, confounding variables, standardised instructions, measures of central tendency. These research methods concepts have all been covered at this point in *The Complete Companion*.

Handouts 34 and 35

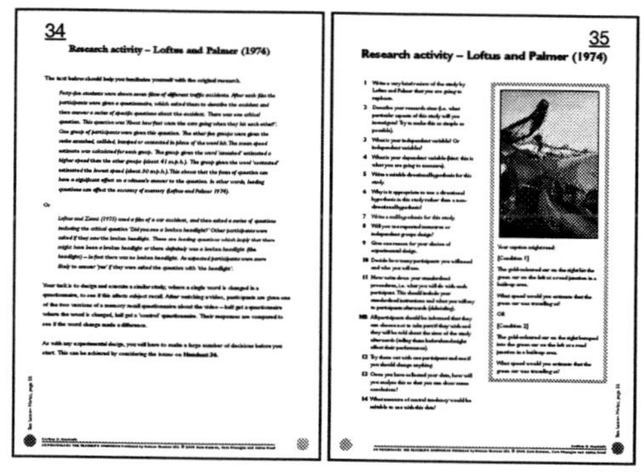
34
Research activity – Loftus and Palmer (1974)

35
Research activity – Loftus and Palmer (1974)

MODULE: **Cognitive Psychology**
SECTION: **Critical Issue: Eyewitness testimony**
TOPIC: **Reconstructive memory**

Use Scooby Doo to examine cultural assumptions

Most teachers will attempt some kind of replication of Bartlett's classic study of the *War of the Ghosts* (see CD for Star Study on PowerPoint), but many students still struggle to understand *why* participants make mistakes when they recall the Native American tale.

The Complete Companion (page 37) explains that, according to Bartlett, 'our past experience, beliefs and expectations shape the way we reconstruct memory' and this task is designed to examine Western beliefs and expectations, specifically about ghosts, in order to contrast them with those on show in Bartlett's story. These beliefs of course come mainly from TV.

The task utilises what is probably the most familiar source of ghost-related material available to anyone growing up in the last 30 years, namely, the cartoon series *Scooby Doo*. If you can get it on video, great. If not, you can virtually guarantee that the bulk of your class will know exactly what the series is all about anyway.

Even a cursory discussion of the series should bring home to students how weird the notion of hippies and talking dogs, in psychadelic campervans, poking around old abandoned tin mines, really would seem to a non-Western observer. The series does, however, probably encapsulate every supernatural cliché available to our culture.

This could simply serve as a brief illustration of cultural expectations concerning the supernatural and how they might affect memory, or you could extend the issue into something more systematic by giving out a version of the table on the next page, with the italics removed, and ask students to discuss and complete.

And so on ....

Of course ideally you want to test non-Westernised native Americans in terms of their memory for episodes of *Scooby Doo*, but you'll probably have trouble rustling up a sample group!

Cont'd ...

...Continued from previous page

Comparing cultural comparisons of the supernatural

Comparison	Story: War of the Ghosts	Cartoon: Scooby Doo
Are ghosts viewed as 'real'?	Yes.	No, ghost is always revealed at the end as a man in disguise.
What do ghosts look like?	Ordinary people (black from mouth?).	Take your pick – floating apparitions, rattling chains, headless cavaliers, etc.
Are ghosts malevolent?	Unclear.	Yes.
Where/when do ghosts appear?	During a fishing trip – daytime?	Gothic castles, abandoned buildings – at night.
How do ghosts move?	Like us e.g. by canoe.	Float or lumber along with both arms raised in front of them.

Demonstration of the effect of schema

Pompi, K.F. and Lachman, R. (1967) *Journal of Experimental Psychology*, 75, 143–50.

This is adapted from an experiment by Pompi and Lachman (1967).

First read or show the following passage to your students.

Chief Resident Jones adjusted his face mask while anxiously surveying a pale figure secured to the long gleaming table before him. One swift stroke of his small sharp instrument and a thin red line appeared. Then an eager young assistant carefully extended the opening as another pushed aside glistening surface fat so that vital parts were laid bare. Everyone present stared in horror at the ugly growth too large for removal. He now knew it was pointless to continue.

Remove the first passage and then display the following list of words.

Which of these words were in the story?

green	scalpel	bare
surface	tomorrow	wind
blood	slow	tumour
stroke	mask	door
nurse	thin	fat

There are three groups of words.

1 Words in the story: surface, stroke, thin, fat, bare.

2 Words not in the story but related to the schema (operations): blood, nurse, scalpel, mask, tumour.

3 Words not in the story and unrelated to schema: green, tomorrow, slow, wind, door.

Students should not recall any of the words unrelated to the schema but might recall a few 'schema words'. This shows that schema affects recall.

If it doesn't work, it may be that they guessed the purpose of the activity and resisted including any schema words!

AS PSYCHOLOGY: THE TEACHER'S COMPANION Published by Nelson Thornes Ltd. © 2004 Sara Berman, Cara Flanagan and Adrian Frost

Research activity: Schema and recall (Bransford and Johnson 1972)

Bransford, J.D. and Johnson, M.K. (1972) Contextual prerequisites for understanding: Some investigations of comprehension and recall. *Journal of Verbal Learning and Verbal Behaviour*, 11, 717–26.

There are many studies which demonstrate the effects of schema on recall. Some of Bartlett's studies are given in the next activity but first here is one of several experiments by Bransford and Johnson on schema.

In the original experiment, there was a piece of text and an illustration, as shown on **Handout 36**. There were five conditions as described below.

Handout 36

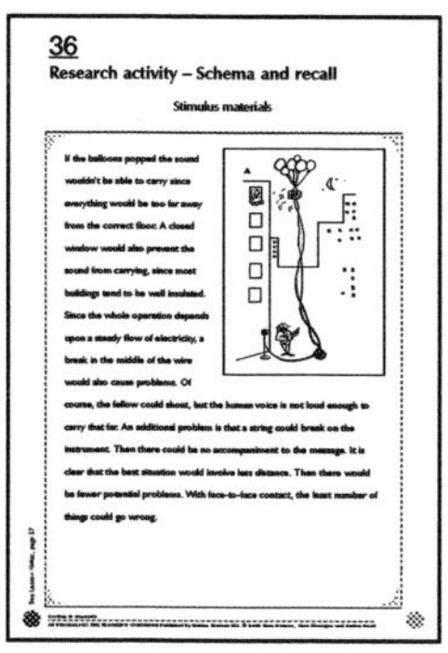

36

Research activity – Schema and recall

Stimulus materials

If the balloons popped the sound wouldn't be able to carry since everything would be too far away from the correct floor. A closed window would also prevent the sound from carrying, since most buildings tend to be well insulated. Since the whole operation depends upon a steady flow of electricity, a break in the middle of the wire would also cause problems. Of course, the fellow could shout, but the human voice is not loud enough to carry that far. An additional problem is that a string could break on the instrument. Then there could be no accompaniment to the message. It is clear that the best situation would involve less distance. Then there would be fewer potential problems. With face-to-face contact, the least number of things could go wrong.

Group 1: No context

Standardised instructions I am going to read a story to you aloud. After I finish reading the story to you, I would like you to recall the story from your memory by writing down what you remember. So please pay close attention to the story.

Standardised procedure Story read aloud to participants, given five minutes to write down their recall. Asked to rate the story for comprehensibility on a scale of 1 to 7 where 7 indicated 'highly comprehensible' and 1 'very incomprehensible'.

Group 2: Context after

Shown 'balloon story context picture' for 30 seconds immediately after the story. 'Actually the story was about the following situation described in this picture. You have 30 seconds to study this picture carefully in order to help you recall the story.'

Group 3: Context before

Shown 'balloon story context picture' for 30 seconds before the story.

Group 4: Partial context

Shown the partial context (not included here) picture before.

Group 5: No context – repetition

Story was repeated twice to assess the effect of repetition.

Handout 37 shows the findings and a graph of these results, plus some questions related to the experiment.

Handout 37

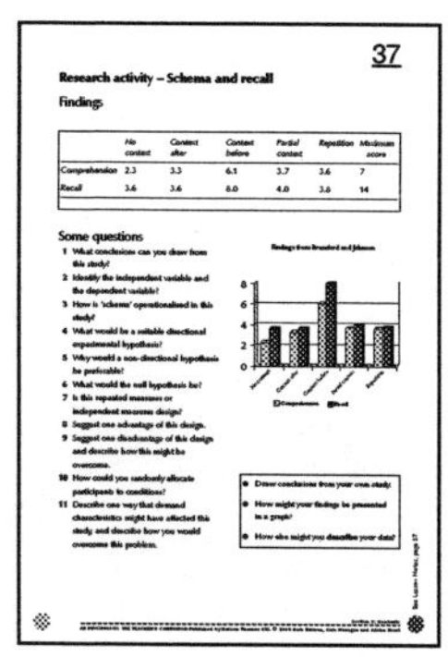

37

Research activity – Schema and recall

Findings

	No context	Context after	Context before	Partial context	Repetition	Maximum score
Comprehension	2.3	3.3	6.1	3.7	3.6	7
Recall	3.6	3.6	8.0	4.0	3.8	14

Some questions

1 What conclusions can you draw from this study?
2 Identify the independent variable and the dependent variable?
3 How is 'schema' operationalised in this study?
4 What would be a suitable directional experimental hypothesis?
5 Why would a non-directional hypothesis be preferable?
6 What would the null hypothesis be?
7 Is this repeated measures or independent measures design?
8 Suggest one advantage of this design.
9 Suggest one disadvantage of this design and describe how this might be overcome.
10 How could you randomly allocate participants to conditions?
11 Describe one way that demand characteristics might have affected this study, and describe how you would overcome this problem.

- Draw conclusions from your own study.
- How might your findings be presented in a graph?
- How else might you describe your data?

You might replicate part of this experiment by dividing your class in three: group 1 have no picture, group 2 are given the picture before and group 3 are given the picture afterwards.

AS PSYCHOLOGY: THE TEACHER'S COMPANION Published by Nelson Thornes Ltd. © 2004 Sara Berman, Cara Flanagan and Adrian Frost

Research activity: Bartlett's studies (1932)

Bartlett, F.C. (1932) *Remembering*. Cambridge: Cambridge University Press.

Bartlett proposed that memory was a social act, reconstructed according to expectations generated by social schema. In order to investigate this hypothesis he selected a variety of stories and drawings which would be foreign to his participants. This would mean that participants would inevitably 'shape' some of the concepts to fit their own expectations, producing new versions different from the original in predictable ways.

Some of Bartlett's stories were *The Art of Lawn Tennis*, *Air Raid on the East Coast* and the well known *War of the Ghosts* (see Star Study on PowerPoint). I confess that for many years I couldn't quite get the point of this story or the research. It may help students to gain a speedier understanding if they consider several of Bartlett's stories and the pictures. The pictures in particular illustrate how schema affect recall.

Some of these stories and pictures are reproduced on **Handouts 38** and **39** (and could be transferred to OHTs).

Handouts 38 and 39

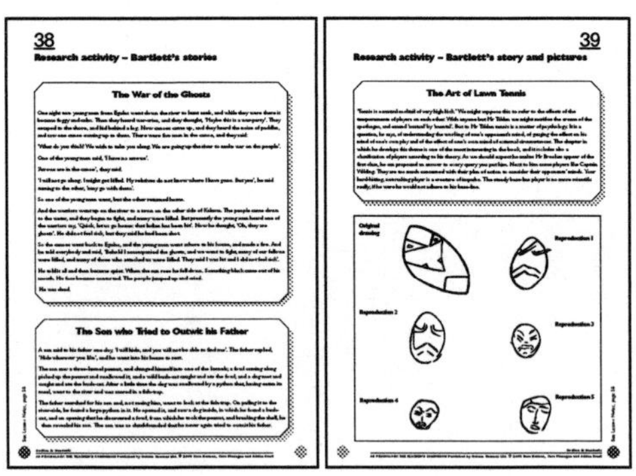

Procedures

In each case read or show these to students and then ask them to repeatedly recall the stories after minutes, hours and days. Bartlett found that initially people reduce the length of each story and tend to produce stereotyped stories. Bartlett expected that participants would soon reach a standard version; however he found that the stories went on evolving, the reproductions very soon becoming fairly fixed but with gradual transformations occuring indefinitely. In other words memory was forever being reconstructed.

Analysis

Compare different versions of the story as recalled by participants. You could ask students for ideas about how to analyse the results.

Or, in order to produce a quantitative analysis, you can identify 'idea units' in the original version and score how accurately these are reproduced in subsequent versions. Findings can be displayed graphically.

Discussion

- If you were a native of the country-of-origin for these stories or a tennis player, would you find it easier to recall these stories? What does that tell us? What things were remembered well? What things were forgotten? What things were changed? Can you offer any explanations?
- What insights does this give you into memory processes?
- Is this a good way to study memory (compared with other methods you have used)? What are its strengths and limitations?

Who do you turn to for support?

Hold a group discussion on the subject of who you would turn to when something really unpleasant happens. Consider how the answer may have been different 5, 10, 15 years ago. Why?

Ask students what they would feel if that person wasn't there. What function does this attachment figure serve?

Stages in development

The Specification requires that students can describe the development of attachments. Many books outline a sequence for development. **Handout 43** jumbles up the material used in *The Complete Companion* to describe these stages but should make sense to anyone familiar with the stages of development.

Handout 43

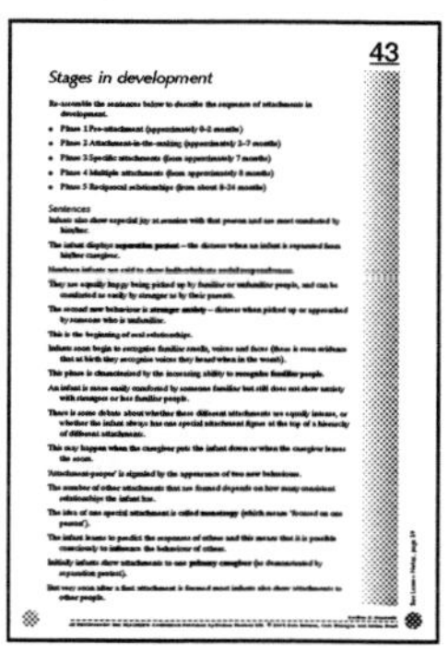
43

Stages in development

The following is the correct version.

Phase 1 Pre-attachment (approximately 0–2 months)

Newborn infants are said to show *indiscriminate social responsiveness*. They are equally happy being picked up by familiar or unfamiliar people, and can be comforted as easily by a stranger as by their parents. However, they soon begin to recognise familiar smells, voices and faces (there is even evidence that at birth they recognise voices they heard when in the womb).

Phase 2 Attachment-in-the-making (approximately 2–7 months)

This phase is characterised by the increasing ability to *recognise familiar people*. An infant is more easily comforted by someone familiar but still does not show anxiety with strangers or less familiar people.

Phase 3 Specific attachments (from approximately 7 months)

'Attachment-proper' is signalled by the appearance of two new behaviours. The infant displays *separation protest* – the distress when an infant is separated from his/her caregiver. This may happen when the caregiver puts the infant down or when the caregiver leaves the room. Infants also show especial joy at reunion with that person and are most comforted by him/her.

The second new behaviour is *stranger anxiety* – distress when picked up or approached by someone who is unfamiliar.

Phase 4 Multiple attachments (from approximately 8 months)

Initially infants show attachments to one *primary caregiver* (as demonstrated by separation protest). But very soon after a first attachment is formed most infants also show attachments to other people. The number of other attachments that are formed depends on how many consistent relationships the infant has. There is some debate about whether these different attachments are equally intense, or whether the infant always has one special attachment figure at the top of a hierarchy of different attachments. The idea of one special attachment is called *monotropy* (which means 'focused on one person').

Phase 5 Reciprocal relationships (from about 8–24 months)

The infant learns to predict the responses of others and this means that it is possible consciously to influence the behaviour of others. This is the beginning of real relationships.

AS PSYCHOLOGY: THE TEACHER'S COMPANION Published by Nelson Thornes Ltd. © 2004 Sara Berman, Cara Flanagan and Adrian Frost

Individual differences in attachment

Ainsworth, M.D.S., Blehar, M.C., Waters, E. and Wall, S. (1978) *Patterns of Attachment: A Psychological Study of the Strange Situation*, Hillsdale, N.J.: Lawrence Erlbaum.

The aim of this worksheet is to increase understanding of the Strange Situation research. Mary Ainsworth worked with John Bowlby in London in the early 1950s. She perceived a need to find a way to measure attachment in order that its effects could be systematically studied. The Strange Situation procedure grew out of her observations of infants and their mothers in Uganda and America. She recognised that infants displayed different kinds of behaviours which were indicative of the way that they were attached.

The Strange Situation classification scheme suggests that there are three types of infant behaviour: secure, insecure/avoidant and insecure/resistant. Of course behaviour doesn't fit quite so neatly into such categories. The three categories are a generalisation of real human behaviour. It may increase student understanding to try to classify the behaviours on **Handout 44**. The descriptions are taken from Ainsworth *et al.* (1978).

These descriptions may be used as a 'standalone' worksheet or as the basis for the role play suggested in the next activity. You might also consult **Handout 44** for descriptions of attachment types.

Answers

- Profile 1 = Group A (Insecure avoidant)
- Profile 2 = subtype B_1
- Profile 3 = subtype A_1
- Profile 4 = subtype C_2
- Profile 5 = Group B (Secure attachment)
- Profile 6 = subtype A_2
- Profile 7 = subtype C_1
- Profile 8 = subtype B_2
- Profile 9 = Group C (Insecure-resistant)

Handouts 44 and 45

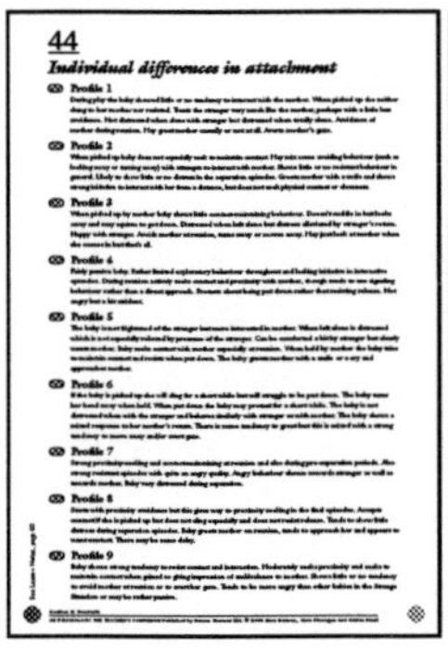
44
Individual differences in attachment

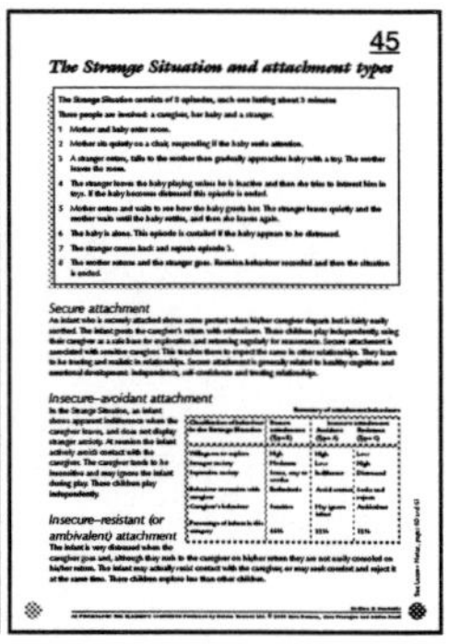
45
The Strange Situation and attachment types

AS PSYCHOLOGY: THE TEACHER'S COMPANION Published by Nelson Thornes Ltd. © 2004 Sara Berman, Cara Flanagan and Adrian Frost

Role play the Strange Situation

Allow your students to try out the Strange Situation for themselves. There is no doubt that anyone who tries to act as, for example, an insecure-resistant infant will not forget the characteristic behaviours!

In Ainsworth's original research observers recorded infant behaviour in terms of five categories:

1 proximity and contact-seeking behaviours;

2 contact-maintaining behaviours;

3 proximity and interaction-avoiding behaviours;

4 contact and interaction-resisting behaviours;

5 search behaviours.

Every 15 seconds the observers made a note of which of the above behaviours was being displayed and also scored the behaviour for intensity on a scale of 1 to 7.

This provides the rest of the class (those who do not act as stranger, caregiver or infant) to practise making observations (and finding out just how hard this is).

Ask for three groups of three volunteers. In each group there should be a caregiver, stranger and infant. Group 1 infant should act as securely attached, group 2 infant should be insecure/avoidant and group 3 as insecure/resistant. The caregiver and stranger do not need to know the type. Characteristic behaviours are given on **Handout 45** (and you might also look at **Handout 44** – answers are given in the previous activity).

Each group should go through the episodes of the Strange Situation as outlined on **Handout 45**.

Observers should design an observation grid, and record behaviours over the 8 episodes.

Analysis

Afterwards class members should compare their results and decide on a way to express these using descriptive statistics (e.g. measure of central tendency, measure of dispersion, graphs).

One possibility is to ask students to work in groups of three or four and average their results. They can present these results in a graph and consider their conclusions (which infant was which attachment type?).

Each group can then present their findings and conclusions to the class.

Handout 45

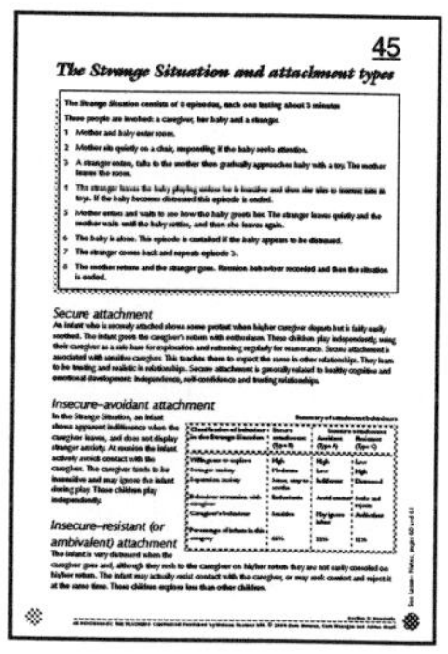
45

The Strange Situation and attachment types

How to make culture your friend

Every examiner comes across hundreds of 'generic' A02 points. They normally surface near the end of an essay and refer to issues such as 'lack of ecological validity' or 'ethical concerns'. They attract credit, but often not much credit.

There's nothing wrong with such points, and indeed there are lists of prompts for such material elsewhere in this book, but they seldom attract more than limited credit, as candidates find it difficult to do much with them in terms of linking them to the question and exploring them in any depth. Students often worry that using generic points will be regarded by examiners as 'cheating', which is not the case. What will matter is the extent to which students use those points to engage with the longer 18-mark questions.

This section takes the 'Daddy' of all generic A02 points and attempts to show how a bit of preparation can substantially beef it up a bit.

'Culture' is a good point to make because, let's face it, there isn't a section of psychology that wouldn't benefit from more cross-cultural research and so 'possibility of culture bias' will always be a valid point, but let's do some work with it as follows.

The box on **Handout 46** contains a standard set of points that can be rote learnt and applied to a wide range of areas. It isn't that easy though, as the candidate has to work to connect the material to the question, especially at the end of the second and third sections. This doesn't require learning, but *thinking* on the part of the candidate.

Handout 46

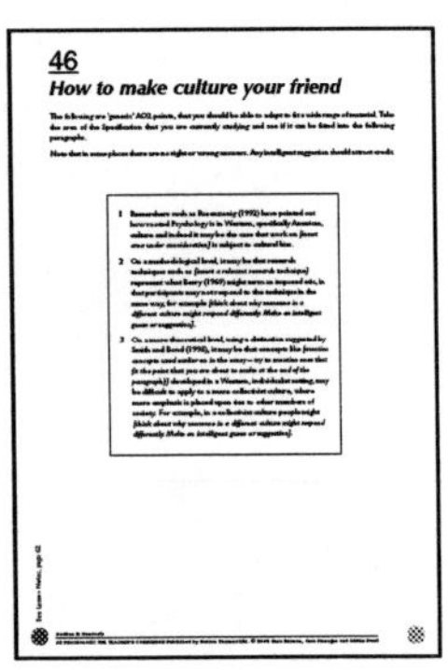
46
How to make culture your friend

Some initial discussion will be required, in order to familiarise students with some quite high-level concepts that have been imported from the 'Issues' section of the A2 paper. Most important however, is practice. If you return to this paragraph at the end of each section or module and ask students to apply it to the material, they will eventually become masters at analysis of material in terms of cultural bias. High-level material will trip off their tongues, especially if they can develop the confidence to make an educated guess at points 2 and 3 on the Handout. A tedious, formulaic, rote-learnt point will start to expand and make a genuine contribution to their argument.

Also, it doesn't matter if they make the same point twice on a paper, as long as it's linked to the material in question.

In terms of the mark scheme, they will be doing several important things.

- Contains reference to three separate researchers*: there is *informed commentary*.
- Makes a distinction between methodological and theoretical issues: there is *reasonably thorough analysis*.
- Links important concepts back to the material under discussion: material is used in an *effective manner*.

*I don't want to leave you with the impression that the key to success is remembering names and dates. It's the grasp of concepts and ideas that matters. See next page for examples.

Cont'd ...

AS PSYCHOLOGY: THE TEACHER'S COMPANION Published by Nelson Thornes Ltd. © 2004 Sara Berman, Cara Flanagan and Adrian Frost

...Continued from previous page

Examples of using the handout

I've (AF) tried to apply the paragraph to four separate areas of the Specification to show how it can work (see **Handout 39**). Cognitive Psychology is, I feel, probably the most difficult area to apply this, but it's always worth 'having a go' and practice definitely brings improvement.

Attachment

Researchers such as Rosenzweig (1992) have pointed out how rooted Psychology is in Western, specifically American, culture and indeed; it may be the case that work on *attachment* is subject to cultural bias.

On a methodological level, it may be that research techniques such as the *Strange Situation* represent what Berry (1969) might term an imposed etic, in that participants may not respond to the technique in the same way, for example, *response to the formal 'laboratory' setting may vary across cultures.*

On a more theoretical level, using a distinction suggested by Smith and Bond 1998, it may be that concepts like *monotropy* developed in a Western, individualist setting, may be difficult to apply to a more collectivist culture, where greater emphasis is placed upon ties to other members of society. For example, in a collectivist culture people might *be more likely to share childcare duties amongst many individuals.*

Causes of abnormality

Researchers such as Rosenzweig (1992) have pointed out how rooted Psychology is in Western, specifically American, culture and indeed it may be the case that work on *the causes of abnormality* is subject to cultural bias.

On a methodological level, it may be that research techniques such as *clinical interviews* represent what Berry (1969) might term an imposed etic, in that participants may not respond to the technique in the same way, for example *people from some cultures may be less willing to discuss personal feelings with a stranger.*

On a more theoretical level, using a distinction suggested by Smith and Bond 1998, it may be that concepts like *depression*, developed in a Western, individualist setting, may be difficult to apply to a more collectivist culture, where greater emphasis is placed upon ties to other members of society. For example, in a collectivist culture people might *be less likely to be depressed as they have more social support.*

Short-term memory

Researchers such as Rosenzweig (1992) have pointed out how rooted Psychology is in Western, specifically American, culture and indeed it may be the case that work on *memory* is subject to cultural bias.

On a methodological level, it may be that research techniques such as *memorising lists of numbers or letters* represent what Berry (1989) might term an imposed etic, in that participants may not respond to the technique in the same way, for example *people from other cultures may be less familiar with this type of task.*

On a more theoretical level, using a distinction suggested by Smith and Bond 1998, it may be that concepts like *working memory* developed in a Western, individualist setting, may be difficult to apply to a more collectivist culture, where more emphasis is placed upon ties to other members of society. For example, in a collectivist culture people might *place less emphasis upon the memory skills of the individual.*

Stress and life events

Researchers such as Rosenzweig (1992) have pointed out how rooted Psychology is in Western, specifically American, culture and indeed it may be the case that work on *life events* is subject to cultural bias.

On a methodological level, it may be that research techniques such as *the Social Readjustment Ratings Scale* represent what Berry (1969) might term an imposed etic, in that participants may not respond to the technique in the same way, for example *many of the life events mentioned may not occur or may be viewed as less important in their culture.*

On a more theoretical level, using a distinction suggested by Smith and Bond 1998, it may be that concepts like *Life Change Units* developed in a Western, individualist setting, may not apply to a more collectivist culture, where more emphasis is placed upon ties to other members of society. For example, in a collectivist culture people might *place more emphasis upon changes to the group rather than to the individual.*

References

Berry, J. (1989) Imposed etics derived emics: the operationalisation of a compelling idea. *International Journal of Psychology*, 24, 721–35.

Rosenzweig, M.R. (1992) Psychological science around the world. *American Psychologist*, 47, 718–22.

Smith, P.B. and Bond, M.H. (1998) *Social Psychology Across Cultures* (2nd Edition). Hemel Hempstead: Prentice Hall Europe.

AS PSYCHOLOGY: THE TEACHER'S COMPANION Published by Nelson Thornes Ltd. © 2004 Sara Berman, Cara Flanagan and Adrian Frost

Revision task: Bowlby's theory of attachment

Handout 47

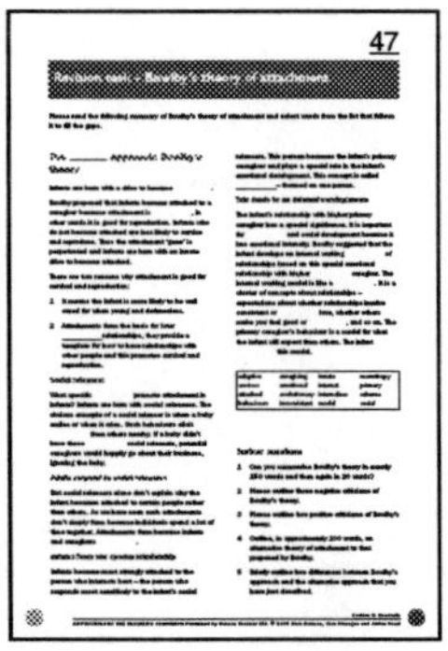

Research activity: Hazan and Shaver love quiz (1987)

Hazan, C. and Shaver, P.R. (1987) Romantic love conceptualised as an attachment process. *Journal of Personality and Social Psychology*, 52, 511–24.

Bowlby's theory of attachment suggests that the infant's relationship with his/her primary caregiver forms the basis of the child's internal working model of relationships. This will affect the child's expectations about what relationships (including romantic ones) will be like. Therefore we would expect a link between early attachments, attitudes about romantic relationships and actual romantic relationships. This is called the *Continuity Hypothesis* and can be taken as support for Bowlby's hypothesis. (Though there is an alternative possibility – that an individual's innate temperament is a key factor in early attachments and in later relationships. This is called the *Temperament Hypothesis*.)

Hazan and Shaver (1987) extended Bowlby's idea that later love relationships should be predictable from knowledge of an individual's early attachment style. In particular, they predicted the consequences shown in the table below.

Hazen and Shaver's study

Hazan and Shaver (1987) tested Bowlby's hypothesis with their 'love quiz'. This was a quiz of nearly 100 questions published in the *Rocky Mountain News*. They received 620 replies to their questionnaire and drew the following conclusions.

Securely attached adults:

- had certain beliefs about relationships (love is enduring);
- reported certain experiences in relationships (e.g. mutual trust);
- were less likely to have been divorced.

	Secure adults	Resistant (anxious) adults	Avoidant adults
Different love experiences	Relationships are positive	Preoccupied by love	Fearful of closeness.
Adults' views of relationships	Trust others and believe in enduring love	Fall in love easily but have trouble finding *true* love	Love is not durable nor necessary for happiness
Memories of the mother–child relationship	Positive image of mother as dependable and caring	Conflicting memories of mother being positive *and* rejecting	Remember mothers as cold and rejecting

Cont'd ...

AS PSYCHOLOGY: THE TEACHER'S COMPANION Published by Nelson Thornes Ltd. © 2004 Sara Berman, Cara Flanagan and Adrian Frost

...Continued from previous page

Insecurely attached adults:

- felt true love was rare, and fell in and out of love easily;
- found relationships less easy;
- were more likely to be divorced.

In terms of attachment style 56 per cent classified themselves as secure, 25 per cent as avoidant and 19 per cent as resistant. Love experience and attitudes towards love (internal working model) were related to attachment type.

In the short version of the quiz on **Handout 48** the questions make assessments as follows:

- Q 1, 2 and 3 assess attachment history.
- Q 4, 5 and 6 assess adult attachment type.
- Q 7, 8 and 9 assess mental models of relationships.

Handout 48

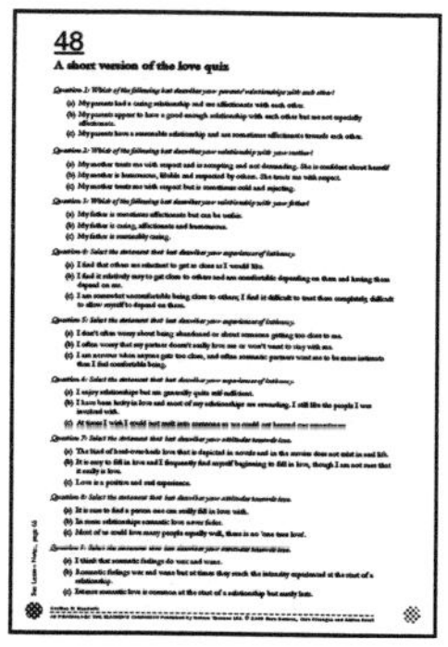
48
A short version of the love quiz

Ethics briefing

This study involves questions that may be related to sensitive information about an individual's early life experiences and which may suggest problematic adult relationships. Always seek informed consent beforehand, where possible, or offer thorough debriefing including the right to withhold individual data. In this case one should emphasise that the suggested correlation between early experience and later relationships is not 100 per cent – there are many individuals who overcome early, unfavourable circumstances. In addition this correlation is not proven.

To work out scores used the table below.

	Question	a	b	c
Part C	1	secure	insecure avoidant	insecure resistant
	2	secure	insecure resistant	insecure avoidant
	3	insecure resistant	secure	insecure avoidant
	Score for part A (the dominant category chosen (secure, insecure-avoidant or insecure-resistant) =			
Part B	4	insecure resistant	insecure avoidant	secure
	5	secure	insecure resistant	insecure avoidant
	6	insecure avoidant	secure	insecure resistant
	Score for part B (the dominant category chosen (secure, insecure-avoidant or insecure-resistant) =			
Part A	7	insecure avoidant	insecure resistant	secure
	8	insecure avoidant	secure	insecure resistant
	9	insecure resistant	secure	insecure avoidant
	Score for part C (the dominant category chosen (secure, insecure-avoidant or insecure-resistant) =			

AS PSYCHOLOGY: THE TEACHER'S COMPANION Published by Nelson Thornes Ltd. © 2004 Sara Berman, Cara Flanagan and Adrian Frost

Is your biological mother your primary caregiver?

This question offers students the opportunity to discuss varying family experiences (e.g. adoption, fostering, separation). And for you to be aware of their different attachment experiences.

Does it matter? What aspects of development might be affected? Positive or negative consequences?

Bowlby's Maternal Deprivation Hypothesis and Attachment Theory

I have done this activity because when I first studied these two theories I was confused about which was which. To be fair there is a significant amount of overlap, which is not surprising since one grew out of the other. I always tell students one way to remember the difference is that I (CF) was born in 1951 (the year Bowlby first published the Maternal Deprivation Hypothesis in his book *Maternal Care and Mental Health*) and in 1969 I went to university (the year he published *Attachment and Loss. Volume 1: Attachment*).

If students encounter some difficulties in determining which belongs where the answers are provided below – not all textbooks are accurate about these two theories.

Handout 49 gives a list of sentences that should be placed in one column or the other.

Handout 49

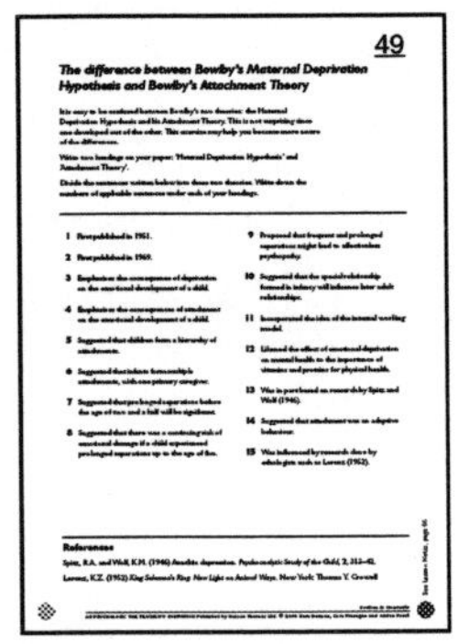

The correct answers to the task given on **Handout 49** are as follows.

Maternal Deprivation Hypothesis: Numbers 1, 3, 7, 8, 9, 12, 13.

Attachment Theory: Numbers 2, 4, 5, 6, 10, 11, 14, 15.

 © 2004 Sara Berman, Cara Flanagan and Adrian Frost

Star Study by Hodges and Tizard (1989)

Hodges, J., and Tizard, B. (1989) Social and family relationships of ex-institutional adolescents. *Journal of Child Psychology and Psychiatry*, 30, 77–97.

This study is named in the Specification, not as an example but a study which may be specified explicitly in an exam question. This means that students must know the full details of the study – though only enough to provide 3 to 4 marks worth of material on aims, procedures, findings, conclusions and criticisms.

Handouts 50 and 51

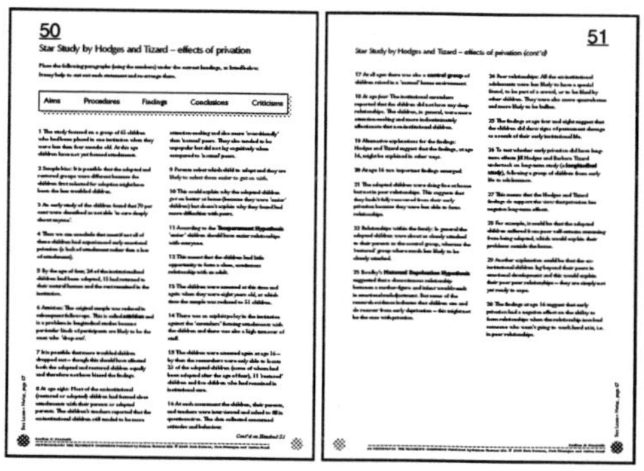
50
Star Study by Hodges and Tizard – effects of privation
Aims | Procedures | Findings | Conclusions | Criticisms
51
Star Study by Hodges and Tizard – effects of privation (cont'd)

Handouts 50 and **51** contains a jumbled version of the study (details of this Star Study are also on PowerPoint).

The correct version from *The Complete Companion* is given below.

Aims

Bowlby's *Maternal Deprivation Hypothesis* suggested that a discontinuous relationship between a mother-figure and infant would result in emotional maladjustment. But some of the research evidence indicates that children can and do recover from early deprivation – this might not be the case with privation. To test whether early privation did have long-term effects Jill Hodges and Barbara Tizard undertook on long-term study (a *longitudinal study*), following a group of children from early life to adolescence.

Procedures

The study focused on a group of 65 children who had been placed in one institution when they were less than four months old. At this age children have not yet formed attachments. There was an explicit policy in the institution against the 'caretakers' forming attachments with the children and there was also a high turnover of staff. This meant that the children had little opportunity to form a close, continuous relationship with an adult. An early study of the children found that 70 per cent were described as not able 'to care deeply about anyone'. Thus we can conclude that most if not all of these children had experienced early emotional privation (a lack of attachment rather than a loss of attachment).

By the age of four, 24 of the institutionalised children had been adopted, 15 had returned to their natural homes and the rest remained in the institution. The children were assessed at this time and again when they were eight years old, at which time the sample was reduced to 51 children. The children were assessed again at age 16 – by then the researchers were only able to locate 23 of the adopted children (some of whom had been adopted after the age of four), 11 'restored' children and five children who had remained in institutional care.

At each assessment the children, their parents and teachers were interviewed and asked to fill in questionnaires. The data collected concerned attitudes and behaviour.

At all ages there was also a *control group* of children raised in a 'normal' home environment.

Findings

At age four: The institutional caretakers reported that the children did not have any deep relationships. The children, in general, were more attention-seeking and more indiscriminately affectionate that non-institutional children.

At age eight: Most of the ex-institutional (restored or adopted) children had formed close attachments with their parents or adopted parents. The children's teachers reported that the ex-institutional children still tended to be more attention-seeking and also more 'over-friendly' than 'normal' peers. They also tended to be unpopular but did not lag cognitively when compared to 'normal' peers.

At age 16 *two important findings emerged*.

1 Relationships within the family: In general the adopted children were about as closely attached to their parents as the control group, whereas the 'restored' group where much less likely to be closely attached.

Cont'd ...

AS PSYCHOLOGY: THE TEACHER'S COMPANION Published by Nelson Thornes Ltd. © 2004 Sara Berman, Cara Flanagan and Adrian Frost

...Continued from previous page

2 Peer relationships: All the ex-institutional adolescents were less likely to have a special friend, to be part of a crowd, or to be liked by other children. They were also more quarrelsome and more likely to be bullies.

Conclusions

The findings at age four and eight suggest that the children did show signs of permanent damage as a result of their early institutional life.

The findings at age 16 suggest that early privation had a negative effect on the ability to form relationships when the relationship involved someone who wasn't going to work hard at it, i.e. in peer relationships. The adopted children were doing fine at home but not in peer relationships. This suggests that they hadn't fully recovered from their early privation because they were less able to form relationships.

Criticisms

Attrition

The original sample was reduced in subsequent follow-ups. This is called *attrition* and is a problem in longitudinal studies because particular kinds of participants are likely to be the ones who 'drop out'. It is possible that more troubled children dropped out – though this should have affected both the adopted and restored children equally and therefore not have biased the findings.

Sample bias

It is also possible that the adopted and restored groups were different because the children first selected for adoption might have been the less troubled children. Parents select which child to adopt and they are likely to select those easier to get on with. This could explain why the adopted children got on better at home (because they were 'easier' children) but doesn't explain why they were found to have had more difficulties with peers. According to the *Temperament Hypothesis* 'easier' children should have easier relationships with everyone. This means that the Hodges and Tizard findings do support the view that privation has negative long-term effects.

Alternative explanations for the findings

Hodges and Tizard suggest that the findings, at age 16, might be explained in other ways. For example, it could be that the adopted children suffered from poor self-esteem stemming from being adopted, which would explain their problems outside the home. Another explanation could be that the ex-institutional children lag beyond their peers in emotional development and this would explain their poor peer relationships – they are simply not yet ready to cope.

Correct answers

Aims	23, 26
Procedures	1, 14, 12, 3, 4, 5, 12, 15, 16, 17
Findings	18, 8, 20, 22, 24
Conclusions	25, 30, 21
Criticisms	6, 7, 2, 9, 10, 11, 27, 19, 28, 29

AS PSYCHOLOGY: THE TEACHER'S COMPANION Published by Nelson Thornes Ltd. © 2004 Sara Berman, Cara Flanagan and Adrian Frost

What is day care?

Discuss with students the nature of day care. Try to define what it is. Consider various forms of care and look at similarities and differences. What day care experiences have they had themselves?

Research activity: Day care interviews

Various activities are suggested below related to day care. Each permits a student to find out more about the process of research design and an opportunity to think more deeply about day care issues.

1 An interview for mothers

Arrange to interview mothers about day care. This is time consuming but teaches students all about interviewing while they collect information about day care.

Design decisions.

- Structured or unstructured interview (probably best to try a mixture).
- What information do you want to find out about day care? For example, where the mother didn't work, then what affected her decision not to work? What are her attitudes about day care (e.g. is it harmful to social or cognitive development?). Students should be encouraged to brainstorm this material.
- Write questions out (see **Handout 32** about questionnaire design).

2 An attitude survey (form of questionnaire survey)

This would enable more data to be collected and might even provide the basis for A2 coursework. Instructions for constructing a Thurstone scale are provided on **Handout 52**. It involves the use of *standard deviation* which might be useful to cover.

Handout 52

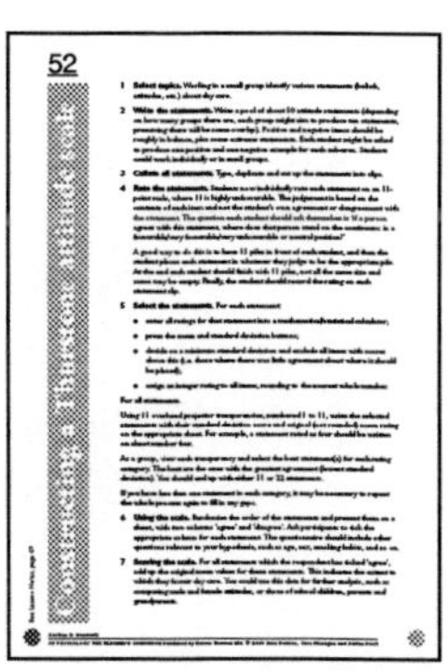
52

Constructing a Thurstone attitude scale

3 A correlational survey: day care and GCSE results

This activity is taken from *The Complete Companion*.

A recent study (Ermisch and Francesconi 2000) found a *negative correlation* between a child's educational attainment and how much the child's mother had been working when the child was under five. In other words the more a mother worked, the less good the educational achievement – or, to put it a different way, a mother who didn't work at all was likely to have a child who did well at school.

Reference

Ermisch, J. and Francesconi, M. (2000) Educational choice, families and young people's earnings. *Journal of Human Resources*, 35(1), 143–76

Instructions for replicating this study are given on **Handout 53**.

Handout 53

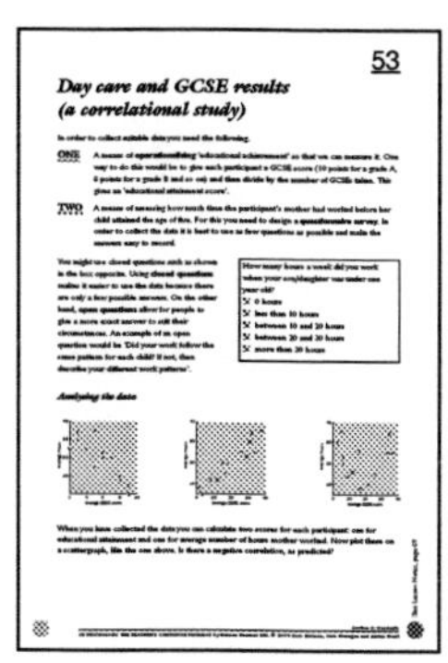
53

Day care and GCSE results (a correlational study)

AS PSYCHOLOGY: THE TEACHER'S COMPANION Published by Nelson Thornes Ltd. © 2004 Sara Berman, Cara Flanagan and Adrian Frost

MODULE: **Developmental Psychology**
SECTION: **Critical issue: Day care**
TOPIC: **The effects of day care on cognitive development**

Why might day care affect cognitive development?

Based on Bowlby's theory, discuss why day care could affect cognitive and social development.

Ask students to use their knowledge of Bowlby's theory of attachment to provide resons why day care would have positive and negative effects on cognitive and social development.

Assessing the quality of day care centres

Despite the fact that most students should have personal experiences of day care (so the statistics suggest) they appear to have little insight into what this involves or how they felt about it – or they are unwilling to discuss events so far back. So it might be helpful to revive their interest in day care or at least familiarise themselves with what happens at a nursery, and at the same time they can try some qualitative research!

There are two approaches to qualitative research.

1 *Grounded theory*. An interview text or any discourse (conversation) is examined. Recurrent and/or important themes are identified, and used to give insight into the topic of study.

2 *Thematic analysis*. Themes or concepts are identified before starting the research. Then responses from an interview or questionnaire are organised according to the themes.

Students might start by looking at advertisements for day care provision that are on the web ('grounded theory') and drawing up a list of the factors that they use to advertise themselves. They should work out some way to rate these.

They could also look at their notes on day care and decide on criteria that are likely to be important (e.g. the number and quality of staff, the activities offered, the physical surroundings. This is thematic analysis.

You might also look at the child care checklist offered on http://www.extension.iastate.edu/Publications/PM1805.pdf

They should now devise their own system of assessing day care providers and produce a report on one or more centres. Such reports can be quantitative (perform a content analysis using the criteria selected) or qualitative (write a commentary related to the criteria selected, but including particular details).

MODULE: **Developmental Psychology**
SECTION: **Critical Issue: Day care**
TOPIC: **The effects of day care on social development**

Reviewing day care evidence

Handouts 54 and **55** provide students with an opportunity to assemble research evidence related to the day care debate, and to explore the kind of evidence they could use in an essay.

This highlights the possibility that they could be asked specifically about effects on cognitive or social development.

Handouts 54 and 55

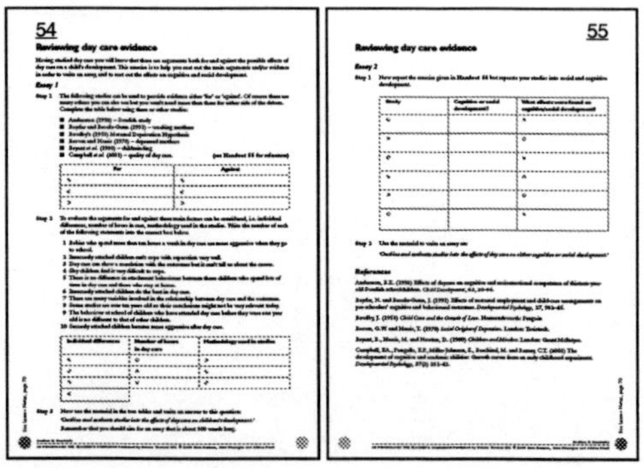

AS PSYCHOLOGY: THE TEACHER'S COMPANION Published by Nelson Thornes Ltd. © 2004 Sara Berman, Cara Flanagan and Adrian Frost

MODULE: **Physiological Pyschology**
SECTION: **Stress as a bodily response**
TOPIC: **The body's response to stressors**

Introduction to stress, including ethics

This has to be done before any mention of stress. The teacher has to stress the class – how this is done will depend on the teacher's ability to 'act' and what else is happening at school. For example, if reports are due out, telling the class that the surprise test they are about to sit will influence the grade that goes on the report. Or if a piece of work is due back, rant and rage to the group about how dreadful it was, how they are all going to fail, etc. After a few minutes of this start to ask named individuals (those who are robust and will cope) how they are feeling. Do this in a cross and angry manner, ask them to describe their physical feelings. At this point one or two of the bright ones might start to see the point. Once the students have described at least one or two stress responses (sweaty palms, butterflies in stomach, faster heart beat – other signs of ANS activity include sweaty armpits, dry mouth, dilated pupils) the teacher 'confesses'. Students are thoroughly debriefed and asked to describe how they feel. This exercise allows the teacher to introduce the physical feelings of stress and explain that students will soon learn why the body responds like this. This approach also allows the discussion of ethics.

The GAS model: Learning to précis information

Learning how to précis information and use it for different purposes. See pages 25–26 of the General Notes.

Handout 1

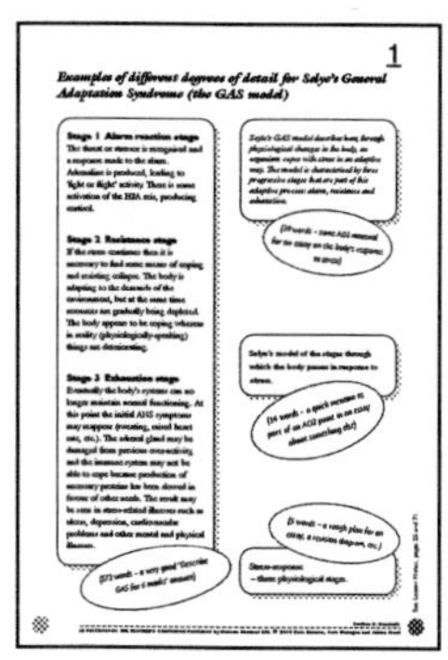

AS PSYCHOLOGY: THE TEACHER'S COMPANION Published by Nelson Thornes Ltd. © 2004 Sara Berman, Cara Flanagan and Adrian Frost

Testing stress responses and cardiovascular activity

You might use resources such as a heart rate monitor, or measure blood pressure. Biodots can be used to measure stress. They are small, self-adhesive, temperature-sensitive discs that indicate temperature by changing colour. Temperature changes are due to changes in the amount of blood flowing through the skin. When a person is tense and stressed their skin blood vessels constrict, reducing blood flow and lowering skin temperature. Yellow, amber or black indicates stress whereas turquoise, blue or voilet is related to relaxation. Biodots can be obtained from: Stresswise, PO BOX 5, Congleton, Cheshire, CW1 1XE. The current price for 100 biodots is £14. Cheques should be made payable to Stresswise. You should allow 28 days for delivery, though they usually arrive within two weeks.

Prepare a leaflet: 'Looking after your heart'

One way of getting students to summarise information effectively is to ask them to produce leaflets (or a PowerPoint display). These can be attractive and slightly more entertaining than producing revision summaries.

A good example is a leaflet on 'How to look after your heart'. These can be based upon the conclusions of psychological research into stress and cardiovascular disorders and could include advice on the following:

- what sort of job to get;
- the importance of family support;
- strategies for coping with stress;
- warning signs, etc.

However, even more fun is the ironic 'How to have a heart attack' leaflet, which brings a shade of black humour to proceedings. This can include advice like 'Leave your job and move far away from family and friends. Relocate to an area of high air-traffic density, where planes fly low over your house at unpredictable intervals. Get a job as an air-traffic controller, preferably on the night shift, and then divorce your partner. To cope with this, drink and smoke lots, but, whatever you do, never, ever tell anyone how you feel or admit that you are not in control of your life'.

Indeed, even if you don't want to create the leaflet, it is an interesting revision activity to ask students to work together to describe the very worst cardiac arrest inducing lifestyle possible. (Remember to get them to concentrate upon psychological, stress-related factors rather than factors such as diet or genes.)

AS PSYCHOLOGY: THE TEACHER'S COMPANION Published by Nelson Thornes Ltd. © 2004 Sara Berman, Cara Flanagan and Adrian Frost

The relationship between stress and physical illness

Stress and the body is a good topic through which to develop student understanding of statistical analysis.

Questionnaires can be used to gather data on levels of stress and illness and the relationship between the two can then be examined. The difficult part is finding ways to quantify stress and illness and thus generate 'scores' for each individual.

One way to quantify stress is to use versions of stress scales typically covered by AS students such as the SRRS or the Hassles and Uplifts scale. These can, however, be problematic, as, for example, many events on the SRRS do not readily apply to AS Level students and complete versions of the latter are not always readily available in texts.

Alternatively, students could develop their own stress scales. This is time consuming, but can be useful as part of an overall critique of existing scales. Students could, for example, develop a life events or a daily hassles scale that *does* relate more specifically relate to AS Level students. (For example, where are computer viruses, spam emails or company 'call waiting' systems on the current scales?)

Illness is perhaps a little easier to quantify as one can use 'days off' as a measure – although, as we know, there are a wide-range of 'non-illness' factors that students regard as justifying a day off !

A simple exercise is to hand out a photocopy of your register (perhaps with the names blanked out) and compare attendance for 'stressful' periods, such as the month preceding exams, and 'non-stressful' periods (if such a time exists). Average attendance can be calculated for each month and plotted on a frequency distribution curve (see graph).

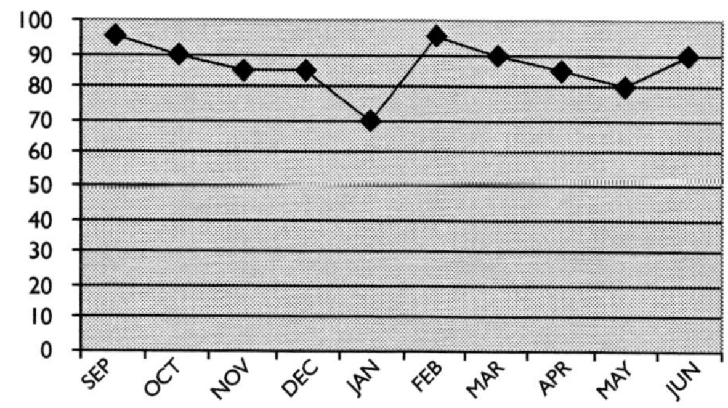

Percentage attendance in Psychology classes over one year

Of course attendance at school/college isn't a particularly valid measure of health and there are a million other variables that could come into play here, but discussion of such limitations should help deepen student understanding.

Another useful source of data is that which underlies the 'Life Expectancy Calculator' on the BBC website at http://www.bbc.co.uk/health/interactivearea/living_100.shtml Here you are asked a range of questions about your family, lifestyle, etc. and your responses are used to calculate your predicted life expectancy. The questions cover everything from sleeping habits to sausage consumption, but some of them relate directly to issues on this section of the Specification, such as personality type, level of social support, etc. It's interesting to 'tweak' these and examine the effect upon overall life expectancy.

The whole thing is based upon extensive, statistically robust research and does give students a real feel for the way in which a multitude of social, cultural, genetic, environmental and psychological factors combine to affect an individual's health and life expectancy. Be warned though! It will at one point calculate your body mass index – you may be surprised at who comes out at overweight! (Well OK, in my (AF) case maybe no-one was surprised.)

AS PSYCHOLOGY: THE TEACHER'S COMPANION Published by Nelson Thornes Ltd. © 2004 Sara Berman, Cara Flanagan and Adrian Frost

MODULE: **Physiological Pyschology**
SECTION: **Stress as a bodily response**
TOPIC: **Stress and physical illness: The immune system**

Quiz: The body's response to stressors

Handout 59

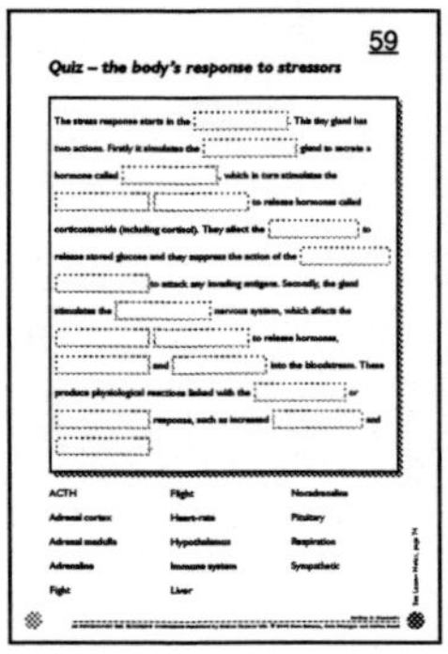
59

Quiz – the body's response to stressors

The stress response starts in the ______. This tiny gland has two actions. Firstly it stimulates the ______ gland to secrete a hormone called ______, which in turn stimulates the ______ ______ to release hormones called corticosteroids (including cortisol). They affect the ______ to release stored glucose and they suppress the action of the ______ ______ to attack any invading antigens. Secondly, the gland stimulates the ______ nervous system, which affects the ______ ______ to release hormones, ______ and ______ into the bloodstream. These produce physiological reactions linked with the ______ or ______ response, such as increased ______ and ______.

ACTH	Flight	Noradrenaline
Adrenal cortex	Heart-rate	Pituitary
Adrenal medulla	Hypothalamus	Respiration
Adrenaline	Immune system	Sympathetic
Fight	Liver	

MODULE: **Physiological Psychology**
SECTION: **Sources of stress**
TOPIC: **Life changes**

A short illness questionnaire

Conduct a short illness questionnaire. For instance ask 'What makes people ill?' 'Why do some people experience more ill health than others?'

AS PSYCHOLOGY: THE TEACHER'S COMPANION Published by Nelson Thornes Ltd. © 2004 Sara Berman, Cara Flanagan and Adrian Frost

A little bit of soap (Using the SRRS)

The best way to teach Holmes and Rahe's 'Social Readjustment Rating Scale' is, of course, to *use* it. Most textbooks give a version of the scale and most students need little encouragement to tot up their own scores. It is given on page 104 of *The Complete Companion*. (This is probably the point in the lesson to make clear that the relationship between scores and likelihood of major illness is not that strong!)

That said, it's not always appropriate to ask students to do this. Whilst we shouldn't shy away from helping students make Psychology relevant to their own experience, asking an entire class to recall 18 months' worth of stressful events will probably open up the odd 'can of worms' that it might not be appropriate to deal with in a lesson.

The solution? Use a group of people whose life histories we know intimately and whose actions we can analyse to our heart's content – soap opera characters.

Any soap will do, but *Eastenders* seems to provide the most tragic bunch of individuals. A cursory trawl through the recent history of any of the major characters will provide evidence of more than enough 'life change' and the chances of their suffering a major illness can be calculated from there. (The curiously robust constitutions of most of the characters shouldn't discredit the theory though!)

This can be approached using handouts such as the example of **Handout 60**, to be used as a light-hearted introduction to the topic.

Handout 60

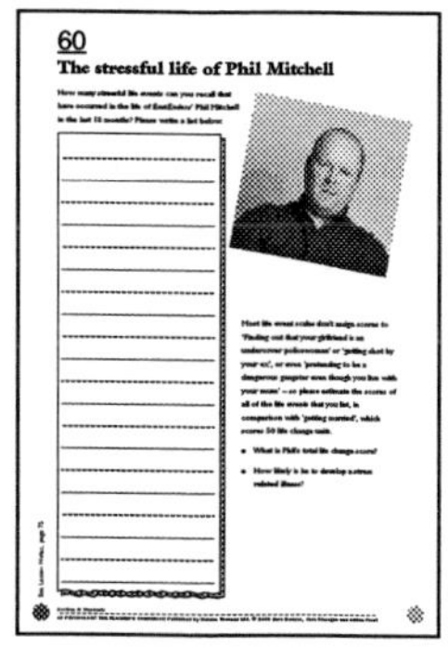
60
The stressful life of Phil Mitchell

I've seen other lecturers use *Eastenders* characters to illustrate various attachment types, as there are some whose life histories we know so well that we can speculate upon how childrearing styles affected their adult personalities. Of course soap operas, with their emphasis upon family bonds and betrayal, are also perfect for discussion of the psychodynamic approach. (Though, in my experience, nothing comes close to the complicated father–son relationship of the Skywalkers in terms of illustrating the Oedipus Complex!)

Don't watch soap operas? – 'Too much marking' will only provide you with a partial excuse here. There are however solutions: one is to allow the ardent soapwatchers in the class to become the experts in this context and to present the material to you. Or, if you want to root a lesson in more concrete stimulus material, character biographies are available on the BBC website.

How well do you know your Star Study?

Rahe, R.H., Mahan, J. and Arthur, R. (1970) Prediction of near-future health-change from subjects' preceding life changes. *Journal of Psychosomatic Research*, 14, 401–06.

Handout 61 gives a version of the Star Study from *The Complete Companion* with 22 mistakes. The version below is the correct version, with errors highlighted.

The actual study:

Star Study on life changes as a source of stress (Rahe *et al.* 1970)

Aim

Rahe *et al.* used the Social Readjustment Ratings Scale to test Holmes and Rahe's hypothesis that the number of life events a person experienced would be positively correlated with illness. Rahe *et al.* aimed in particular to study a 'normal' population as distinct from the populations previously studied of individuals who were already ill in hospital.

Procedures

A version of the SRRS was given to all the men aboard three US Navy Cruisers, a total of over

Cont'd ...

...Continued from previous page

2700 men. The men filled the questionnaire in just before a tour of duty, noting all the life events experienced over the previous 6 months.

An illness score was calculated on the basis of the number, type and severity of all illnesses recorded during the tour of duty (about 7 months). Rahe *et al.* didn't include sick bay visits that appeared to be due to a desire to get out of work (because the individual wasn't actually ill).

Findings

An LCU score and an illness score was calculated for each man. Rahe *et al.* found a positive correlation between these scores of +0.118. A positive correlation is one where both co-variables increase together. The number 0.118 expresses how closely the co-variables varied together. 0.118 is not a very strong correlation but given the number of participants it is significant.

Conclusions

The findings support the hypothesis of a link or positive correlation between life changes/events and physical illness. It is possible that the link is stress: life changes cause stress and we know that stress causes illness. Therefore life changes are sources of stress. Both positive and negative events are included in the SRRS so we see that it is change rather than negativity that is important. It is the overall amount of 'psychic energy' required to deal with an event that creates stress.

Handout 61

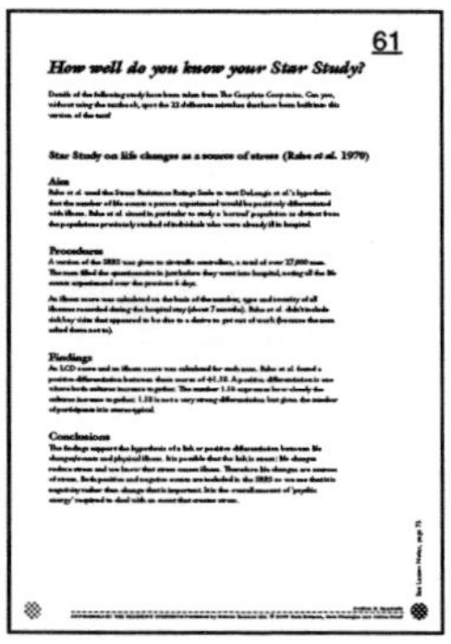
61
How well do you know your Star Study?

Assess the hassles in your life

Adapted from Schafer, W. (1992) *Stress Management for Wellness* (2nd edition). Harcourt Brace Jovanovich.

Handout 62 provides a questionnaire that is relevant to students and permits them to assess their daily hassles. The score can be correlated with a 'health score'. Discuss how you might calculate such a score, how would you operationalise health, e.g. counting days of absence. (See discussion on page 75.)

Correlational data can be plotted on a scattergraph. If this is done on Excel you will be given the correlation coefficient.

Handout 62

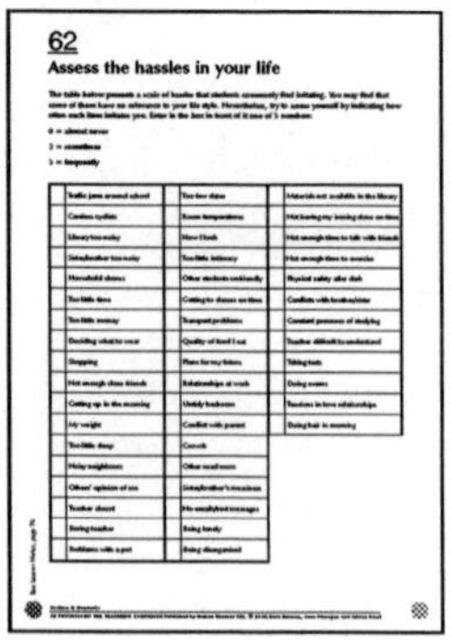
62
Assess the hassles in your life

AS PSYCHOLOGY: THE TEACHER'S COMPANION Published by Nelson Thornes Ltd. © 2004 Sara Berman, Cara Flanagan and Adrian Frost

Is school more stressful than work?

Discuss the question of whether attending school and undergoing examinations are more stressful than attending paid work. For students who have part-time jobs you could discuss what causes them stress at work.

Make those monkeys do some work for you!

Brady, J.V. (1958) Ulcers in executive monkeys. *Scientific American*, 199, 95–100.

Everyone always remembers Brady's controversial 'Executive Monkey' study and it seems to crop up on a large number of student papers, whatever the question is.

Each year this causes a major headache for examiners on Unit 2, as they have to decide whether or not the study is relevant to the question asked. For example, if the monkeys are referred to as 'executives', can they automatically be taken as relevant to questions on 'workplace stressors' or does the candidate have to make the link explicit? Can the study be relevant to questions on the immune system or cardiovascular disorders? and so on ...*

The simple answer to these questions is – the study can be used in all sorts of places, *as long as you make it relevant by clearly linking the material to the question*. The best way to decide where the study can be used is to remind students of two things: the details of the study and the details of the Specification. Both of these are included in **Handouts 63** and **64**, which requires students to consider the issue of where Brady's study can be used.

Handouts 63 and 64

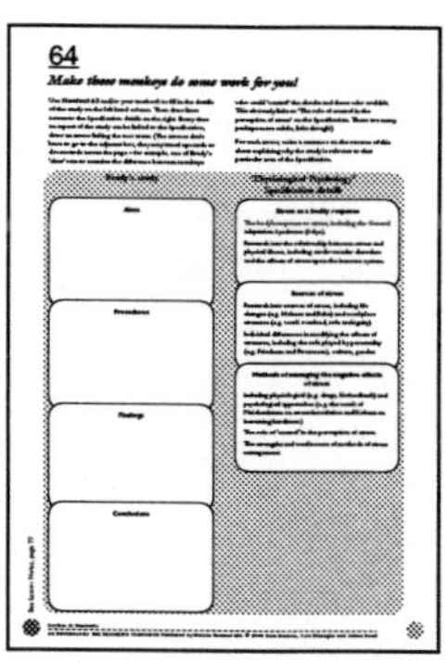

(The other approach is, of course, not to teach Brady at all. It's a classic, but then students often get confused about when to use it and it isn't required by the Spec. Loathe as I (AF) am to 'dump' a classic, memorable study, which is great for 'animal ethics' in the second year, perhaps they may be better off using other material?)

*In answer, the study can contribute to a 'workplace' essay, though the link to 'executives' in the workplace has to be made clear. For the latter questions, as the monkeys were examined for stomach ulceration, the student will have to work *really* hard to make a link to the immune system or CHD. They might be better advised opting for studies more firmly rooted in these particular areas.

References

Holmes, T.H. and Rahe, R.H. (1967) The social readjustment rating scale. *Journal of Psychosomatic Research*, 11, 213–18

Friedman, M. and Rosenman, R.H. (1959) Association of specific overt behaviour pattern with blood and cardiovascular findings. *Journal of the American Medical Association*, 169, 1286–96.

Kobasa, S.C. (1979) Personality and resistance to illness. *American Journal of Community Psychology*, 7, 413–23.

Meichenbaum, D. (1985) *Stress Inoculation Training*. New York: Pergamon.

Selye, H. (1950) *Stress*. Montreal: Acta.

AS PSYCHOLOGY: THE TEACHER'S COMPANION Published by Nelson Thornes Ltd. © 2004 Sara Berman, Cara Flanagan and Adrian Frost

MODULE: **Physiological Psychology**
SECTION: **Sources of stress**
TOPIC: **Individual differences: The role of personality**

What type are you? Type A or type B questionnaire

Friedman, M. and Rosenman, R.H. (1974) Type A behaviour and your Heart. New York: Knopf.

Friedman and Rosenman (1974) investigated the relationship between personality type and CHD. They used the Jenkins Activity Survey to measure personality type. The questionnaire on **Handout 65** (with scoring on **Handout 66**) is a modified version of the JAS (modified for 16 to 18 year old students).

Students can also find out whether they are Type A or Type B by taking a test online: http://discoveryhealth.queendom.com. The website gives a description of Type A behaviours and will also score your questionnaire for you and tell you a little bit about your personality. Takes about 10 to 15 minutes.

Handouts 65 and 66

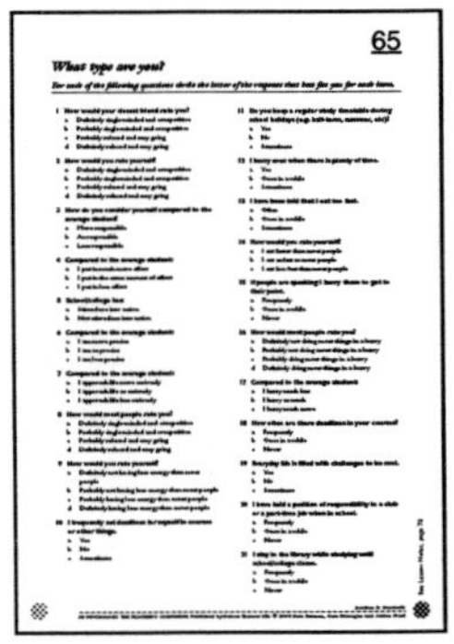

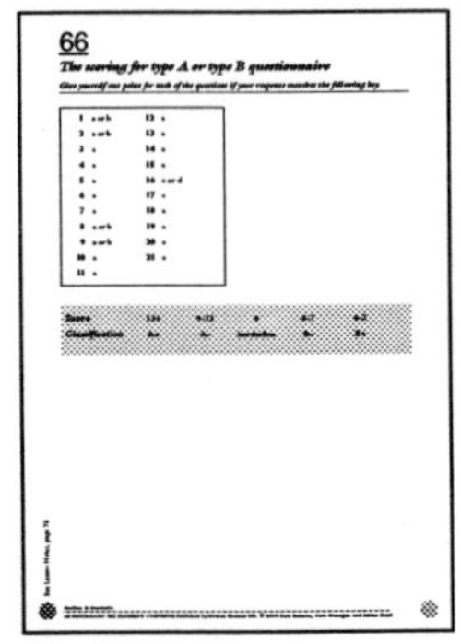

MODULE: **Physiological Psychology**
SECTION: **Sources of stress**
TOPIC: **Individual differences: The role of culture**

Ideas for discussion on stress and culture

This tends to be an area where students perform badly in the exam. Like the cognitive model of abnormality, this is a topic that students will only stray into if enticed by a more popular sub-question further along the paper.

As always, start with the Specification, which says the following.

'Individual differences in modifying the effects of stressors, including the role played by personality (e.g. Friedman and Rosenman), culture, gender.'

There are several factors to note here.

1. There's no requirement for a Star Study here, as research is not specifically asked for, so no 'APFCC' question can be set. This means that specific details of research can be used to illustrate and deepen points, but they aren't specifically required for full marks.
2. Students need to be aware that their culture material could be used in questions that ask about 'individual differences' but don't specifically mention culture.
3. There is considerable overlap between the areas of personality, culture and gender. Friedman and Rosenman's study concerned *Western men* with Type A *personalities* – such material could be usefully employed for any question in this area – though candidates would, of course, have to make it relevant to the question.
4. The term 'culture' will be interpreted very widely by examiners encompassing, for example, subcultures and work-place cultures – though again candidates would, of course, have to make it relevant to the question.

The next step is to look at past questions (Try http://www.aqa.org.uk/qual/gceasa/psyA_assess.html for past papers). Which should lead you to questions like the following from May 2003.

- 'Outline the role of culture in modifying the effects of stressors.'

Cont'd ...

AS PSYCHOLOGY: THE TEACHER'S COMPANION Published by Nelson Thornes Ltd. © 2004 Sara Berman, Cara Flanagan and Adrian Frost

...Continued from previous page

Several factors are worth noting.

1 Note the link to 'modifying the effects of stressors' – lifted straight from the Specification. Lots of candidates slipped up here. They presented examples of differences between cultures (such as variations in poverty, climate, etc.), but did not link this to the effects of stressors.

2 The question is quite broad – description of any number of cultural factors is creditworthy, providing the link to stress is made. In other years the question could, for example, specifically ask for two factors.

In terms of implications for teaching, this means the following.

1 Emphasis upon cultural factors/differences, with research being used to support such points.

2 Clear need to link such cultural factors to 'modifying the effects of stress'.

The 'size and shape' of this section is thus something like the following.

Cultural difference	Role in modifying the effect of stressors
1	
2	
3	

It may be best to 'go deep' on three factors, perhaps providing discussion and one or two bits of research evidence for each, rather than extend the list any further.

A good list of factors to start with might be the following.

- Individual/collectivist cultures.
- Social support – e.g. family, religion.
- Diet and lifestyle.

All of these are addressed in *The Complete Companion*.

In general, this is a difficult area to 'kick-start' and I find that initial discussion needs something quite structured, like the following, to get it going:

'Questions for the board' on culture and stress

1 What is a 'culture'?

2 In what way do people from one culture differ from those in another?

3 What are individualist and collectivist cultures? Can you think of examples of each? (If you have covered 'Attachment' already, look back at those notes for clues.)

4 In what way might living in each of these cultures make life more or less stressful?

5 If people are stressed, what types of social support can they turn to? How would these vary from culture to culture?

6 How might diet and lifestyle affect stress? How do these vary from culture to culture?

Fantasy island

When we taught Plato's *Republic* for AS Level Philosophy, one of my (AF) colleagues used to get students to design their own 'perfect' political systems in order to deepen student understanding of Plato's proposed model.

Similarly, a Psychology colleague of mine asks students to draw islands, which are administered by psychologists of a particular theoretical persuasion. Society upon such islands could be run according to particular sets of psychological principals, so presumably toilet training is particularly important on the Isle of Freud, whereas strict reinforcement timetables will be in place at Behavioural Beach.

This sort of approach is exemplified in **Handout 67** on stress and culture.

Handout 67

Cont'd ...

MODULE: **Physiological Psychology**
SECTION: **Sources of stress**
TOPIC: Individual differences: The role of culture

...Continued from previous page

I've asked students to design nursery systems in order to promote cognitive or social development or societies that prevent the onset of eating disorders; indeed any aspect of the Specification which emphasises environmental factors is ripe for 'If psychologists ruled the world' type conjecture. I know that such speculation has gone out of fashion a bit since the days of 'Brave New World' and 'Walden Two', but students like the opportunity to 'play God' and apply their psychological knowledge.

Of course, it is even more entertaining to speculate upon systems specifically designed to *hinder* psychological development ... much more fun to be the architect of 'Phillip Larkin World'!

MODULE: **Physiological Psychology**
SECTION: **Sources of stress**
TOPIC: Individual differences: The role of gender

Personal reactions to stress

Discuss with students what their individual reactions to stress tend to be. When you get stressed, what do you do? Do boys and girls behave differently? What things increase or decrease your stress responses?

Compare male and female behaviour on stress task (wordsearch)

This exercise can be used for all sorts of investigations of stress. It shows how a relatively simple task can still cause stress – as seen by an increase in pulse rate. There are various tasks that can be chosen but there must be two almost identical versions: one that can be completed in the time limits and one that is impossible to complete no matter how much time there is. Half the class do the possible task and the other half (unknown to them) attempt the impossible one. Pulse rates should be taken before and after the task and the difference calculated for each student. These results can be illustrated in a graph, although it is worth remembering that some pulse rates might decrease after the task so make allowances for negative numbers. It is always interesting discussing with students why such a simple task causes them so much stress. It is also interesting finding out why some students pulse rates actually decrease! (For some, merely being part of an experiment is stressful (ethical issues?) and once they find out that 'all' they have to do is a wordsearch they relax.)

Aim

To investigate the effects of stress when completing a simple task.

Hypothesis

1 Participants completing an impossible task (Wordsearch 1) will have a greater increase in their pulse rates than those who are completing a possible task (Wordsearch 2).

2 Male participants will have a greater increase on the impossible task than female participants. (Can only be done if you have enough of each in your class.)

Method

Independent groups design. Each participant has his or her pulse rate taken at the start of the experiment. (NB there needs to be enough experimenters for the number of participants, unless tested individually; experimenters should practise taking pulses – either manually or using a pulse monitor.) Instructions to all participants along the lines of: 'research has suggested a link between health and the ability to solve puzzles, so we will be taking your pulse rate at the start of this task'.

Participants are given either the possible or the impossible task with the instructions written on the top. After the allotted time (e.g. five minutes), all wordsearches are collected in and pulses taken again. Participants thanked and debriefed.

Cont'd ...

AS PSYCHOLOGY: THE TEACHER'S COMPANION Published by Nelson Thornes Ltd. © 2004 Sara Berman, Cara Flanagan and Adrian Frost

...Continued from previous page

Results

Calculate the difference in pulse rate for each participant.
The data could be summarised as follows.

	Possible task Males	Possible task Females	Impossible task Males	Impossible task Females
Mean				
Median				
Mode				
Range				
Standard deviation				

(The measure of central tendency will depend on the data collected; if there is an extreme value then the mean might not be appropriate.) Illustrate the data on a graph.

Discussion

Students should be encouraged to consider why there is (or is not) a difference between the two groups, in terms of the body's response to stress. They could also look at research into daily hassles, which is relevant here.

Wordsearch 1 is impossible (only one word can be found – CAT – seven lines down on the right, counting back four letters). Wordsearch 2 is the possible version. A copy is shown below, showing where the words are.

Handouts 68 and 69

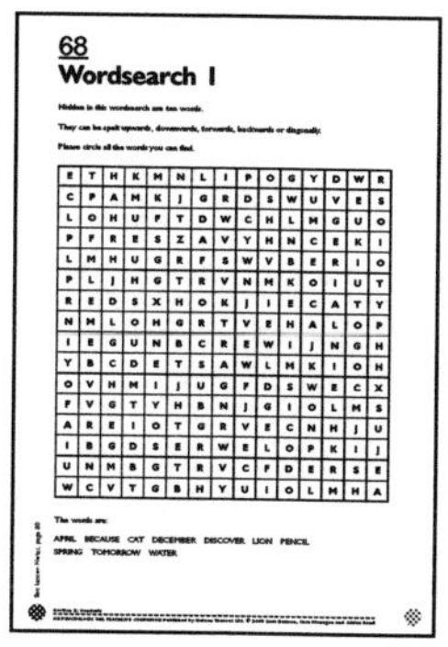

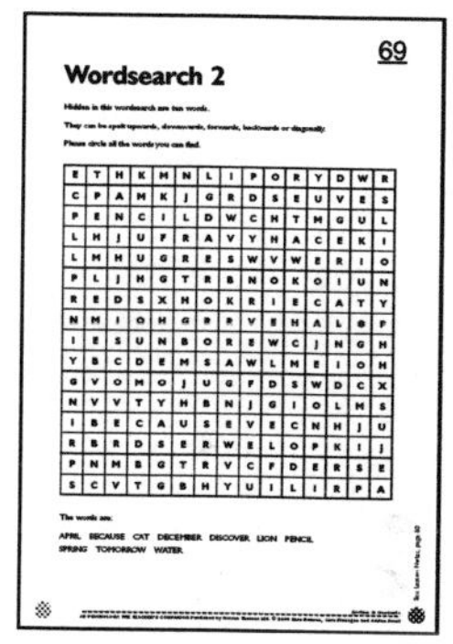

E	T	H	K	M	N	L	I	P	O	R	Y	D	W	R
C	P	A	M	K	J	G	R	D	S	E	U	V	E	S
P	E	N	C	I	L	D	W	C	H	T	M	G	U	L
L	H	J	U	F	R	A	V	Y	H	A	C	E	K	I
L	M	H	U	G	R	E	S	W	V	W	E	R	I	O
P	L	J	H	G	T	R	B	N	O	K	O	I	U	N
R	E	D	S	X	H	O	K	M	I	E	C	A	T	Y
N	M	I	O	H	G	R	M	V	E	H	A	L	O	P
I	E	S	U	N	B	O	R	E	W	C	J	N	G	H
Y	B	C	D	E	T	S	A	W	L	M	E	I	O	H
G	V	O	M	I	J	U	G	F	D	S	W	D	C	X
N	V	V	T	Y	H	B	N	J	G	I	O	L	M	S
I	B	E	C	A	U	S	E	V	E	C	N	H	J	U
R	B	R	D	S	E	R	W	E	L	O	P	K	I	J
P	N	M	B	G	T	R	V	C	F	D	E	R	S	E
S	C	V	T	G	B	H	Y	U	I	L	I	R	P	A

Have a nice day! Evaluating methods of stress management

In exams many students show little awareness of the fact that, when they are required to assess or evaluate the merits of psychological theories or research, such evaluation can be positive in nature and that, in fact, positive criticisms are potentially worth just as much, in terms of marks, as negative ones.

This section of the Specification specifically requests that stress management methods are viewed in terms of strengths as well as weaknesses. Other areas are not so specific, but this doesn't mean that positive criticisms won't be rewarded. Indeed there are only two sections (here and in the first section of Individual Differences) that specifically state a 'direction' for evaluation, in terms of 'limitations' or 'weaknesses' – otherwise positive critiques will often prove just as useful – though, as always, students should read the question carefully!

Despite this, many students can view the evaluative demands of the exam as a request to 'put the boot in' to whatever research is under discussion. This not only leads to rather 'shallow' evaluation, but deprives candidates of further avenues to explore and thus further sources of marks.

This activity is designed to reinforce the notion that evaluation and discussion is about more than just 'moaning about' the work of psychologists.

Aim

The basic idea is, for an entire lesson, or homework essay, or mock exam, to require students *only* to provide positive evaluative points.

For example, on this section of the Specification, students are often well able to point out issues such as addiction, side-effects and over prescription, when discussing drugs as a method of combating stress, but, in their haste to reach such material, often fail to point out that psychotherapeutic drugs can, and do, make people *feel* better. Indeed, many would point to drug therapies and our enhanced understanding of brain chemistry as one of the most significant and least ambiguous advances made in the field of Psychology over the past century. This activity is, however, equally applicable to other areas of the Specification.

Whilst it seems unlikely that students will in an exam restrict themselves entirely to such a positive approach, a requirement to focus entirely upon positive evaluative points will encourage students to address issues that they can often neglect in their haste to 'criticise' material.

AS PSYCHOLOGY: THE TEACHER'S COMPANION Published by Nelson Thornes Ltd. © 2004 Sara Berman, Cara Flanagan and Adrian Frost

MODULE: **Physiological Psychology**
SECTION: **Critical issue: Stress management**
TOPIC: **Psychological approaches to stress management**

Research activity: Hardiness and stress

Kobasa's view of hardiness is that individuals who are 'hardy' are better able to cope with stress. One Japanese study (M. Kosaka 1996, see http://www.websitemk.jp/papers/hard96.html) tested this prediction by assessing Hardiness at Time 1 and then assessing stress response three months later. You may not want to wait this long! Kosaka found a negative correlation (as one would expect) between hardiness and stress.

1 Assess hardiness

Use questionnaire from *The Complete Companion*, which is printed on **Handout 70**, or use an online questionnaire.
http://www.mhhe.com/socscience/hhp/corbin11e/labs/cor_18B.htm

Handout 70

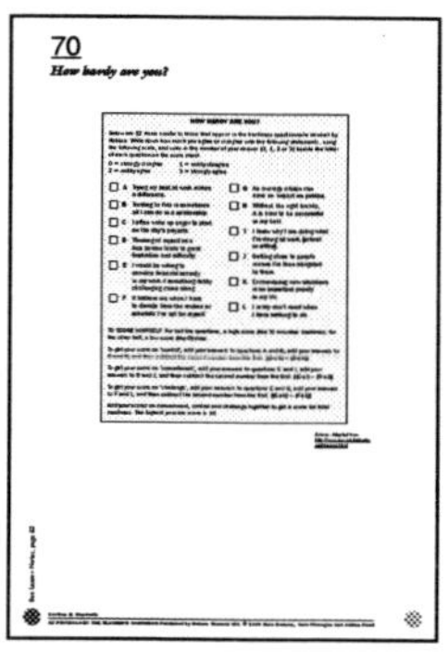
70
How hardy are you?

2 Assess stress

Professional Life Stress Test (needs a bit of interpretation to be used with students).
http://www.hcc.hawaii.edu/intranet/committees/FacDevCom/guidebk/teachtip/stress-t.htm

Or use the Hassles scale on **Handout 62**.

Or try http://docinthebox.com/strscalc.html

3 Calculate correlation coefficient

A simple way to do this is to use Excel. You enter the pairs of scores onto an Excel worksheet, and then Excel calculates the coefficient and plots a scattergraph! The different versions of Excel do this differently so it's difficult to provide instructions.

If you wish to calculate the coefficient manually, there are instructions in the coursework material on the CD (from *The A2 Complete Compansion*).

Stress management star rating system

An activity to review the stress management systems studies and assess their comparative strengths and weaknesses by trying to establish criteria for making such comparisons. This should increase understanding and evaluative abilities.

Handout 71

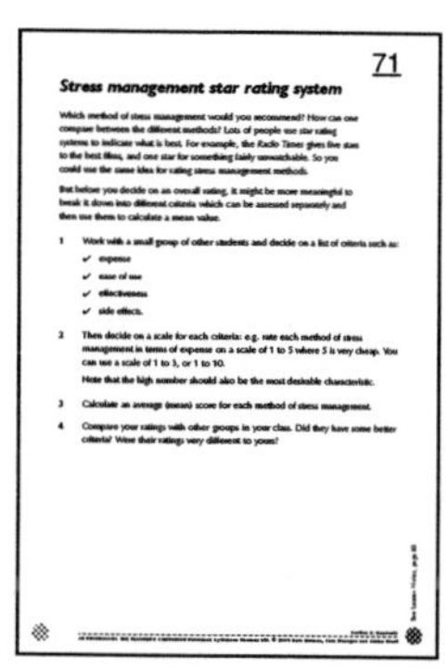
71
Stress management star rating system

Is control related to stress?

One of the central concepts related to role of control in stress is Rotter's research on internal and external locus of control. He suggested that locus of control is about where you place the responsibility (or blame) for things that happen to you. Locus of control moderates the perception of stress.

Some people have an internal locus of control. This means that they believe they are responsible for the things that happen to them. They control their world – for good or bad. This means they can feel good when they succeed and means they feel bad when things go wrong ('the buck stops here'). If you are experiencing something unpleasant and know you can stop it (perceived control) this reduces your sense of distress.

As an introduction to this, students might try the very short (but commonly used) scale by Pearlin and Schooler: The Pearlin Mastery Scale (Pearlin, L.I. and Schooler, C. [1978] The structure of coping. *Journal of Health and Social Behavior*, 19, 2–21.)

Mastery scale

Which of the following statements apply to you? For each statement write down 'very true', 'somewhat true', 'don't know', 'not true'.

1 I have little control over the things that happen to me.

2 What happens to me in the future mostly depends on me.

3 There is little I can do to change many of the important things in my life.

4 There is really no way I can solve some of the problems I have.

5 I can do just about anything I really set my mind to do.

6 Sometimes I feel that I am being pushed around in life.

7 I often feel helpless in dealing with the problems of life

Discussion

Discuss how control may be related to stress, and why it might be related to stress. As to *why* control is related to stress ... no answer appears to have been offered.

What can you control?

There are numerous websites for stress management companies and trainers. The big message is to learn to control what you can control and let the rest go. One activity suggested for doing with a group is as follows.

Ask the members of the group to try and make themselves angry. (Emotions are the hardest to control.) Now ask them to think of only the colour green for one minute. (Thoughts are easier to control but it is still difficult to do so for the entire time.) Now ask them to raise their right arm. (Actions are easy to control.)

What this exercise illustrates is that actions are the easiest to control. In fact if you 'move joyfully' actions can have a positive effect on our emotions!

AS PSYCHOLOGY: THE TEACHER'S COMPANION Published by Nelson Thornes Ltd. © 2004 Sara Berman, Cara Flanagan and Adrian Frost

Research activity: Rotter's locus of control questionnaire

People who have an internal locus of control should experience less stress and thus, presumably, less illness. You can correlate a score on a Locus of Control scale with some measure of health (for example, number of days off school) or devise a short questionnaire to assess health more reliably. Internals have also been found to be more active at solving mental problems (Lefcourt 1976), less likely to smoke (Coan 1973), more likely to engage in physical exercise (Walker 1973).

References

Coan, R.W. (1973) Personality variables associated with cigarette smoking. *Journal of Personality and Social Psychology*, 26, 86–104.

Lefcourt, H.M. (1976) *Locus of Control: Current Trends in Theory and Research*. Hillsdale, NJ: Lawrence Erlbaum.

Walker, T.G. (1973) Behaviour of temporary members in small groups. *Journal of Applied Psychology*, 58, 144–6.

Procedure

Handout 72 provides a questionnaire to assess locus of control. This questionnaire is Rotter's I-E scale.

Handout 72

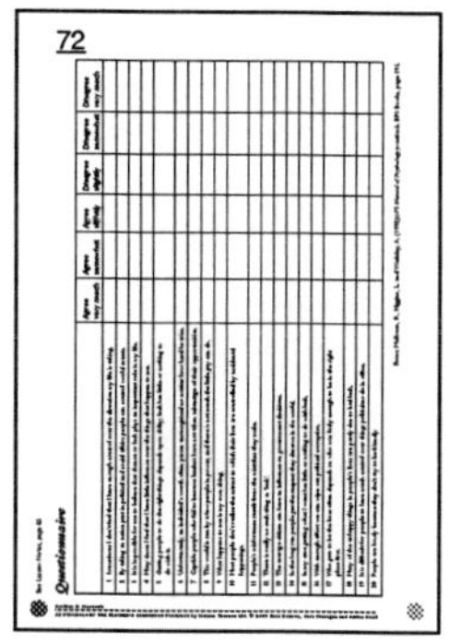

To score the scale

Score internal statements as follows (question numbers 2, 3, 5, 7, 9, 11, 12, 13, 14, 15, 16, 20)

Give each statement a score between 1 and 6, where the answer 'agree very much' = 1 and 'disagree very much' = 6

Score external statements as follows (question numbers 2, 3, 5, 7, 9, 11, 12, 13, 14, 15, 16, 20)

Give each statement a score between 1 and 6, where the answer 'agree very much' = 6 and 'disagree very much' = 1

Add up total score. Scores range from 20 to 120. A low score indicates an internal locus of control so there should be a *positive* correlation between score and number of days off school.

AS PSYCHOLOGY: THE TEACHER'S COMPANION Published by Nelson Thornes Ltd. © 2004 Sara Berman, Cara Flanagan and Adrian Frost

What is abnormality?

Try a challenging topic for debate: 'There is no such thing as abnormality' or 'Normality is simply the absence of abnormality', 'Are you normal?'.

Recognising abnormal behaviour

Handout 76

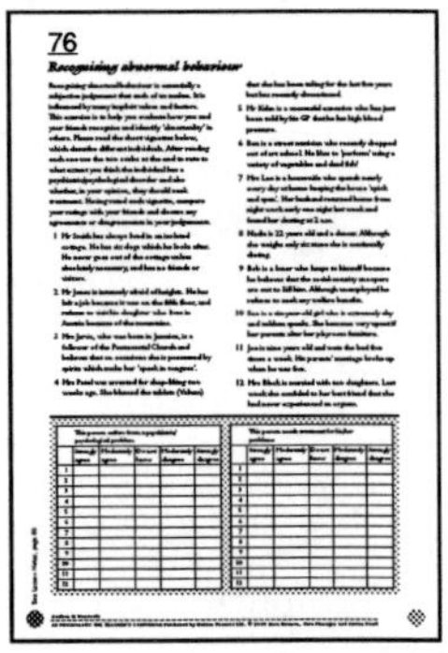
76

Recognising abnormal behaviour

Handout 76 is a way of getting students to think about what they mean by 'abnormality'.

Whose line is it anyway?

This activity is designed to encourage students to use, and think about, the four methods of defining abnormality given on the Specification. It will hopefully encourage class discussion, as well as broaden students' understanding of the term 'abnormality'.

After some brief introduction/note-taking concerning the four approaches, students are asked, individually or in small groups, to consider the table on **Handout 77**.

Handout 77

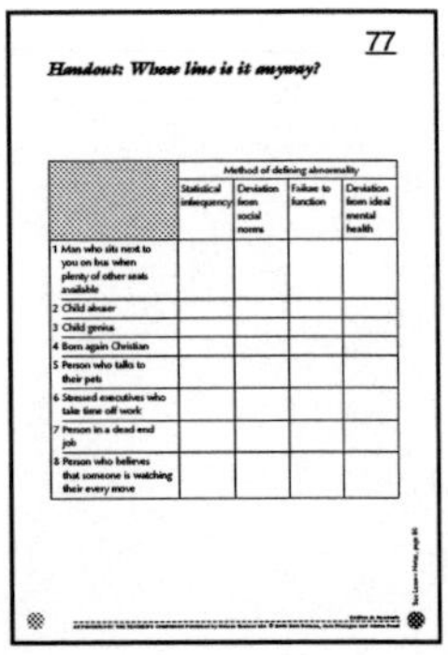
77

Handout: Whose line is it anyway?

	Method of defining abnormality			
	Statistical infrequency	Deviation from social norms	Failure to function	Deviation from ideal mental health
1 Man who sits next to you on bus when plenty of other seats available				
2 Child abuser				
3 Child genius				
4 Born again Christian				
5 Person who talks to their pets				
6 Stressed executives who take time off work				
7 Person in a dead end job				
8 Person who believes that someone is watching their every move				

Students are required to place a tick or a cross in each box, depending upon whether, in their judgement, the person in question would be deemed abnormal according to each of the definitions of abnormality, i.e. where would each 'draw the line' between normal and abnormal?

Subsequent discussion normally raises many of the issues that would become AO2 evaluation, such as social desirability, problems with quantification, context, cultural relativism, etc.

At the end of the activity, students should hopefully have a clearer idea of the four different approaches and their limitations.

AS PSYCHOLOGY: THE TEACHER'S COMPANION Published by Nelson Thornes Ltd. © 2004 Sara Berman, Cara Flanagan and Adrian Frost

MODULE: **Individual Differences**
SECTION: **Defining psychological abnormality**
TOPIC: **Cultural relativism**

Culture-bound syndromes

This section concerns the following part of the Specification:

'Limitations associated with these attempts to define psychological abnormality (including cultural relativism).'

One way of introducing cultural relativism is to illustrate the fact that what is abnormal in one culture, and is named, doesn't even 'exist' in another culture.

Culture-bound syndromes

- *Amok*: wild, aggressive behaviour, which only lasts a short time and is usually found in males. During an episode the person attempts to kill or injure others. This disorder is found in Southeast Asia.
- *Brain fag*: found mainly in West Africa among students who are about to take university or school exams. The symptoms are an inability to concentrate, headaches, difficulty in learning and eye-strain.
- *Koro*: a southern Chinese anxiety disorder in which the male believes that his penis is slowly shrinking and retracting into his abdomen and that he will die when the retraction is completed.
- *Latah or imu*: a syndrome usually found among women in Japan. The person imitates other people's behaviour to an excessive degree without any self-control. They copy others' movements and speech, are very compliant and can be commanded to do things that they would not normally do (such as swear).
- *Pibloqtoq or pibloktoq*: found among people who live within the Artic Circle. It involves an uncontrollable desire to take off all one's clothes and go outside.
- *Susto*: depression, apathy and the inability to sleep, usually among children in the Andes who believe it is due to 'the evil eye'.
- *Witiko*: the person goes off ordinary food and begins to feel depressed and anxious; this often develops into acts of murder and cannibalism. It is found among Canadian Indians.

Other culture-bound syndromes have been identified, for example: Boufee delirante aigue (Haitian); Hsieh-ping (Chinese); Mal ojo (Mexican–American); Shinkeishitu (Japanese); Negi-negi (African).

Don't run amok with cultural relativism

Culture-bound syndromes (as outlined in the Starter activity above), whilst no doubt extremely disturbing for those afflicted, can often raise a smile in the classroom, but it pays not to 'run amok' with such material. Close examination of the Specification indicates that the usefulness of this material is strictly limited.

Many student essays are packed with detail on flaming footballs, retractable penises, burning blankets and so on, but descriptions of cultural variations are of limited value unless linked to limitations of definitions.

The syndromes described would probably be judged abnormal in any culture and thus pose little problem for many of the definitions – they are judged abnormal and mentally unhealthy in all cultures.

Many students present such descriptive material, but to get any real credit, their material must be linked back to the original definitions of abnormality. All of these definitions have problems when used across cultures and this section demands an examination of these.

It's often difficult for students to get a clear handle on any kind of structure here. **Handout 78** may provide this.

Handout 78

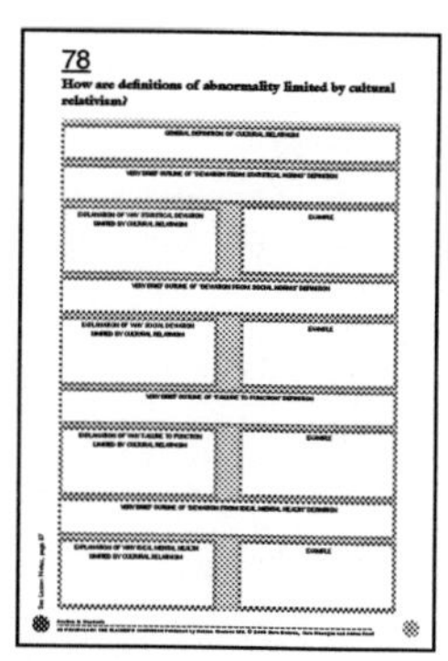
78
How are definitions of abnormality limited by cultural relativism?

Case study for a biological therapist

Students might work in groups and then discuss the case study given in **Handout 79** as a class.

The possible biological causes of Adam's behaviour are as follows:

- *Genetic.* He has inherited the manic-depression (bi-polar depression) from his father.
- *Biochemical substances.* In this case the consumption of a large quantity of alcohol could affect his behaviour – although not abnormal (yet) too much alcohol can lead to a variety of mental disorders.
- *Physical trauma.* The head injury he received playing rugby might have contributed to his mental health.

Students could also look at the aspects of Adam's life that this approach would *ignore*, such as his relationship with his mother (Freud); learning to use alcohol in the same way that his father did (behaviourist); feelings of inadequacy (cognitive).

This activity is very good preparation for the A2 Approaches question, as well as for thinking about the biological model. It could be repeated for the other models.

Handout 79

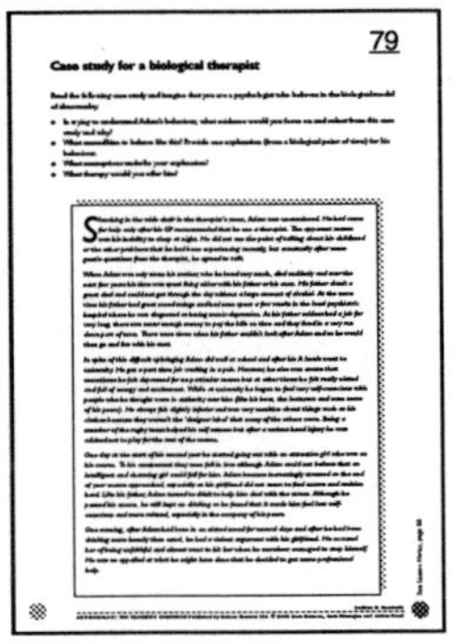
79

Case study for a biological therapist

Modelling models (or how to fill your classroom with memory cues)

This activity doesn't really belong anywhere but can be fitted in anywhere. I (AF) did this a few years back at the very end of term, when, as part of their feedback, students asked to do 'something with glitter'. This urge to regress to infant school is sometimes hard to resist in the classroom. Everyone who has ever given out a handout with any kind of diagram knows how hard it is to stop certain students from colouring it in and 'the need to colour' is a definitely a glaring omission from the lower levels of Maslow's Hierarchy of Needs. Sometimes I have just given in to this and organised colouring competitions using Thunderbirds colouring books, but such urges can be more constructively used to fill the classroom with memory cues.

Basically, I just collected together materials and asked students to create visual reminders of key psychological terms. Best not to restrict student creativity on this. Once you get them started, their ideas will probably be better than yours, but here's a few of the ones that stick in my mind (so they obviously worked).

1. A mobile made from a coat hanger with words like 'Asda' and 'Sainsbury's' hanging from it (the 'multi-store' model).
2. A lovely picture of several elephants walking along in a line with 'Conforming to Social Norms' written underneath it.
3. The nicely succinct 'Pills don't teach skills' on a big poster for methods of stress management.
4. A portrait of a student's mother with speech bubbles saying 'Do this …', 'Don't do that … ' – for 'interference' theories of forgetting. (One for the psychodynamic approach I think.)
5. A drawing of a red-haired man with a large snail on his shoulder (we never did work that one out).

Someone at a meeting once told me that they constructed models of the multi-store model using cereal packets and toilet rolls. A marble, representing 'stimuli', was passed along the tubes from store to store. Presumably there was only room for seven marbles in the first box.

This is a nice end of term activity, as long as it is handled right and no-one feels they are being overly patronised.

AS PSYCHOLOGY: THE TEACHER'S COMPANION Published by Nelson Thornes Ltd. © 2004 Sara Berman, Cara Flanagan and Adrian Frost

Get your dreams analysed online

I (AF) used to teach a bit of Philosophy as well, and I always told strangers that I was a Philosophy teacher, because I found that if I ever mentioned Psychology, I got one of two responses: 'Ooh, we better watch out, you'll be analysing us' or, even worse: 'Really, I had this dream and in it ...'. It might be a personal thing, but I think there's nothing more tedious than other people's dreams.

There does, however, seem to be a definite interest amongst most students in the meaning of dreams, and, I think, possibly many of them are slightly disappointed that there isn't more of that sort of thing in the AS Level (along with serial killers).

I always find myself at a loss for anything to say with regard to student dreams. The internet does, however, offer a solution. There are a number of sites, which will offer 'meanings' for various types of dream content. Some function just as dictionaries, others dress the whole thing up a bit more and ask you to register and then submit dreams for a more individual 'interpretation'.

I normally use http://freakydreams.com but there's plenty of other sites out there. I typed 'Free dream interpretation' into Google and got lots of results. (Like everything else on the net, you have to play around a bit: 'Online dream analysis' proved far less fruitful.)

This doesn't seem to be the most rigorously scientific area of the internet, and as with most parts of the web, you are seldom more than two clicks away from sites of an alternative, if not downright dodgy, nature, but if you can find a dream dictionary you are happy with, it could provide an interesting ten-minute introduction to the concept of dream analysis. I can't imagine Freud would be too impressed though ...

Make your own projective tests

This has got to be the recipe for a perfect lesson, combining as it does cutting, sticking and repressed sexual tension.

I (AF) always teach projective tests as part of the psychodynamic approach, as it gives students something slightly more structured in terms of therapeutic technique and enables them to see how Freud's initial ideas were developed by others.

It can be hard to find more than one or two examples from such tests in textbooks, as these areas often contain only a single illustrative image. You will do better by looking on the internet, where the whole set of Rorscharch inkblots can be found, as well as the 'Blacky the Dog' (an example is shown on the right) and 'Thematic apperception test' images.

Websites come and go, but you could try:

http://www.deltabravo.net/custody/rorschach.htm

http://schatz.sju.edu/psychtest/projectiveppt/sld001.htm

Example of image used in projective tests

Blacky the Dog

Cont'd ...

AS PSYCHOLOGY: THE TEACHER'S COMPANION Published by Nelson Thornes Ltd. © 2004 Sara Berman, Cara Flanagan and Adrian Frost

MODULE: **Individual Differences**
SECTION: **Biological and psychological models of abnormality**
TOPIC: The psychodynamic model

...Continued from previous page

Once your students have seen enough examples, they can then start to create their own. Rorschach inkblots are easy; just splash some paint around and then fold and unfold the paper. More interesting is the creation of images similar to those above, perhaps by creating collages of magazine images. This is more difficult than it looks. Students will need to bear the following in mind.

1 The image must contain figures with whom the viewer can *identify*. They can be human or, as in 'Blacky The Dog', animal, but human is probably best. There can more than one such figure, indeed choice of with whom to identify may be a vital part of the process.

2 The feelings and motivations of the figures should be *ambiguous*. That ecstatic girl from the shampoo ad leaves us in no doubt as to her state of mind and therefore she might not be that useful as she leaves us little space to 'project' our own emotions.

3 The relationship between the figures and the activity in which they are indulging should be open to *multiple interpretations*. For example, one thing to watch out for is age. The examples on the previous page could be husband and wife or father and daughter or mother and son.

4 The material could hint at *key unconscious conflicts* – not just to do with sex, but also power, control, family, insecurity, etc. (See bed and knife/blindfold above).

The above can often be achieved by carefully juxtaposing two or more magazine images.

Students could then have a go at developing a scoring system for their test. This will be much harder and the exercise will probably do little more than illustrate how difficult it is to score responses to such tests objectively.

As usual, you have to be careful that these sort of exercises don't 'open up a can of worms' with some students, but the completed tests will look very nice on the wall!

MODULE: **Individual Differences**
SECTION: **Biological and psychological models of abnormality**
Topic: The behavioural model

What do you expect?

The handout prepared for this activity is designed to kick start discussion in this area, with little prior knowledge required of students. It does, however, rest a little upon the assumption that this is not the first approach to abnormality that has been covered.

Handout 80

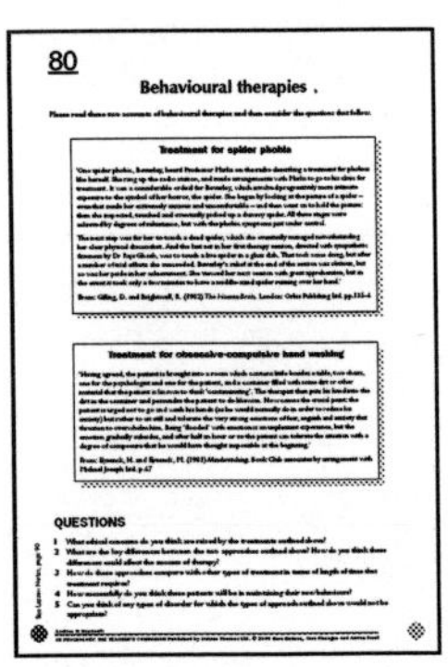
80

Behavioural therapies

Treatment for spider phobia

Treatment for obsessive-compulsive hand washing

QUESTIONS

Suggested 'answers' to questions on handout and discussion prompts

1 Patient needs to be briefed well, so can give informed consent. High levels of arousal/distress possible. Approaches vary in extent to which patient exercises control over events.

2 First approach involves far more rapid (and distressing) exposure to feared stimulus? Less control over events exercised by patient.

3 Quicker than drug therapy or lengthy psychoanalysis? (Cognitive approach also viewed as 'fast-acting' though?)

4 Effect might diminish once removed from lab setting and positive reinforcement from therapist, therefore high chance of relapse?

5 Psychotic, as opposed to neurotic, disorders? Disorders with no clearly identifiable behavioural component? Genetic/physiological/neurochemical disorders?

AS PSYCHOLOGY: THE TEACHER'S COMPANION Published by Nelson Thornes Ltd. © 2004 Sara Berman, Cara Flanagan and Adrian Frost

MODULE: **Individual Differences**
SECTION: **Biological and psychological models of abnormality**
TOPIC: **The cognitive model**

Abnormality is caused by faulty thinking

The cognitive model assumes that thinking, expectations and attitudes (i.e. cognitions) direct behaviour. Mental illness is the result of disordered thinking. The issue is not the problem itself, but the way you *think* about it. Faulty and irrational thinking prevents the individual behaving adaptively. Examples of faulty thinking include maladaptive assumptions about oneself (thinking that there are perfect solutions to everything) and upsetting thoughts (fleeting images that go through one's mind without conscious control). Such thoughts lead one to failure and depression.

Can you identify the 'faulty' thinking in the excerpts below? Each is from a book written by a woman who has suffered from a mental disorder. Look for what is implied, as well as that which is stated directly.

Handout 81

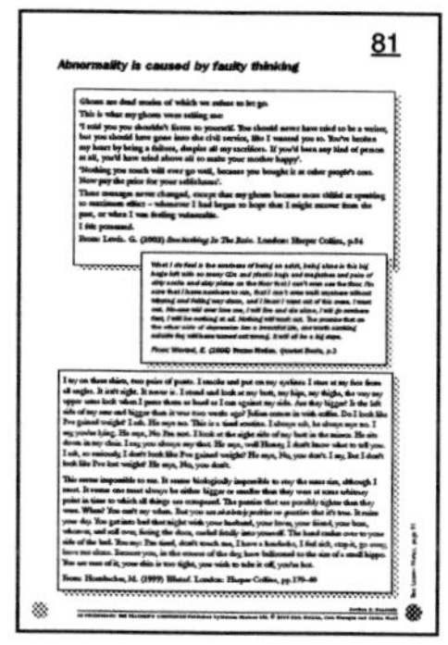

81

Abnormality is caused by faulty thinking

The question is, why are you a werewolf?

This activity provides an overview of the model of abnormality. Divide the class into four or more groups. Assign each group a 'perspective', drawn from one of the four main approaches outlined on the Specification i.e. medical, behavioural, psychodynamic and cognitive.

Ask each group to develop a list of key assumptions, perhaps as part of a research activity. Or, alternatively, just give them **Handout 82**. This is intentionally very basic, as trying to apply theoretical assumptions is quite a difficult skill. It probably pays to keep it simple at first and then build it up as you go along.

Handout 82

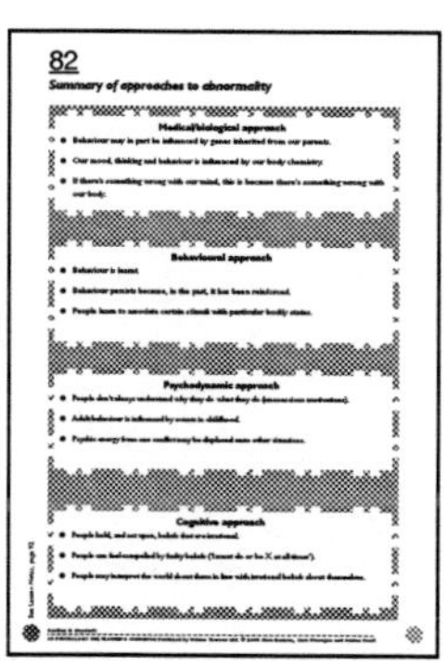

82

Summary of approaches to abnormality

Medical/biological approach

Behavioural approach

Psychodynamic approach

Cognitive approach

Present yourself as a range of 'patients' and ask for suggestions, explanations, proposed treatments, etc. from them, which are to be drawn from their assigned approach. You could draw upon statements such as the following.

I can't sleep at night.

I am lazy and don't do my job properly.

I am a werewolf.

I drink beer and get into fights on Saturdays.

The FBI are watching my every move.

My psychology teacher hates me.

And so on ...

I (AF) always worry about being light-hearted on mental health issues, but it does help to have an accessible, jargon-free start to this activity. You can then move onto more serious stuff such as 'I don't eat enough to maintain a healthy bodyweight'.

This can be used in a variety of ways, with varying degrees of structure.

Rather than just use it once, I used to roll it out whenever I had five minutes, or the moment was right. Last term I had a student who was going to see Justin Timberlake live at Birmingham and we all discussed the outing using various different perspectives. ('Justin Timberlake is a good performer' is an irrational belief. 'Justin increases hormone activity' and so on.)

Cont'd ...

AS PSYCHOLOGY: THE TEACHER'S COMPANION Published by Nelson Thornes Ltd. © 2004 Sara Berman, Cara Flanagan and Adrian Frost

...Continued from previous page

At other points, I only allowed students to give in homework late if they could provide me with an excuse from a psychodynamic perspective such as 'Oedipal resentment displaced onto an alternative authority figure'. ('You castrated me, so you're not getting my coursework'.)

Like many of the other activities in this pack, this works best if used little and often as part of routine discussion. Once students get used to it, it becomes no problem to ask for a comment from the 'cognitive table' or a medical explanation from the back row. It doesn't take much time and provides a structured way to elicit comment from those who don't normally say much in class.

It's dead easy for them just to say 'That's an irrational belief' all the time, but, with practice, their responses will deepen. Also, students will become better at applying psychological approaches to other areas of the Specification, such as stress or attachment and thus open up further A02 discussion areas, when they are stuck for something to say on an 18-mark question. You'll also reap the reward when you come to cover the 'Approaches' section of the A2 paper, as they'll have had plenty of practice.

Revise the models of abnormality

You can print all the statements on separate cards and give them to students (either individually or as a small group), or they can read them on the handout. Then they need simply write the correct number in the correct box. It makes marking quick and simple. Once they have got the box completed correctly, they can write out the statements in full.

Handout 83

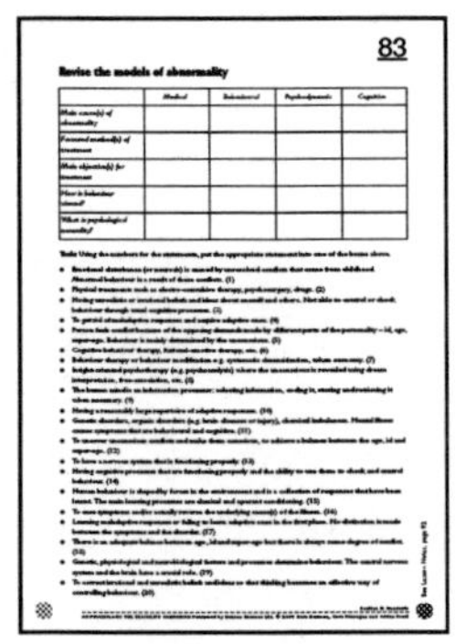

Correct answers

	Medical (biological)	Behavioural	Psychodynamic	Cognitive
Main cause(s) of abnormality	11	17	1	3
Favoured method(s) of treatment	2	7	8	6
Main objective(s) for treatment	16	4	12	20
How is behaviour viewed?	19	15	5	9
What is psychological normality?	13	10	18	14

Compare and contrast the different models of abnormality

There are no 'right' answers provided as I'm not sure there are any – most are moot points at best!

Handout 84

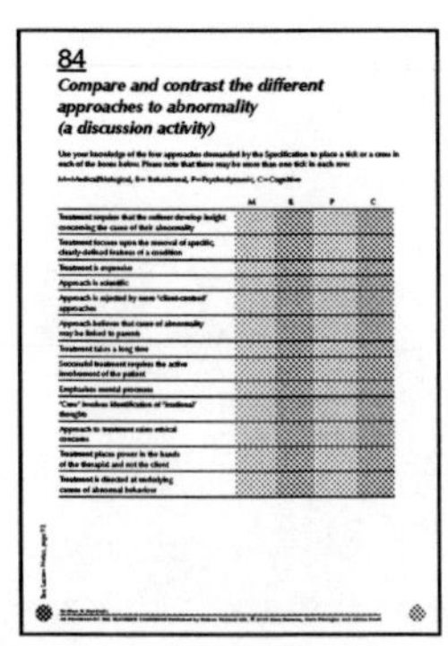

AS PSYCHOLOGY: THE TEACHER'S COMPANION Published by Nelson Thornes Ltd. © 2004 Sara Berman, Cara Flanagan and Adrian Frost

Debate on the cause of eating disorders

Introduce the challenging topic of whether the media is to blame for eating disorders in girls.

Ask groups to prepare arguments either for or against, plus to be ready to respond to counter-arguments made by other groups.

'Diet diaries': The trouble with food

This video (originally shown on C4, available from Richmond College www.rutc.ac.uk) is made up of five case studies; it may not be necessary to show all at one time, but to use them to illustrate different types of eating disorders when teaching them. The first is a young woman with bulimia, the second is a woman with anorexia, the third is of a man with a serious hate of food (some slightly graphic language), the fourth is an athlete who controls her food with exercise. The last combines two cases that are not explicitly eating disorders: a woman who is constantly on a diet and has been for 20 years and two teenagers who are obese.

Only the first two cases have been included in **Handout 85**. Note: the questions on this worksheet are based entirely on the video and can be answered simply by watching the video. An alternative approach would be to ask questions that require students to use their own knowledge. For example:

> Which model/theory of eating disorders best explains the cause of Sarah M's anorexia? Use evidence from the video to support your case …

Handout 85

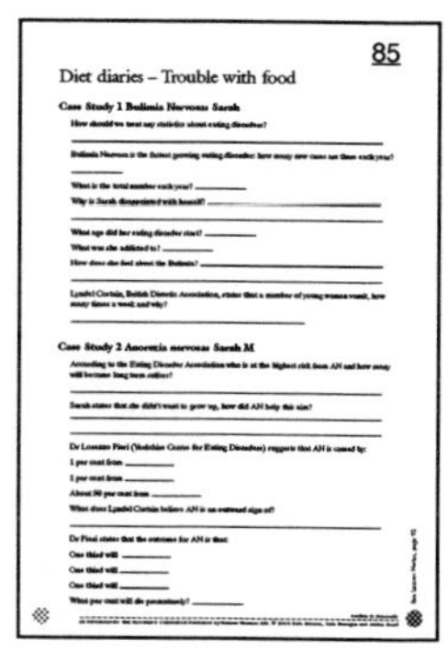
85

Diet diaries – Trouble with food

Do the figures support the biological explanation of anorexia?

This exercise is designed to sharpen student skills in the interpretation of statistical data and to encourage care in the conclusions that are drawn from it. It's a difficult exercise and students may well need leading through it, because for students who can't 'see' the problems with the data, it can be difficult to provide them with a structured path to their own conclusions. Some Vygotskian 'scaffolding' is often required!

Handouts 86 and 87

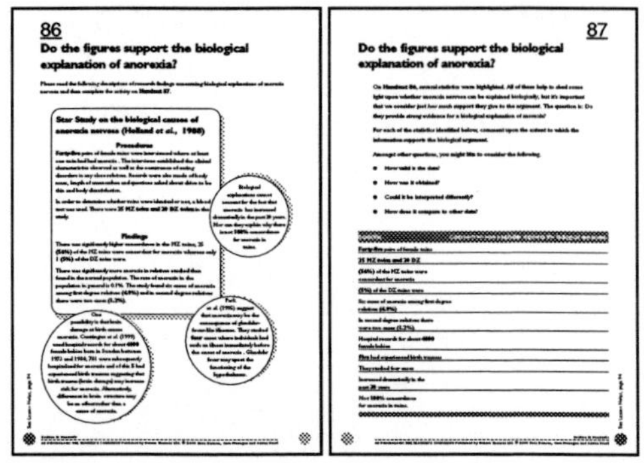
86
Do the figures support the biological explanation of anorexia?

87
Do the figures support the biological explanation of anorexia?

Suggested 'answers'/discussion prompts

Statistics	Suggested comments/prompts
Forty-five pairs of female twins	A reasonable size sample group? Difficult to find participants for this study? No males? Other issues concerning representativeness of sample groups?
25 MZ twins and 20 DZ	Reasonably equal balance between the two allows comparison
56% of the MZ twins were concordant for anorexia	A significant figure, especially compared to DZ twins Note that twins not reared apart, so is there a signifi cant role for environmental factors?
5% of the DZ twins were concordant for anorexia	See above
Six cases of anorexia among first degree relatives (*4.9%*)	Looks a low figure, but is nearly 50 times higher than level for general population (0.1 per cent)
In second degree relatives there were two cases (*1.2%*)	Again, much higher than 0.1%, but figure based on very small number of participants.
Hospital records for about *4000* female babies	A large sample group! – but only 781 had anorexia
Five had experienced birth traumas	This is 0.64 per cent of the 781 who had anorexia. If expressed as '99.36% of anorexics did *not* have birth trauma', it looks very different.
They studied *four* cases	Small sample group?
Increased dramatically in the past *30* years	Evidence against bio approach? Unless we put it down to increased awareness and diagnosis of biologically caused condition.
Not *100%* concordance for anorexia in twins	Possible evidence for role of environmental factors in 'triggering' a biological condition.

References

Cnattingius, S., Hultman, PhD, C.M., Dahl, M. & Sparén, P. (1999) Very pre-term birth, birth trauma, and the risk of anorexia nervosa among girls. *Archives of General Psychiatry*, 56, 634–8.

Holland, A.J., Sicotte, N. & Treasure, J. (1988) Anorexia nervosa: Evidence for a genetic basis. *Journal of Psychosomatic Research*, 32, 561–572.

Park, R.J., Lawrie, J.M. & Freeman, C.P. (1995) Post-viral onset of anorexia nervosa. *British Journal of Psychology*, 166, 386–9.

AS PSYCHOLOGY: THE TEACHER'S COMPANION Published by Nelson Thornes Ltd. © 2004 Sara Berman, Cara Flanagan and Adrian Frost

Research activity: Body image

Garner, D.M., Garfinkel, P.E., Schwartz, D. and Thompson, M. (1980) Cultural expectations of thinness in women. *Psychological Reports*, 47, 483–91.

Garner *et al.* (1980) conducted a kind of cross-cultural study in that they compared desirable female bodies from different historical periods as well as considering changes in attitudes towards dieting. Their study revealed changing sociocultural pressures on eating disorders in Western society in the last 20 years; ideal female body shape and attitudes towards dieting had changed.

They used a form of indirect observation by using photographs of women taken during a 20-year period – centrefolds from *Playboy* magazine and contestants and winners of the Miss America pageant in the years from 1959 to 1978. They also looked at articles about dieting in six popular women's magazines.

The photographs show that there has been a gradual but definite change in the preferred shape for women toward a more angular and thinner physique. In addition to weight changes, bust and hip measurements became smaller. According to this data, 69 per cent of *Playboy* centrefolds and 60 per cent of Miss America participants from 1959 to 1978 had weights 15 per cent or less of the average weights for their age and height.

Moreover, in the 1970s the pageant winners even weighed significantly less than the other contestants. Meanwhile, actuarial statistics published in 1979 showed that the average female weight for the population had increased during that 20-year period. During that same period, they also found an increase in the number of diet articles in six popular women's magazines.

This suggests a growing disparity between actual body sizes and the cultural standard, and a parallel increase in the culture's interest in and attention to dieting, thinness and appearance in women. Garner *et al.* concluded that this changing sociocultural pressure has had an enormous impact on women and this, together with family expectations and individual characteristics, determines the causes of eating disorders.

Procedure

You could conduct a similar study using the data on Miss America pageant winners provided on **Handouts 88** and **89**.

Handouts 88 and 89

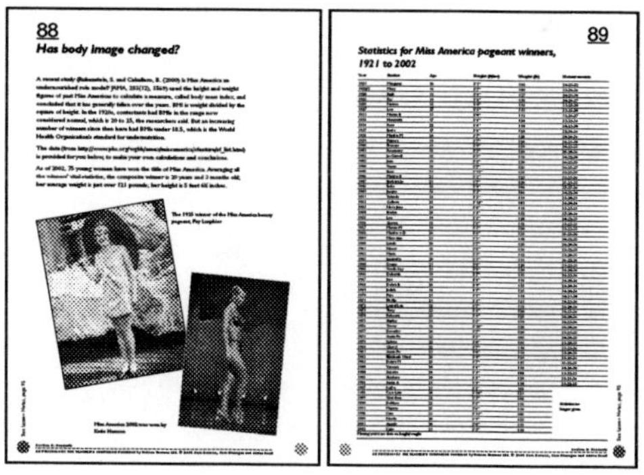

MODULE: **Indvidual Differences**
SECTION: **Critical issue: Eating disorders**
TOPIC: **Biological explanations of bulimia nervosa**

How *not* to write a questionnaire on attitudes to eating disorders

The questionnaire given in **Handout 90** is clearly appalling!

Handout 90

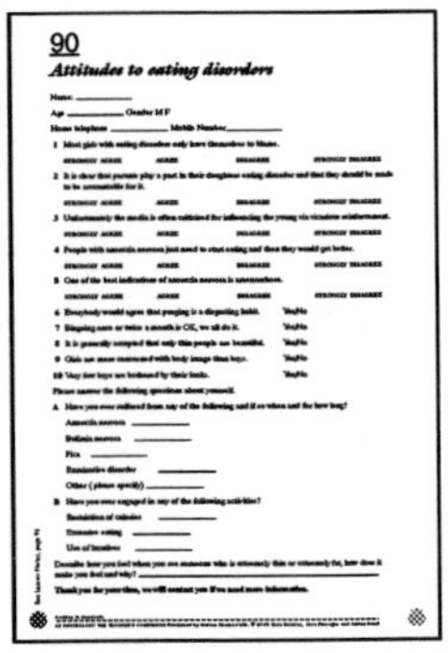
90
Attitudes to eating disorders

You might like to allow students to identify the flaws in the questionnaire themselves. Or you could suggest to them that they consider some or all of the following criteria.

- Offensive questions.
- The use of jargon that lay people might not understand.
- The forced choice (not allowing for a 'don't know' or 'neither agree nor disagree').
- Ethical issues (confidentiality, anonymity, consent to be contacted at a later day).
- Questions that are in fact two questions in one.
- And so on ...

You might look at **Handout 32** for information on constructing questionnaires.

MODULE: **Indvidual Differences**
SECTION: **Critical issue: Eating disorders**
TOPIC: **Psychological explanations of bulimia nervosa**

Analysis of eating disorders

In *The Complete Companion* excerpts from young people experiencing eating disorders were printed to enable students to get a more rounded picture of what it really involves. This offers an excellent opportunity for students to try out some qualitative analysis.

They will need access to the internet (to collect their own case histories) or they can use **Handout 91** which is taken from *The Complete Companion*. Useful website addresses are given in the table of contents.

There are two approaches.

1 *Grounded theory*. An interview text or any discourse (conversation) is examined. Recurrent and/or important themes are identified, and used to give insight into the topic of study.

Ask student to examine case histories and compile a list of the five most important characteristics of anorexia and/or bulimia. Then compare these criteria with the DSM lists.

2 *Thematic analysis*. Themes or concepts are identified before starting the research. Then responses from an interview or questionnaire are organised according to the themes.

Start with the DSM list of characteristics and record how frequently these are found in case histories (a *content analysis*). Also produce a qualitative record by '*giving voice*' recording particular examples of characteristics to illustrate them.

Handout 91

91
A qualitative analysis of eating disorders

AS PSYCHOLOGY: THE TEACHER'S COMPANION Published by Nelson Thornes Ltd. © 2004 Sara Berman, Cara Flanagan and Adrian Frost

Beans in a jar

Jenness, A. (1932) The role of discussion in changing opinion regarding matter of fact. *Journal of Abnormal and Social Psychology*, 27, 279–96.

Jenness' (1932) experiment using beans in a jar to demonstrate conformity is a popular piece of coursework for students and one that lends itself nicely to an introduction to majority influence.

Fill a jar with beans (ambiguous stimulus – can use smarties, pasta shells – whatever) and ask people to provide estimates. In order to determine whether their behaviour is influenced by others you need to ask the students to write their answers on pieces of paper where previous students have recorded theirs (make up some story about conducting research and you have already collected some data). Some of the pieces of paper should have high estimates (group 1), others should have low estimates (group 2). You can make these estimates extreme or or not.

Participants in each condition should differ in terms of their mean estimates, as a consequence of conforming to the estimates they see.

Research activity: Conformity on a general knowledge quiz

You can use this either as a means of testing conformity with your students or they can design the stimulus material and use it to conduct research of their own.

You will need a general knowledge questionnaire as provided on **Handout 95**.

Handout 95

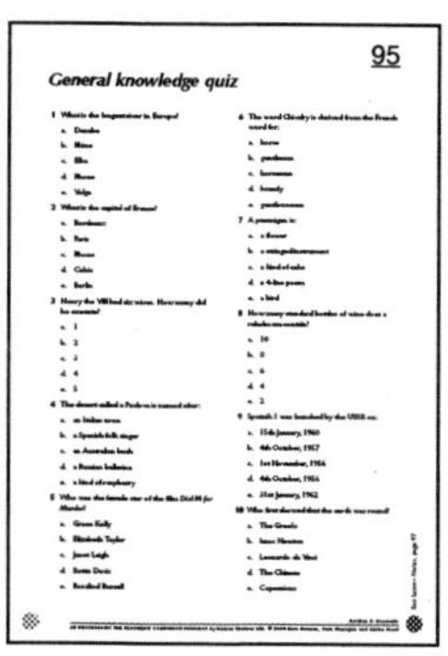

Procedure

Produce two answer sheets, one 'dirty' and one clean. The 'dirty' answer sheet should have about five ticks after each question written in various styles so it looks as if they are written by other participants. Experimenter says to participants, 'I'm sorry about the other answers, I ran out of questionnaires and the photocopier broke. Please ignore them and give your answer.'

Analysis

You could use a table like the one below and the Mann-Whitney test for independent measures to analyse the results (see 'Coursework' on the CD for instructions to do the Mann–Whitney test).

The correct answers for the quiz are:

1e 2b 3b 4d 5a 6c 7e 8c 9b 10a

Question with wrong answers	Number of people giving wrong answer	
	Clean version	'Dirty' version
3		
4		
6		
8		
9		

Cont'd ...

...Continued from previous page

Alternative design

Crutchfield, R.S. (1955) Conformity and character. *American Psychologist*, 10, 191–8.

Produce a questionnaire with ambiguous (unclear) questions and unambiguous ones. If you want inspiration look at http://familygames.com/features/quizzes/dayquiz.html or http://www.freequizzes.co.uk/pubquiz.htm. In order to distinguish between clear and unclear studies you will need to do a *pilot study*.

Crutchfield (1955) compared participants' performance on different kinds of questions and found 30 per cent conformity when the question was clear-cut but 80 per cent conformity when the answer was ambiguous.

Produce a 'dirty' answer sheet. On two ambiguous and two unambiguous questions the majority should have indicated the wrong answer.

Do participants conform more in the ambiguous condition?

Analysis

Separate ambiguous (uncertain) questions versus unambiguous (certain) ones, as in the table below.

Use a Wilcoxon test for repeated measures (see 'Coursework' on CD for instructions for how to do the Wilcox test).

Participant	**Number of wrong answers**	
	Ambiguous	**Unambiguous**
1		
2		
3		
4		
5		

Role play: Asch (1956)

Asch, S.E. (1956) Studies of independence and conformity: A minority of one against a unanimous majority. *Psychological Monographs*, 70 (Whole no. 416).

There are two possibilities.

1 If you have a situation where one student is absent, brief the rest of the class on Asch's experiment and enlist them as confederates. In the next lesson when the absent student returns, run the experiment by showing the stimulus lines and comparison line (these are provided for you on the handouts – but need to be transferred to cards or OHTs). On 12 out of 18 trials everyone should give the wrong answer. Interview the 'absent' students about what he/she felt and debrief (you have to chose your absent student carefully).

2 Role play Asch's experiment with one true participant and all confederates, or with one confederate who gives the right answer. Students love doing this and, even though it may seem chaotic, it helps embed the procedures clearly and also may give them some insight into why people did conform and into ethical issues.

Cont'd ...

AS PSYCHOLOGY: THE TEACHER'S COMPANION Published by Nelson Thornes Ltd. © 2004 Sara Berman, Cara Flanagan and Adrian Frost

...Continued from previous page

Handouts 96–101

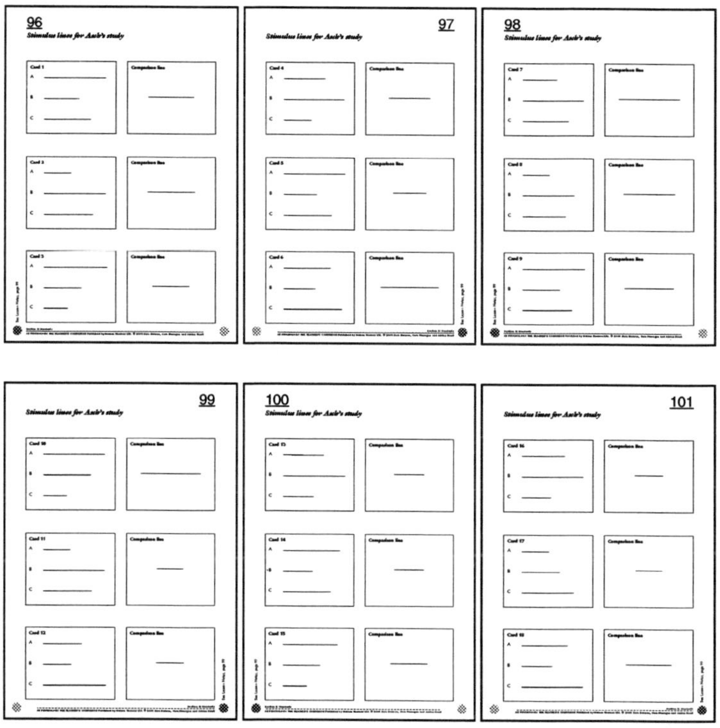

The correct answers are:

1C	2C	3B	4A	5B	6C	7A	8B	9C
10A	11A	12B	13C	14B	15B	16C	17A	18A

The confederates should give right answers on 6 critical trials e.g. 1, 3, 7, 8, 11, 15.
Therefore their answers would be:

1C	2B	3B	4C	5A	6B	7A	8B	9A
10C	11A	12A	13B	14A	15B	16B	17C	18C

MODULE: **Social Psychology**
SECTION: **Conformity and minority influence**
TOPIC: **Minority influence**

Research activity: Nemeth and Brilmayer (1987)

Clark, R.D. III and Maass, A. (1990) The effects of majority size on minority influence. *European Journal of Social Psychology*, 25, 99–117.

Nemeth, G.J. and Brilmayer, A.G. (1987) Negotiation versus influence. *European Journal of Social Psychology*, 17, 45–56.

Nemeth and Brilmayer (1987) did a study of minority influence where a mock jury was asked to consider the compensation to give to a person injured in a ski accident. In each group there was a confederate who was told to argue for a more extreme figure. There were two conditions: one where the confederate did not budge from his original position, and the second where the confederate was more flexible and adjusted his figure slightly towards the group mean. The study found that majority opinion shifted more when the minority confederate was more flexible.

Procedures

When replicating this study you will have to give each participant individual instructions (see **Handouts 103** and **104**) and tell them to keep them private. On these instructions is an explanation of the claim being made and a space where

Cont'd ...

AS PSYCHOLOGY: THE TEACHER'S COMPANION Published by Nelson Thornes Ltd. © 2004 Sara Berman, Cara Flanagan and Adrian Frost

...Continued from previous page

each participant should fill in what compensation they would regard as reasonable. Collect these in before the beginning of the experiment. At the end ask everyone to record individually what compensation they now think is acceptable.

Group size should be relatively small in order for a minority effect to occur at all. Clark and Maass (1990) found that when there was a majority of 8 or 12 there was no minority effect (which is important when considering juries). There was an effect when the majority was four (as in Moscovici *et al.*'s original study).

You will need at least two groups, but can have more groups of either group 1-type or group-2 type. Print instruction slips as required.

Handouts 102 and 103

102
Instructions for participants

103
Instructions for participants

Analyse findings

Findings should be analysed for each participant by working out the difference between their original figure and figure after discussion (presuming that their new figure was closer to the group norm – you could calculate this to check). Then work out the mean difference for members of group 1s and group 2s. The differences should be greater for group 2s.

You could analyse the findings for each group separately and discuss reasons for differences (e.g. some minority confederates might have been more or less effective – for what reasons?).

MODULE: **Social Psychology**
SECTION: **Obedience to authority**
TOPIC: **Obedience to authority**

How far would you go?

Introduce a challenging topic for debate on the nature of obedience: 'How do you know how far you would go? Would you electrocute a stranger if asked?'

Introduction to obedience

Orne, M.T. (1962) On the social psychology of the psychological experiment: With particular reference to demand characteristics and their implications. *American Psychologist*, 17, 776–83.

The teacher asks the class to do something, e.g. 'For today I'd like you to sit in alphabetical order' and then continues asking them to do more and more strange and meaningless things. This is to see just how far they will go. I (SB) have had a class of 20 students standing on their desks carefully tearing pieces of file paper into strips, then into squares, then scattering them on the ground, then getting down, picking them all up, handing them to the next person until they were thrown in a bin – and doing this whole pointless exercise three times! It makes the point well, how far will they obey me and why? We then have fun discussing what they definitely won't do.

Cont'd ...

...Continued from previous page

Way to introduce the topic

Ask the class to do strange things, e.g. get them to sit in a row according to birthdays; lots of chat relaxes them.

Then ask them all to stand behind their chairs, on their desks, with some A4 paper, tear it carefully into strips, drop every fourth strip on the floor, all those with birthdays between March and June get down and pick up paper, etc. Nothing dangerous or embarrasing but keep going until someone asks 'Why?' It's extremely interesting to see how far they will obey totally absurd requests.

You can then discuss why they obey. What was it about the situation, my role, their role, socialisation process of school behaviour. This is quite a fun way to lead into Milgram.

It also allows a discussion of the ethics of what the teacher did.

This can also lead to discussion of Orne's research on demand characteristics. Social psychology of experiments is one spread in *The Complete Companion* (pages 192–193).

Orne (1962) observed that people behave in quite unusual ways if they think they are taking part in a psychology experiment. For example, in one experiment he asked participants to add up columns of numbers on a sheet of paper and then tear the paper up and repeat this again. If people believed this was part of a psychology experiment some were willing to continue the task for over six hours! This led Orne to develop the idea of *demand characteristics*. People taking part in an experiment want to please an investigator and want their performance to be helpful. This results in people sometimes being over-cooperative and behaving in quite a different way than they would normally – normally no one would tear up paper for six hours. This means that my experiment told us little or nothing about behaviour in real life. A demand characteristic acts as a confounding variable.

The Rolf Harris school of teaching

We used to have visiting speakers who informed us of the different 'learning styles' – visual, acoustic and kinaesthetic. I (AF) never really got the psychology song, or the lesson conducted by a mime, off the ground – but I do make quite a lot of use of visual learning, mainly because I like doodling on the Board.

Some kind of visual approach is useful for the Social Influence section of the Specification, because it helps students to keep track of what's going on in the studies.

Research like that of Asch, Crutchfield or Moscovici can get very confusing for students over time, as they try to keep track of varying stimulus material, majorities, minorities, confederates, dissenters and experimenters. I always find it best to draw the varying conditions on the Board, even if I only use stick men. (I've never got a 'bluey-green' pen for Moscovici though.) Little speech bubbles can be added and I do genuinely find that it helps the students to remember material.

If you're not big on drawing, get the students to do it for you. Some students just like to draw, and can be relied upon to produce excellent visual aids and revision material. A surprising amount of material can be crammed into one image (see the Milgram example below).

Some students really like this approach, others groan, especially if asked to copy material down. Here's some ideas for a slightly more structured approach:

1 *A good little task for the 'Strange Situation'*. Draw lots of 'empty' baby heads, distribute to students and ask them to draw facial expressions which convey the different attachment types. Others have to guess which attachment type each baby is. This gets a laugh, but reinforces the material as well.

Cont'd ...

...Continued from previous page

2 *Ask students to produce cartoons*. Get a big compilation book of cartoons. Books of newspaper cartoons like 'Peanuts' or 'Calvin and Hobbes' work best, as they contain hundreds of images of the same people, drawn at about the same size, wearing the same clothes in each frame. Photocopy lots of different figures and then cut out and stick them onto a sheet of A3 paper. This is time consuming, but you only have to do it once.

Photocopy this A3 'resource sheet' and distribute to students. Ask them to cut out figures and stick on paper, and then they have to add speech bubbles of their own. This works well with two characters where they have to debate a particular issue, with each figure holding a particular viewpoint and the argument alternating between the two viewpoints, so that you end up with something like 'Calvin and Hobbes debate the ethics of Milgram's research', with one character presenting criticisms and the other presenting counterpoints. This really helps the students to produce balanced argument, discussion and debate, rather than rote learnt AO2 points.

Once you've got the sheets, you only have to rustle up scissors and glue anytime you want to use the exercise. (In my experience groups like the exercise so long as they are only ever asked do it once or twice.) The results look great if photocopied onto coloured card and it is guaranteed that other staff will ask to photocopy your mastersheet.

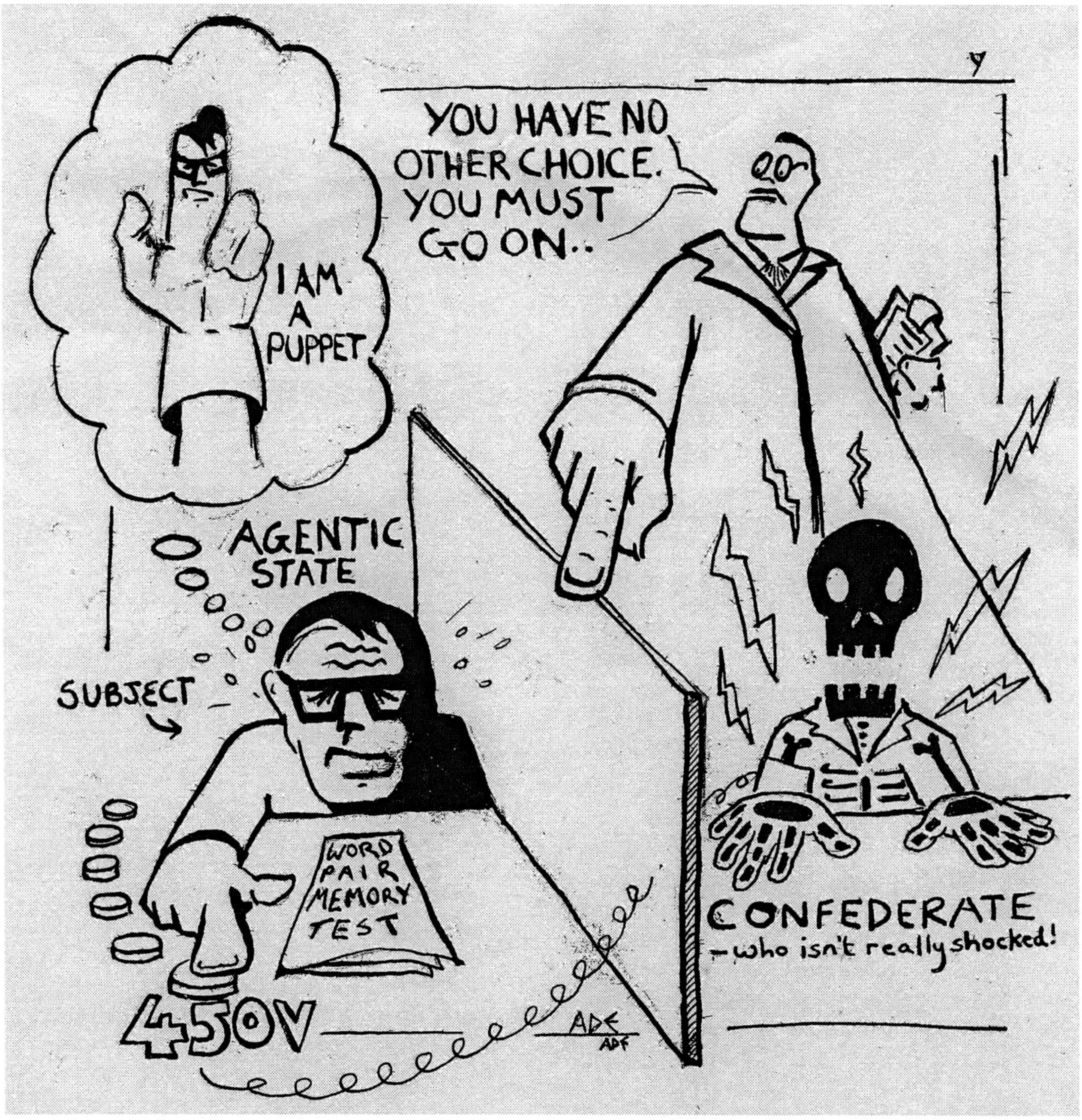

Is it better to be obedient or resistant?

Discuss with your class which is more important: obedience or resistance to obedience?

Turning obedience into resistance

Some of the participants in Milgram's study said they were glad to have participated because it taught them something of personal importance – that they should be careful about obeying authority mindlessly. This is one value of such research – that we may generally learn ways to reduce mindless obedience and create individuals who think more carefully about their actions and their responsibility for these actions, i.e. they learn how to resist obedience to authority. The topic 'resistance to obedience' is really 'obedience' turned inside out!

You can make life very easy for your students by giving them the opportunity to work out resistance to obedience for themselves, simply take anything you have learned for 'obedience' and rephrase it for 'resistance'.

For example:

'Why do people obey authority?'

'One reason is because they think the responsibility is taken by the authority figure, i.e. the Agentic shift'.

'Why do people resist authority?

'One reason is that people learn to take responsibility for themselves, i.e. the autonomous state'.

'What does Milgram's study tell us about obedience?'

'It tells us that most people were willing to obey authority even when they knew they were causing harm to another person'.

'What does Milgram's study tell us about resistance?'

'It tells us that some people (quite a few) do not obey mindlessly; they are not in an Agentic state'.

AS PSYCHOLOGY: THE TEACHER'S COMPANION Published by Nelson Thornes Ltd. © 2004 Sara Berman, Cara Flanagan and Adrian Frost

EV or not EV? That is the question

This is a very difficult area of study. It's very easy for students (or even staff!) to get tied up in knots on this one.

However, it is easy to apply a few simple rules to clear this area up. These include the following.

1. Only the terms used on the Specification will be used in the exam.
2. If the Specification says 'e.g.' – you don't *have* to cover it.
3. Follow the Specification rather than any textbook.
4. Always work out the 'size and shape' of your required knowledge before you start revising.

The Specification for Social Psychology says the following:

'Issues of experimental and ecological validity associated with such research'.

And that's it ...

Let's see how those rules apply:

We have two terms to master – 'experimental validity' and 'ecological validity'.

The textbook I've just picked up has also highlighted terms such as internal/external validity, generalisability, various types of reliability, etc. These might be useful in expanding our understanding of the two key terms, but they can't be specifically mentioned as part of the question, even if useful as part of the answer, because of rule one above.

So, if you get confused about the relationship between internal, external, experimental and ecological validity – don't worry about it. Just concentrate upon the two terms demanded by the Specification. If it mentions other things in the textbook that you are unhappy with, this is OK, as long as you are happy with the terms on the Specification (see rule three above).

Next, we have to relate the terms to 'such' research, which means obedience research in this case. The Specification gives the examples of Milgram, Hofling and Meeus and Raajmakers, but we can ignore the examples if we wish (even Milgram! – see rule two above).

Let's say we'll stick to Milgram and Hofling. Their methods and settings contrast nicely, opening up a few issues for discussion and we'll need two pieces of research anyway, in case a longer question asks for studies in the plural.

So we've got two types of validity and two pieces of research. We have to know what the two types of validity are, so some kind of definition is required, and we have to know how these terms are 'associated' with research, so some kind of exploration of the terms in the context of the research is also required.

Students often mock when I (AF) tell them that the first thing to do is work out the 'size and shape' of their knowledge, but this is the first thing I always do in teaching a new topic. I reckon that this area looks something like this:

	MILGRAM	**HOFLING**
EXPERIMENTAL VALIDITY (Definition)	YES / NO	YES / NO
ECOLOGICAL VALIDITY (Definition)	YES / NO	YES / NO

Cont'd ...

AS PSYCHOLOGY: THE TEACHER'S COMPANION Published by Nelson Thornes Ltd. © 2004 Sara Berman, Cara Flanagan and Adrian Frost

...Continued from previous page

So there's the shape, now for the size. The exam board could perhaps legitimately ask a question concerning how one type of validity was associated with one piece of research, but the teams of teachers and examiners that rigorously check such exams would probably regard this as far too limiting. More likely is a question asking for a range of research studies or both types of validity.

In this context, a reasonable size paragraph in each section above would appear appropriate, even for an 18-mark question, especially when one considers that a third of the response will deal with A01 description.

We now have a clearly-structured diagram to fill in and revise that should leave us covered if this difficult area comes up. So, some forward planning, thorough knowledge of the Specification and an understanding of a few of the 'rules and regs.' has hopefully made the area much more manageable.

The structure above has driven the activity in **Handout 104**.

Handout 104

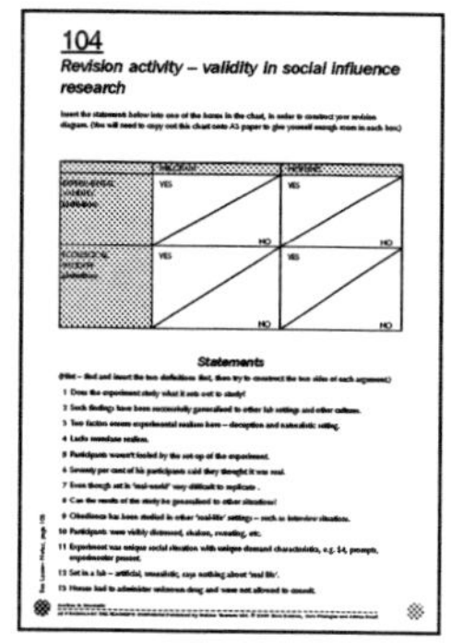
104
Revision activity – validity in social influence research

Answers to task

	MILGRAM	HOFLING
EXPERIMENTAL VALIDITY (Definition) 1	YES: 6, 10 / NO: 5	YES: 3 / NO: 13
ECOLOGICAL VALIDITY (Definition) 8	YES: 2 / NO: 4,11,12	YES: 9 / NO: 7

Ranking ethical issues

Ask the class to divide into small groups and instruct each group to rank ethical issues in order of importance. Discuss the results.

Alternatively, students could be asked to rank ethical issues in the context of psychological studies.

Is it ethical?

The suggested activity relates to the newspaper article 'A trauma I'd totally forgotten' which is on the CD. It permits students to think about the impact of research from a participant's point of view. In this case the researchers found the 'participant' after going through some hospital records. The participant, Peter Moss, was unaware he was a disturbed child until he took part in this research 35 years later. They started the research, thus triggering old memories, etc. but when the funding ran out they had to stop and lost interest, leaving him in the lurch without any answers to his questions. It illustrates the dilemma between doing the research and possibly finding out something important, or not doing anything but risking learning nothing at all. The article also introduces the concept of funding.

It may be heplful to read about Socially Sensitive Research in an A2 textbook as a background to this discussion.

The Donny and Marie approach: Debate on justifying Milgram

This is a technique for developing students A02 skills in analysis. (Please note, this kind of exercise can be done without any reference to early 1970s family supergroups, but it kinda loses something if it is.)

The majority of students can produce both A01 and A02 material and, when work is marked, it is often the case that a 'pattern' of such material will emerge. It can be useful to sketch those patterns in discussion with students.

The following patterns will probably be quite common.

Example 1

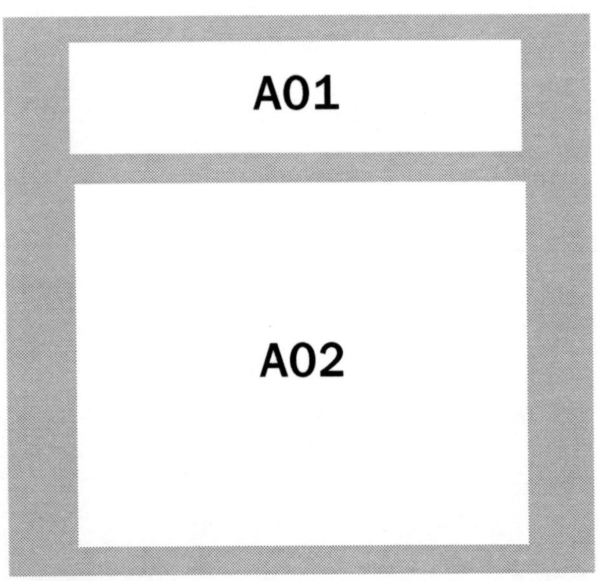

This is a common pattern, especially amongst students new to this sort of assessment. It can get high marks, but the student has to make sure that they get the balance right between the two, and, more importantly, it might be hard to get the discussion material to 'engage' with the content outlined at the beginning.

Cont'd ...

 © 2004 Sara Berman, Cara Flanagan and Adrian Frost

...Continued from previous page

Example 2

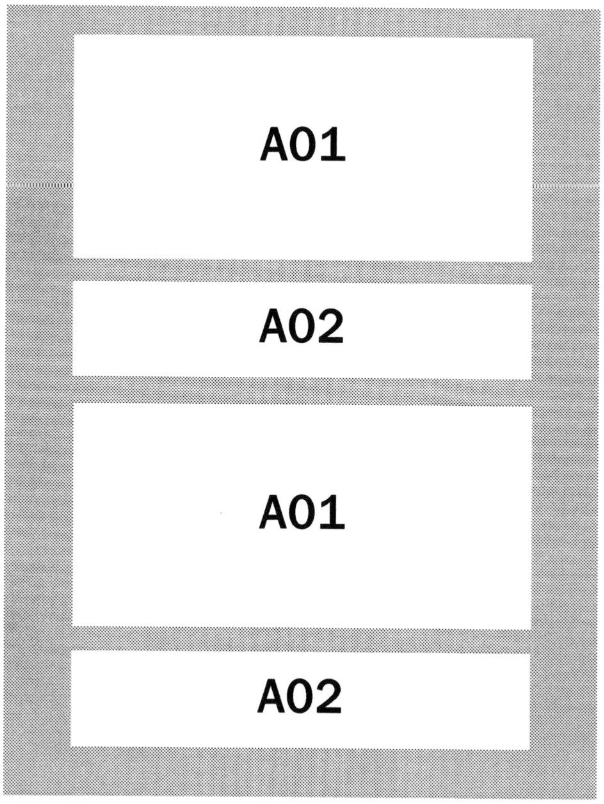

Here, the candidate has made sure that they evaluate the material that they have revised, but the A02 material looks a little 'tacked on', rather than driving the essay.

Example 3

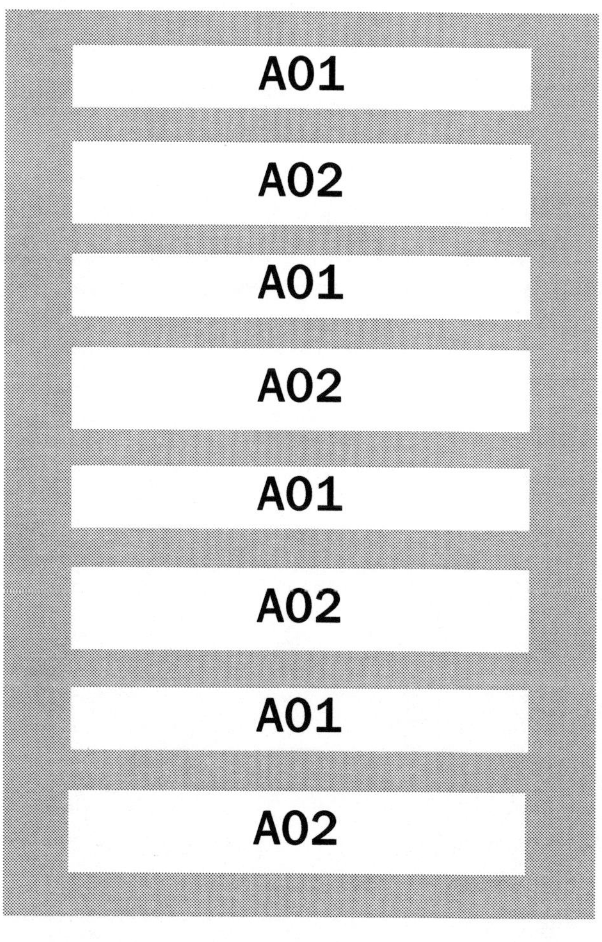

A better essay, however, might look like this.

Rather than being covered in large lumps, the A01 material has been 'sliced' into smaller chunks, and these chunks have been individually discussed. This 'picking apart' of material is the key to analysis.

Each piece of A01 material has been integrated into a discussion. Indeed, in a very good essay, such material will be so fully integrated, that it could be difficult to identify individual sections of text as separate A01 or A02 material.

Cont'd ...

...Continued from previous page

One way to promote this style of writing, is to present it as a dialogue. For example, in this section of the Specification, many students will present the ethical case against, for example, Milgram or Zimbardo, and then have little to add in terms of discussion. If that case can be sliced up into several parts and students encouraged to question each section as it arises, a more meaningful discussion may arise. I often refer to this as the 'Donny and Marie' approach.

It is thus called because Donny and Marie Osmond used to sing a song which began 'I'm a little bit country, you're a little bit Rock 'n' Roll'. The song would proceed with the pair singing alternate lines. The 'Country' of one, contrasting with the 'Rock 'n' Roll' of the other.

(This lesson usually starts with a debate concerning the sheer level of unhipness of the lecturer's musical references. It certainly needs some description of the performance before the point can be made, but then that is what makes it memorable. Kylie and Jason might make an only slightly less dated alternative.)

One side of the argument is presented as 'Donny'. Students are asked to play the role of 'Marie', by providing a consistent counterpoint to the material offered. For those concerned that this will actually involve singing, the activity takes place using something like **Handout 105**. One half is given, the other half has to be added by the student. The argument thus proceeds through point and counterpoint. This type of balanced argument and analysis should get more marks than straightforward 'lumps' of AO2 points.

Thus hopefully, points that would have been placed in an unconnected cluster of AO2 material at the end of a paragraph or an essay are now be fully integrated into a flowing argument ...

Completed example	
'DONNY'	'MARIE'
Criticism of Milgram's research	Defence of Milgram's research
Experiment involved *deception*, e.g. ● false set of objectives ● role of confederate in deception ● only one electric shock ever given (15 V to teacher as a 'test').	● Milgram (1974) had to use deception or would be no point to study.
● Deception was 'disrespectful to participants' – Kelman (1972).	● 'Deception is harmless, trivial and short-lived' – Elms ● 'Many are impressed by a clever deception' – Christensen (1988)
● Participants couldn't give *informed consent* as they weren't told what to expect. ● Newspaper ad didn't mention electrocution.	● Afterwards, 84 per cent of participants said they were glad to have taken part.
● Milgram was suspended by the American Psychological Association.	● Milgram was reinstated in the APA after an investigation and became President.
● Milgram's participants were *not protected from harm* – Baumrind (1964).	● Extensive debriefs and follow-up studies were undertaken.
● Short-term distress and emotional arousal. ● Long-term damage to self-esteem?	● During the debrief, obedient participants were informed that they were 'normal'. ● 'There is no evidence of anyone ever suffering long-term damage from participation in a psychology experiment' – Elms (1982)
● Given the range of ethical concerns, these experiments should never have been undertaken.	● 'Jarred people out of their complacency' – Milgram ● 'A momentous and meaningful contribution to knowledge' – Erikson (1968)

Cont'd ...

 © 2004 Sara Berman, Cara Flanagan and Adrian Frost

...Continued from previous page

Handout 105

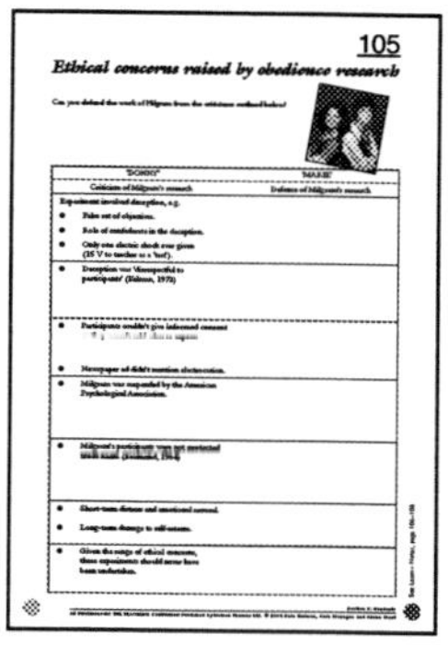
105
Ethical concerns raised by obedience research

References

Baumrind, D.(1964) Some thoughts on ethics of research: after reading Milgram's behavioural study of obedience. *American Psychologist*, 19, 421–3.

Christensen, L. (1988) Deception in psychological research: When is its use justified? *Personality and Social Psychology*, 14, 665–75.

Elms, A.C. (1982) Keeping deception honest: justifying conditions for social scientific research strategies. In T.L. Beuchamp and R. Faden (Eds.) *Ethical Issues in Social Science Research*. Baltimore, MD: Johns Hopkins University Press.

Erikson, M. (1968) The inhumanity of ordinary people. *International Journal of Psychiatry*, 6, 278–9.

Kelman, H.C. (1972) The rights of the subject in social research: An analysis in terms of relative power and legitimacy. *American Psychologist*, 27, 989–1016.

Milgram, S. (1974) *Obedience to Authority: An Experimental View*. New York: Harper & Row.

Role play an ethics committee

Arrange for small groups of students to design their own studies to test conformity, minority influence or obedience. Each study should then be considered by an 'ethics committee' to determine whether they feel it is acceptable.

Alternatively the ethics committee could look at studies that have been done and consider whether they, had they been given the opportunity, would have found this acceptable.

The ethics committee will need a set of guidelines (these can be downloaded from http://www.bps.org.uk/documents/Code.pdf).

AS PSYCHOLOGY: THE TEACHER'S COMPANION Published by Nelson Thornes Ltd. © 2004 Sara Berman, Cara Flanagan and Adrian Frost

Work out an ethical code

Ask students to work out their own ethical codes before looking at BPS guidelines. Try to apply these codes to psychological studies.

The BPS ethical guidelines quiz

Handout 106

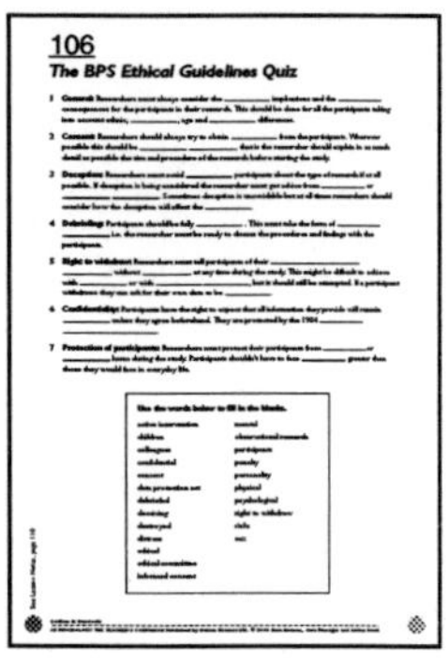
106
The BPS Ethical Guidelines Quiz

Answers

1 *General:* Researchers must always consider the ethical implications and the psychological consequences for the participants in their research. This should be done for all the participants taking into account ethnic, personality, age and sex differences.

2 *Consent:* Researchers should always try to obtain consent from the participants. Wherever possible this should be informed consent, that is the researcher should explain in as much detail as possible the aim and procedure of the research before starting the study.

3 *Deception:* Researchers must avoid deceiving participants about the type of research if at all possible. If deception is being considered the researcher must get advice from colleagues or ethical committees. Sometimes deception is unavoidable but at all times researchers should consider how the deception will affect the participants.

4 *Debriefing:* Participants should be fully debriefed. This must take the form of active intervention, i.e. the researcher must be ready to discuss the procedures and findings with the participants.

5 *Right to withdraw:* Researchers must tell participants of their right to withdraw, without penalty, at any time during the study. This might be difficult to achieve with children or with observational research, but it should still be attempted. If a participant withdraws they can ask for their own data to be destroyed.

6 *Confidentiality:* Participants have the right to expect that all information they provide will remain confidential unless they agree beforehand. They are protected by the 1984 Data Protection Act.

7 *Protection of participants:* Researchers must protect their participants from mental or physical harm during the study. Participants shouldn't have to face risks greater then those they would face in everyday life.

AS PSYCHOLOGY: THE TEACHER'S COMPANION Published by Nelson Thornes Ltd. © 2004 Sara Berman, Cara Flanagan and Adrian Frost

Examples of different degrees of detail for Selye's General Adaptation Syndrome (the GAS model)

Stage 1 Alarm reaction stage
The threat or stressor is recognised and a response made to the alarm. Adrenaline is produced, leading to 'fight or flight' activity. There is some activation of the HPA axis, producing cortisol.

Stage 2 Resistance stage
If the stress continues then it is necessary to find some means of coping and resisting collapse. The body is adapting to the demands of the environment, but at the same time resources are gradually being depleted. The body appears to be coping whereas in reality (physiologically-speaking) things are deteriorating.

Stage 3 Exhaustion stage
Eventually the body's systems can no longer maintain normal functioning. At this point the initial ANS symptoms may reappear (sweating, raised heart rate, etc.). The adrenal gland may be damaged from previous over-activity, and the immune system may not be able to cope because production of necessary proteins has been slowed in favour of other needs. The result may be seen in stress-related illnesses such as ulcers, depression, cardiovascular problems and other mental and physical illnesses.

(172 words – a very good 'Describe GAS for 6 marks' answer)

Seyle's GAS model describes how, through physiological changes in the body, an organism copes with stress in an adaptive way. The model is characterised by three progressive stages that are part of this adaptive process: alarm, resistance and exhaustion.

(39 words – some AO1 material for an essay on the body's response to stress)

Selye's model of the stages through which the body passes in response to stress.

(14 words – a quick mention as part of an AO2 point in an essay about something else)

(5 words – a rough plan for an essay, a revision diagram, etc.)

Stress-response
– three physiological stages.

See Lesson Notes, pages 25 and 71

AS PSYCHOLOGY: THE TEACHER'S COMPANION Published by Nelson Thornes Ltd. © 2004 Sara Berman, Cara Flanagan and Adrian Frost

2

'How to say something intelligent, when you have nothing to say'

Mentally scan the following lists to see if they provide you with anything useful.

There are various different ones. Not all of the points will work all of the time, but most will provide you with something. This is no replacement for solid, detailed revision – but it will help.

THE FIVE Es

- ✏ Evidence – Is there any? What sort? How good is it? Is there any conflicting evidence?
- ✏ Ethics – Any concerns here? Why?
- ✏ Enemies – You wouldn't use the term 'enemies', but are there any conflicting viewpoints? What would other approaches say?
- ✏ Extrapolation – Who were the participants? Can such results be extrapolated across species/cultures? Why not?
- ✏ Ecological validity? – If using experiments, there are almost certainly going to be problems in this area.

THE FOUR Fs

- ✏ Friends – Any other research which supports the conclusions drawn here?
- ✏ Foes – Any other research which doesn't support the conclusions drawn here?
- ✏ Findings – What research findings are there? What approach do they support?
- ✏ Freud – In 50 years and 40-odd volumes, he had something to say about practically everything. Try inserting the key word from the title into the following sentence and see if it works; 'Freud viewed … as being governed by unconscious sexual forces'.

THE TWO Is

- ✏ Individual differences – Are these taken into account. Would different types of people behave differently? Gender? Culture? Personality Type?
- ✏ Intuitive Appeal – Do the conclusions 'feel right'? Does the research have 'face validity'?

See Lesson Notes, page 27

AS PSYCHOLOGY: THE TEACHER'S COMPANION Published by Nelson Thornes Ltd. © 2004 Sara Berman, Cara Flanagan and Adrian Frost

Examplar mark sheet

QUESTION (30 minutes total)	STUDENT MARKER COMMENT	TEACHER COMMENT
1) Describe two ways in which personality may modify the effects of stressors (3+3 marks)		
Are the two ways clearly signposted?	*Yes - A/B + Hardiness*	3
Does each one contain a clear explanation, a link to some research and an example?	*Not much detail on hardiness?*	**agreed**
Mark/3 for first way		2
Mark/3 for second way		1
2) Outline findings of research into life changes (6 marks)		
Often people wander off into areas like 'aims' or 'procedures' here. Has the answer kept to 'Findings' throughout?	*No, lots of time wasted on procedure*	**good findings though!**
Does the answer stick to 'life changes' or does it stray into 'daily hassles' as well?	*Some daily hassles - no marks for them!*	✓
Have they picked up on the fact that they can use the findings of more than one study here?	*Yes - Navy research mentioned as well*	**Well done!**
Mark/6 for relevant findings		4
3) Outline and evaluate research into the workplace as a source of stress (18 marks)		
If Brady's Monkeys or temperature/rioting material has been used, has it been linked to the workplace?	*Monkeys yes Riots no*	**Take care on this**
Is the AO1 material 'accurate and detailed', 'Generally accurate but less detailed', 'basic' or 'muddled'?	*Generally accurate less detailed*	✓
Mark/6 for AO1		3
Once you have highlighted all the A01 and A02 material, is there roughly twice as much AO2?	*Not much A02*	**See below**
Has any of the 'Research Methods' material we covered last month been used for A02?	*Yes - lack of control*	**Well done!**
Is the commentary 'reasonable', 'basic' or 'superficial'?	*basic*	✓
Mark/12 for AO2		5
TOTAL/30		15
GRADE (A=22,B=19,C=17,D=14,E=12)		D
	COMMENT *Better than mine! Shame you messed up the last Qu!*	COMMENT **Good A01 material - Concentrate on developing discussion next time!**

LESSON FEEDBACK

1. Use the markscheme to decide how long answers should be.

2. Make sure that all points refer back to the questions

See Lesson Notes, page 30

AS PSYCHOLOGY: THE TEACHER'S COMPANION Published by Nelson Thornes Ltd. © 2004 Sara Berman, Cara Flanagan and Adrian Frost

4

Marking

Topic area..

Title of work..

AO1 – Description or 'what they know about the subject'

Tick the number that best fits the AO1 content of the essay.

	6-mark question	*3-mark question*	*2-mark question*
Accurate and detailed	6	3	2
	5		
Generally accurate, less detailed	4	2	
	3		
Basic, lacks detail, muddled	2	1	1
	1		
Nothing to credit/wrong	0	0	0

AO2 – Commentary/evaluation or the 'however' section

Tick the boxes that best fit the AO2 content of this essay, decide whether it is in the higher or lower range of the box, reach an average mark.

Marks	***Comments*** ***'This shows/suggests'***	***Analysis*** ***i.e. main arguments***	***Use*** ***'So what?'***
Top 12–11 10–9	Good Tells you a lot	Reasonably thorough	Material is used effectively (can't put 'so what?' after any statement)
Middle 8–7 6–5	Reasonable Tells you something	Some analysis: not always clear, bit limited	Can put 'so what?' after a few statements
Bottom 4–3 2–1	Doesn't really tell you a lot: superficial	Pretty basic	Material not used very well: can put 'so what?' after lots of statements.
Nothing	–	–	–

Marks: AO1 = ☐

AO2 = ☐

Total = ☐

See Lesson Notes, page 30

AS PSYCHOLOGY: THE TEACHER'S COMPANION Published by Nelson Thornes Ltd. © 2004 Sara Berman, Cara Flanagan and Adrian Frost

The 'Star Studies'

Guidance for using the 'Star Studies' table

1 These are the areas in which students could be asked an APFCC (aims, procedures, findings, conclusions, criticisms) question. It's not a list of the 'only' studies that they need to know, but these are the only studies that they can be asked about for this particular question format.

2 The column on the right is only for guidance.

3 See 'How to work out what to teach' (General Notes pages 21–23) for guidance on coverage of studies that might be useful beyond these 'Star Studies'.

	APFCC questions will be asked *only* in the following *topic* areas:	Candidates are not required to know more than *one* APFCC study in any topic area. An example for each topic area is listed below (from *The Complete Companion*)
Cognitive psychology	Encoding in STM	Jacobs (1887)
	Capacity in STM	Jacobs (1887)
	Duration in STM	Peterson & Peterson (1959)
	STM	Can use any study of STM
	Encoding in LTM	Can use study of encoding in STM which includes LTM
	Duration in LTM	Bahrick *et al.* (1975)
	LTM	Can use any study of LTM
	Flashbulb memory	Brown & Kulik (1977)
	Repression	Williams (1994)
	Emotional factors in forgetting	Can use study of repression or flashbulb memory
	Reconstructive memory	Bartlett (1932)
	Eyewitness testimony	Loftus & Palmer (1974)
Developmental psychology	Secure/insecure attachments	Ainsworth *et al.* (1978), Van Ijzendoorn & Kroonenberg (1988)
	Cross-cultural variation	Van Ijzendoorn & Kroonenberg (1988)
	Individual differences	Can use study of secure/insecure attachments or cross-cultural variation
	Effects of deprivation/separation	Bowlby (1944)
	Related to Bowlby's maternal deprivation hypothesis	Can use study of long-term effects of deprivation
	Effects of privation	Hodges & Tizard (1989)
Physiological psychology	Stress and cardiovascular disorders	Kvantz *et al.* (1991)
	Stress and the immune system	Kiecolt-Glaser *et al.* (1995)
	Stress and physical illness	Can use study of cardiovascular disorder or the immune system
	Life changes	Rahe *et al.* (1970)
	Workplace stressors	Marmot *et al.* (1997)
	Sources of stress	Can use study of life changes or workplace stressors
Individual differences	Biological explanations of anorexia	Holland *et al.* (1988)
	Psychological explanations of anorexia	Becker *et al.* (2000)
	Biological explanations of bulimia	Kendler *et al.* (1991)
	Psychological explanations of bulimia	Cotts and Barrios (1986)
	Biological/psychological explanations of eating disorders	Can use any of above studies
Social psychology	Conformity/majority influence	Asch (1956)
	Minority influence	Moscovici *et al.* (1969)
	Obedience	Milgram (1963)

See Lesson Notes, page 34

AS PSYCHOLOGY: THE TEACHER'S COMPANION Published by Nelson Thornes Ltd. © 2004 Sara Berman, Cara Flanagan and Adrian Frost

6

Template 1: *Star Study and other research*

Research on:

....

Key definition ....

1

2

3

Do not write your answers in full sentences – be brief

The notes you make will help you answer *three* kinds of exam questions:

1 APFCC

2 findings or conclusions from research

3 part (c) questions.

Star study ....

Aims

●

●

●

Procedures

●

●

●

Findings

●

●

●

Conclusions

●

●

●

Criticisms

1

●

●

●

2

●

●

●

Other research

Study 1

Findings

●

●

Conclusions

●

●

Criticism (elaborate your criticism)

●

●

●

Study 2

Findings

●

●

Conclusions

●

●

Criticism (elaborate your criticism)

●

●

●

See Lesson Notes, page 35

AS PSYCHOLOGY: THE TEACHER'S COMPANION Published by Nelson Thornes Ltd. © 2004 Sara Berman, Cara Flanagan and Adrian Frost

Template 2: *Other research*

Research on:

....

Key definition ....

1

2

3

Do not write your answers in full sentences – be brief

The notes you make will help you answer *two* kinds of exam questions:

1 findings or conclusions from research

2 part (c) questions.

Other research

Study 1

Findings

●

●

Conclusions

●

●

Criticism

●

●

●

Study 2

Findings

●

●

Conclusions

●

●

Criticism

●

●

●

Study 3

Findings

●

●

Conclusions

●

●

Criticism

●

●

●

See Lesson Notes, page 35

AS PSYCHOLOGY: THE TEACHER'S COMPANION Published by Nelson Thornes Ltd. © 2004 Sara Berman, Cara Flanagan and Adrian Frost

8

Template 3: *Explanations*

Explanation of:

....

Do not write your answers in full sentences – be brief.

Key definition ....

1

2

3

Explanation ....

-
-
-
-
-
-

Criticisms

1

-
-
-

2

-
-
-

Research studies (which support or challenge)

Study 1

Findings

Conclusions

Study 2

Findings

Conclusions

See Lesson Notes, page 35

 © 2004 Sara Berman, Cara Flanagan and Adrian Frost

Template 4: *Explanations*

Explanations of:

....

Key definition ....

1

2

3

Explanation 1 ....

-
-
-
-
-
-

Criticisms

1

-
-
-

2

-
-
-

Explanation 2 ....

-
-
-
-
-
-

Criticisms

1

-
-
-

2

-
-
-

See Lesson Notes, page 35

AS PSYCHOLOGY: THE TEACHER'S COMPANION Published by Nelson Thornes Ltd. © 2004 Sara Berman, Cara Flanagan and Adrian Frost

10

Template 5: *Evaluation summary sheet*

TOPIC

Strengths and/or supporting evidence

•

•

•

Limitations, disadvantages and/or evidence against

•

•

•

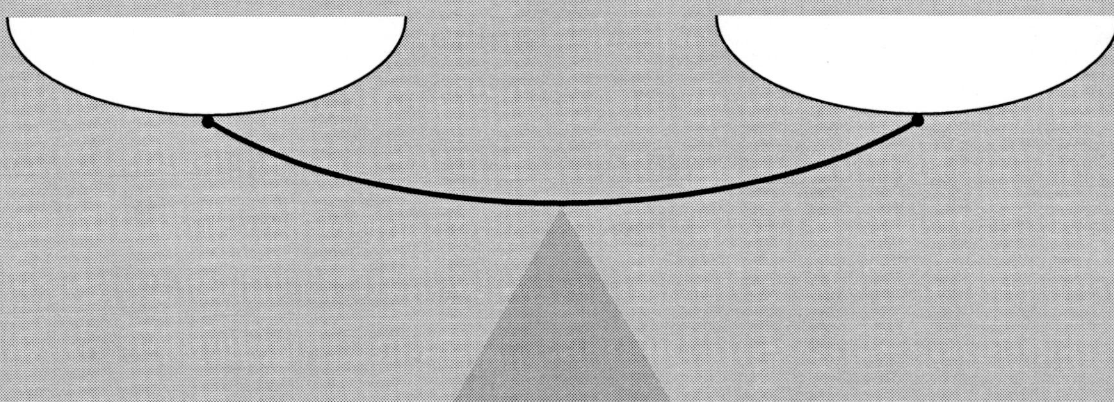

My conclusion is, on balance, that

See Lesson Notes, page 35

AS PSYCHOLOGY: THE TEACHER'S COMPANION Published by Nelson Thornes Ltd. © 2004 Sara Berman, Cara Flanagan and Adrian Frost

Research activity – Peterson and Peterson (1959)

Do you think that Peterson and Peterson's results are right? Do you think that your STM would last longer than 18 seconds? Why don't you try it? Adapt the standardised instructions from this study and try it out on some participants. (If you act as the participant this might be produce unfair results because you would try really hard to remember the letters while counting backwards because you know the aim of the experiment. What you need are some naive participants who don't know the experimental aims! This is called a *single blind design*, because the experimenter knows the aim but the participants don't.)

Whenever conducting research you must behave as a proper psychologist and make sure that you treat any participants with respect. You must inform them of your aims beforehand, if possible, or tell them afterwards what the aims were. Do not bring psychology into disrepute!

Instructions from Peterson and Peterson:

Please sit against the back of your chair so that you are comfortable. You will not be shocked during this experiment. In front of you is a little black box. The top or green light is on now. The green light means we are ready to begin a trial. I will speak some letters and then a number. You are to repeat the number immediately after I say it and begin counting backwards by 3s (4s) from that number in time with the clock ticking that you hear. I might say ABC 309. Then you say, 309, 306, 303, etc. until the bottom or red light comes on. When you see this red light you stop counting immediately and say the letters that were given at the beginning of the trial. Remember to keep your eyes on the black box at all times. There will be a short rest period and then the green light will come on again and we will start a new trial.

Analysis

Summarise findings using *descriptive statistics*:

- Mean, mode or median to show average recall at each retention interval. This can be done for individuals or for the whole class. For example:

	3	6	9	12	15	18 secs
Number of trigrams correctly recalled						
Mean						

- Transfer this data to a bar chart.

Discussion points

1. What can you conclude from your findings about the duration of STM?
2. What can you conclude about trace decay theory?
3. What changes could you make to improve the design of this study?
4. Is this an experiment? What is the IV and DV?
5. Are there any ethical issues that should have been considered?
6. If so, how could you deal with them?
7. If all the participants were students, how might this affect the validity of the findings?
8. What sampling technique did you use?
9. Why would a double blind design be a good thing?
10. Write a hypothesis for this study.

See Lesson Notes, page 37

AS PSYCHOLOGY: THE TEACHER'S COMPANION Published by Nelson Thornes Ltd. © 2004 Sara Berman, Cara Flanagan and Adrian Frost

See Lesson Notes, page 37

Stimulus material

Nonsense trigram	Count backwards from	Retention interval	RECALL	Nonsense trigram	Count backwards from	Retention interval	RECALL	Nonsense trigram	Count backwards from	Retention interval	RECALL
WRT	303	3		FVJ	233	15		DMP	294	6	
TGK	476	15		GKX	576	12		LKJ	487	12	
JDL	289	6		WBK	109	3		GFL	582	15	
WPB	495	18		GDQ	344	6		CGB	497	9	
GPS	628	3		MBN	790	18		QKL	453	3	
DKC	675	9		DKG	278	9		DTK	692	15	
HPQ	382	6		VWQ	497	6		FSC	230	6	
FKM	369	12		NBV	265	18		XNT	359	15	
KZW	286	15		CMX	311	18		MWZ	479	18	
JBQ	286	18		PGR	205	3		QKL	427	9	
RWN	854	12		KGR	900	15		WVB	592	12	
MPL	298	9		KNT	326	3		RPF	609	9	
DFK	155	3		LWB	189	18		KFD	238	3	
CWP	429	18		MBP	472	9		MCC	495	9	
SPD	978	6		CSK	939	15		CLF	199	12	
RFV	359	12		KGF	128	12		RGJ	270	6	

AS PSYCHOLOGY: THE TEACHER'S COMPANION Published by Nelson Thornes Ltd. © 2004 Sara Berman, Cara Flanagan and Adrian Frost

Spot the mistakes – a Revision exercise for Bahrick *et al.* (1975)

Below are details of a classic study of duration in LTM. Can you spot the three deliberate mistakes inserted into each section?

You may like to test your own memory by reading over this study in a textbook first and then attempting to identify the mistakes.

Star Study on duration in LTM (Bahrick *et al.* 1975)

Aims

Some studies have looked at the duration of memory over time but have found that memories fade. It is possible that memories actually last a lot longer than was found in these studies. The problem is that the information that people were asked to remember was not very interesting, and that's why it was forgotten. In real life people have lots of things they do remember over a long time, but these things tend to be from another culture. This study aimed to investigate VLTM in a laboratory setting where the things to-be-remembered were of personal significance. The study also aimed to compare verbal and acoustic LTM.

Procedures

Nearly 400 participants aged 7 to 17 were tested. There were various tests, including:

1 A free-recognition test where they were asked to list all the names that they could remember of individuals in their graduating class.

2 A photo recognition test consisting of 50 photos, some of which were from the participant's high school yearbook.

3 A name recognition test for ex-boyfriends.

There was also a photo matching test, a name matching test and a photo cueing test.

Conclusions

Participants who were tested within 15 years of graduation were about 90 per cent accurate in identifying faces and names (i.e. visual and verbal recognition). After 48 hours, this increased to about 80 per cent for name recognition and 70 per cent for photo recognition.

Free recall was less good. After 5 years this was about 60 per cent accurate dropping to 30 per cent after 48 years.

Findings

There is evidence of very long-term memories up to 57 years after graduation, though there is some loss of memory over time. People remembered the names (visual recall) almost as well as the faces (verbal recall). Recall was better than recognition. This suggests, that in real life our memories contain a vast amount of information but we are not always able to recall it. When given a recognition test this represses our memory and we can remember it (VLTM). Therefore our vast store of memory is there but not always easily accessed.

See Lesson Notes, page 39

 © 2004 Sara Berman, Cara Flanagan and Adrian Frost

14

Correct version of Bahrick *et al.*

The altered areas are highlighted by underlining.

Star Study on duration in LTM (Bahrick *et al.* 1975)

- ***Aims***

Some studies have looked at the duration of memory over time but have found that memories fade. It is possible that memories actually last a lot longer than was found in these studies. The problem is that the information that people were asked to remember was not very interesting, and that's why it was forgotten. In real life people have lots of things they do remember over a long time, but these things tend to be personally important. This study aimed to investigate VLTM in a natural setting where the things to-be-remembered were of personal significance. The study also aimed to compare verbal and visual LTM.

- ***Procedures***

Nearly 400 participants aged 17 to 74 were tested. There were various tests, including:

1 A free-recall test where they were asked to list all the names that they could remember of individuals in their graduating class.

2 A photo recognition test consisting of 50 photos, some of which were from the participant's high school yearbook.

3 A name recognition test for ex-school friends.

There was also a photo matching test, a name matching test and a photo cueing test.

- ***Findings***

Participants who were tested within 15 years of graduation were about 90 per cent accurate in identifying faces and names (i.e. visual and verbal recognition). After 48 years, this declined to about 80 per cent for name recognition and 70 per cent for photo recognition.

Free recall was less good. After 15 years this was about 60 per cent accurate dropping to 30 per cent after 48 years.

- ***Conclusions***

There is evidence of very long-term memories up to 57 years after graduation, though there is some loss of memory over time. People remembered the names (verbal recall) almost as well as the faces (visual recall). Recognition was better than recall. This suggests, that in real life our memories contain a vast amount of information but we are not always able to recall it. When given a recognition test this jogs our memory and we can remember it (VLTM). Therefore our vast store of memory is there but not always easily accessed.

See Lesson Notes, page 39

 © 2004 Sara Berman, Cara Flanagan and Adrian Frost

Research activity – immediate memory span

Set 1

8	1	4									
7	5	3	1								
2	6	5	3								
7	3	8	2	9							
0	5	0	2	4	7	6					
1	8	3	2	3	5	9	8				
4	6	4	8	7	7	3	4	1			
2	6	3	9	7	1	6	4	0	8		
8	5	1	7	3	9	6	2	8	4	5	
8	2	7	6	5	8	3	4	8	9	7	3

Set 2

F	N	P										
R	M	T	S									
W	P	F	Q	H								
X	W	O	Q	D	M							
F	P	I	H	K	S	R						
F	Y	U	M	T	J	R	L					
X	F	P	G	E	M	J	K	A				
L	J	E	F	S	H	T	P	G	Z			
W	N	T	J	C	X	F	O	T	R	W	G	
P	N	E	G	Z	S	O	E	R	W	G	S	B

Set 3

Lion	Boat	Plug									
Walk	Sand	Leaf	Star								
Suit	Look	Stab	Path	Cart							
Junk	Lone	Game	Call	Wood	Head						
Wall	Place	Drug	Desk	Lamb	Lawn	Tins					
Hats	Pick	Gift	Dive	Book	Tree	Hair	This				
Clay	Both	Nail	Door	Hope	Earl	Feel	Cope	Plum			
Soft	Fall	Shop	True	Free	Pail	Twig	Lord	Flat	Milk		
Logs	Time	Lake	Girl	Moon	Foot	Duck	Pens	Earn	Bird	Cake	
Play	Band	Fake	Slug	Ball	Face	Coat	Bark	Live	Sift	Lick	Pond

See Lesson Notes, page 40

AS PSYCHOLOGY: THE TEACHER'S COMPANION Published by Nelson Thornes Ltd. © 2004 Sara Berman, Cara Flanagan and Adrian Frost

16

Research activity – Baddeley (1966)

Word lists for testing STM

List A

man, cab, can, cad, cap, mad, max, mat, cat, map

Recall list for A:

max, map, man, mat, can, cab, cad, mad, cap, cat

List B

pit, few, cow, pen, sup, bar, day, hot, rig, bun

Recall list for B:

pen, few, sup, bun, pit, bar, rig, day, hot, cow

List C

great, large, big, huge, broad, long, tall, fat, wide, high

Recall list for C:

broad, long, wide, great, fat, large, big, huge, high, tall

List D

good, warm, hot, safe, tame, damp, strong, foul, old, late

Recall list for D:

old, strong, good, warm, late, hot, safe, foul, tame, damp

Word lists for testing LTM

List A

pad, did, dig, din, pan, dip, pal, pat, dim, par

Recall list for A:

pal, pat, dim, pad, par, did, dig, dip, pan, din

List B

cot, hit, mop, sad, run, bow, dab, way, tug, fur

Recall list for B:

way, cot, tug, hit, mop, fur, dab, sad, run, bow

List C

little, small, tiny, short, thin, less, few, low, rare, mini

Recall list for C:

little, mini, small, tiny, rare, low, short, thin, few, less

List D

cold, game, snip, fair, bump, hope, match, thread, neat, wrong

Recall list for D:

game, hope, snip, neat, bump, match, thread, wrong, cold, fair

See Lesson Notes, page 41

AS PSYCHOLOGY: THE TEACHER'S COMPANION Published by Nelson Thornes Ltd. © 2004 Sara Berman, Cara Flanagan and Adrian Frost

Visual stimuli for Brandimote *et al.* replication

Pair no.	Composite image	Part of composite
1	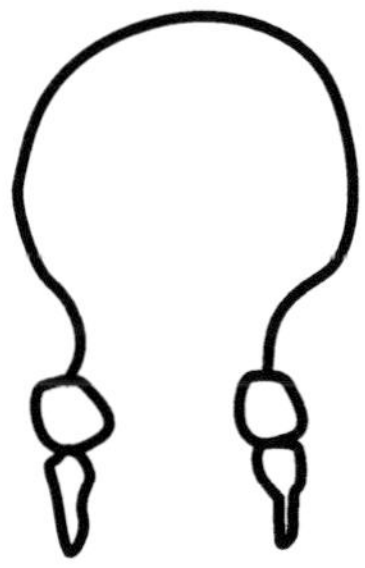	
2	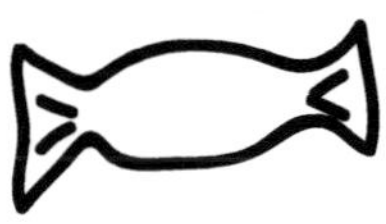	
3		
4		
5		
6		

See Lesson Notes, page 42

 © 2004 Sara Berman, Cara Flanagan and Adrian Frost

18

Serial position curve – *test materials*

List 1	List 2	List 3	List 4	List 5
door	table	bench	couch	watch
tulip	bush	flower	lawn	chair
France	Canada	Germany	Denmark	Africa
blanket	bottle	tape	cushion	stamp
cry	wince	wink	shrug	giggle
bird	shout	flood	brass	apple
cliff	back	year	salute	scout
pace	angle	floor	water	foot
curls	nose	hand	toe	dish
leaf	sail	knife	spoon	fork

See Lesson Notes, page 43

AS PSYCHOLOGY: THE TEACHER'S COMPANION Published by Nelson Thornes Ltd. © 2004 Sara Berman, Cara Flanagan and Adrian Frost

Serial position curve –
recording the findings

Record your findings by putting a tick in the correct box. For example, if you remembered the first three words in list 1 on **Handout 18** and the last two words in list 1, then put a tick in boxes 1, 2, 3, 9 and 10.

Do this for all five lists on **Handout 18**.

The next step is to add up the total number of words for each row. This will give you the total number of words that you remembered, that relates to their position in the list.

Finally, you can illustrate the data on the graph below.

Serial position of word list	List number					Total number of words recalled
	1	2	3	4	5	
1						
2						
3						
4						
5						
6						
7						
8						
9						
10						

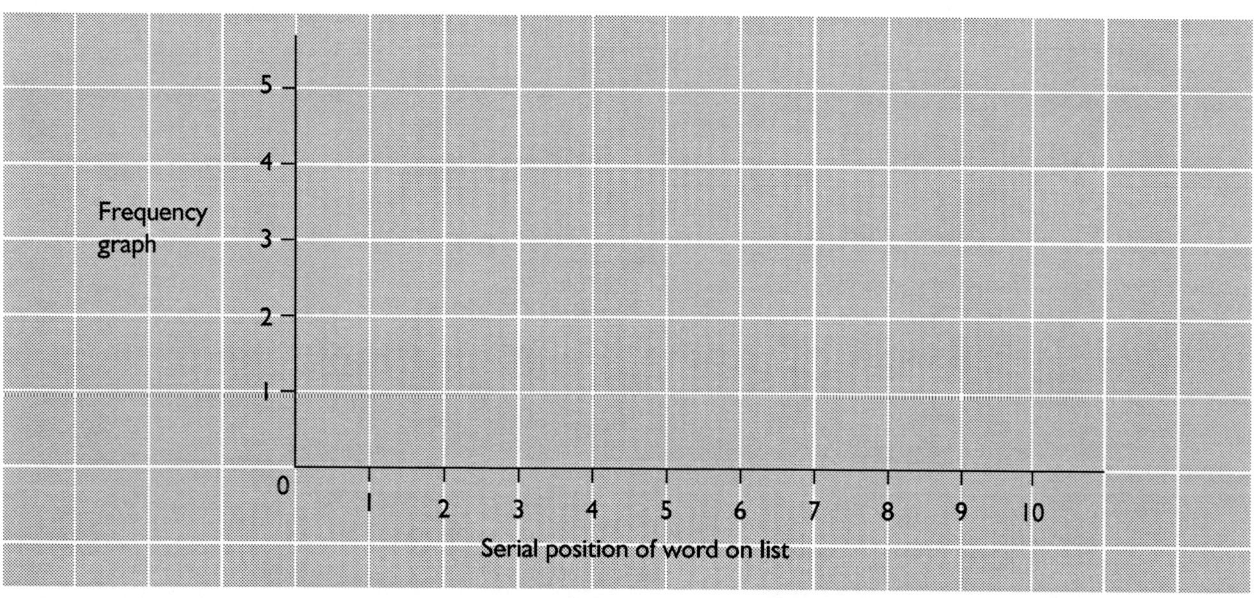

Adapted from Baddeley, A. (1982) *Your Memory: A User's Guide*. Penguin.

See Lesson Notes, page 43

AS PSYCHOLOGY: THE TEACHER'S COMPANION Published by Nelson Thornes Ltd. © 2004 Sara Berman, Cara Flanagan and Adrian Frost

20

Working memory – stimulus materials

Thirty-two six-letter sequences to be made into cards.

BYTJHZ	HJZTBY	JQBZHT	QRYBJZ
RBYTQJ	TZBJRQ	JHZBYT	BJRYZH
HQRBZT	RTYZJH	JBHTZQ	ZHQBJR
QBHRTY	YZHBJR	ZBTHJQ	HJYRTZ
ZHYJRB	HJQZBT	BYHTRJ	BRJYZT
HZYTRJ	TYZHBQ	JYHTQB	BRTHYQ
JYZRQH	ZHBTYJ	QRBTHZ	BRHJQY
BQHRYT	HRJYRZ	TRBYQJ	YBTHJR

See Lesson Notes, page 44

AS PSYCHOLOGY: THE TEACHER'S COMPANION Published by Nelson Thornes Ltd. © 2004 Sara Berman, Cara Flanagan and Adrian Frost

Working memory – sentence verification task

Practice sheet

HA	A is followed by H	Is this true?	YES/NO
AY	A is not followed by Y	Is this false?	YES/NO
AB	A does not follow B	Is this false?	YES/NO
AR	A is followed by R	Is this false?	YES/NO
YA	A precedes Y	Is this true?	YES/NO
QA	A does not precede Q	Is this true?	YES/NO

See Lesson Notes, page 44

AS PSYCHOLOGY: THE TEACHER'S COMPANION Published by Nelson Thornes Ltd. © 2004 Sara Berman, Cara Flanagan and Adrian Frost

22

Working memory – sentence verification task

Test item	Sentence	Verification	Circle YES/NO	Recall six letters	Tick if correct
AB	A follows B	Is this true?	YES/NO		
AJ	A does not follow J	Is this true?	YES/NO		
AW	A is followed by W	Is this true?	YES/NO		
AC	A is not followed by C	Is this true?	YES/NO		
YA	A follows Y	Is this true?	YES/NO		
CA	A does not follow C	Is this true?	YES/NO		
QA	A is not followed by Q	Is this true?	YES/NO		
HA	A is followed by H	Is this true?	YES/NO		
AJ	A follows J	Is this false?	YES/NO		
AB	A does not follow B	Is this false?	YES/NO		
AR	A is followed by R	Is this false?	YES/NO		
AY	A is not followed by Y	Is this false?	YES/NO		
BA	A follows B	Is this false?	YES/NO		
WA	A does not follow W	Is this false?	YES/NO		
JA	A is not followed by J	Is this false?	YES/NO		
WA	A is followed by W	Is this false?	YES/NO		
AH	A precedes H	Is this true?	YES/NO		
AB	A does not precede B	Is this true?	YES/NO		
AR	A is preceded by R	Is this true?	YES/NO		
AC	A is not preceded by C	Is this true?	YES/NO		
YA	A precedes Y	Is this true?	YES/NO		
QA	A does not precede Q	Is this true?	YES/NO		
HA	A is preceded by H	Is this true?	YES/NO		
RA	A is not preceded by R	Is this true?	YES/NO		
AR	A precedes R	Is this false?	YES/NO		
AQ	A does not precede Q	Is this false?	YES/NO		
AW	A is preceded by W	Is this false?	YES/NO		
AJ	A is not preceded by J	Is this false?	YES/NO		
CA	A precedes C	Is this false?	YES/NO		
HA	A does not precede H	Is this false?	YES/NO		
YA	A is preceded by Y	Is this false?	YES/NO		
QA	A is not preceded by Q	Is this false?	YES/NO		

See Lesson Notes, page 44

AS PSYCHOLOGY: THE TEACHER'S COMPANION Published by Nelson Thornes Ltd. © 2004 Sara Berman, Cara Flanagan and Adrian Frost

RUBY

NILE

EMERALD

BEAR

AMAZON

DATSUN

MONKEY

APPLE

MERCEDES

DIAMOND

LEMON

DOG

DANUBE

PEAR

MINI

AMETHYST

SAPPHIRE

LION

FORD

FOX

GANGES

THAMES

AUDI

BANANA

See Lesson Notes, page 46

AS PSYCHOLOGY: THE TEACHER'S COMPANION Published by Nelson Thornes Ltd. © 2004 Sara Berman, Cara Flanagan and Adrian Frost

24

Levels of processing research activity

Analysing the findings

Construct a table to display your findings. For each participant record how many words they recalled from each category. You can illustrate the findings using a bar chart (graph) showing the totals for each condition.

To construct your stimulus material

You need to include ten 'shallow' questions (e.g. 'is the word in capital letters?'), then ten phonetic questions (e.g. 'Does the word rhyme with ...') and then ten semantic questions on meaning (e.g. 'is the word something ...'). Use the words on **Handout 25**. For each word instructions are given as to how you can make it into a rhyme (phonetic) or semantic question. You must decide which 10 words to use for each condition (shallow, phonetic, semantic).

Having decided on 30 questions, you next need to decide a word order. If you just presented the questions in bunches (ten shallow, ten phonemic, ten semantic), this might alert participants to the purpose of the questions. It is also likely that they might simply remember the most recent words best. Therefore questions should be **randomly** distributed. In addition, one must have a balance of questions that have 'yes' answers and those that have 'no' answers. (We don't want all the questions to have the answer 'yes'.)

Bearing this in mind, one way to construct the final questionnaire is to write the three conditions (shallow, phonemic, semantic) on 30 slips of paper (ten of each) and place them in one pile. In another pile have 30 slips of paper, 15 that say 'yes' and 15 that say 'no'. For each word in the table draw two slips of paper, one from each pile and then write the appropriate question. This ensures random distribution of types of question across 30 questions.

For example, the first line of the table says:

Speech	*Each*	*A form of communication*

A shallow question with the answer 'yes' one would put: SPEECH. Is the word in capital letters?

Or, answer 'no': SPEECH. Is the word in small print?

A phonemic question with the answer 'yes' one would put: Speech. Does the word rhyme with 'each'?

Or, answer 'no': Speech. Does the word rhyme with 'tense?'

A semantic question with the answer 'yes' one would put: Speech. Is the word a form of communication?

Or, answer 'no': Speech. Is the word something to wear?

Finally you need a list of 60 words for a subsequent recognition test.

Conducting the experiment

Write a set of standardised instructions for the investigator to use, and to ensure that standard procedures are followed. Phase 1 is giving the questionnaire out, and asking participants to answer the questions. Phase 2 is an unexpected test of recall using the recognition test.

See Lesson Notes, page 46

AS PSYCHOLOGY: THE TEACHER'S COMPANION Published by Nelson Thornes Ltd. © 2004 Sara Berman, Cara Flanagan and Adrian Frost

Stimulus words for levels of processing research activity

Craik and Tulving constructed the stimulus material for their study using the table below. Note that the nouns selected are all similar in terms of familiarity. This is to ensure that no word is especially distinctive and therefore more memorable. Using words that are similar is a form of **experimental control**.

Word	Rhyme question	Semantic question	Word	Rhyme question	Semantic question
Speech	Each	A form of communication	Bear	Hair	A wild animal
Brush	Lush	Used for cleaning	Lamp	Camp	A type of furniture
Cheek	Teak	A part of the body	Cherry	Very	A type of fruit
Fence	Tense	Found in the garden	Rock	Stock	A type of mineral
Flame	Claim	Something hot	Earl	Pearl	A type of nobility
Flour	Sour	Used for cooking	Pool	School	A type of game
Honey	Funny	A type of food	Week	Peak	A division of time
Knife	Wife	A type of weapon	Boat	Rote	A mode of travel
Sheep	Leap	A type of farm animal	Pail	Whale	A type of container
Copper	Stopper	A type of metal	Trout	Bout	A type of fish
Glove	Shove	Something to wear	gram	Tram	A type of measurement
Monk	Trunk	A type of clergy	Wool	Pull	A type of material
Daisy	Crazy	A type of flower	Clip	Ship	A type of office supply
Miner	Liner	A type of occupation	Juice	Noose	A type of beverage
Cart	Start	A type of vehicle	Pond	Wand	A body of water
Clove	Rove	A type of herb	Lane	Pain	A type of thoroughfare
Robber	Clobber	A type of criminal	Nurse	Curse	Associated with medicine
Mast	Past	A part of a ship	Lark	Park	A type of bird
Fiddle	Riddle	A musical instrument	State	Crate	A territorial unit
Chapel	Grapple	A type of building	Soap	Rope	A type of toiletry
Sonnet	Bonnet	A written form of art	Jade	Raid	A type of precious stone
Witch	Rich	Associated with magic	Sleet	Feet	A type of weather
Roach	Coach	A type of insect	Rice	Dice	A type of grain
Brake	Shake	A part of a car	Tire	Fire	A round object
Twig	Big	A part of a tree	Child	Wild	A human being
Grin	Bin	A human expression	Dance	Stance	A type of physical activity
Drill	Fill	A type of implement	Field	Shield	Found in the countryside
Moan	Prone	A human sound	Floor	Sore	A part of a room
Claw	Raw	A part of an animal	Glass	Pass	A type of utensil
Singer	Ringer	A type of entertainer	Tribe	Scribe	A group of people

See Lesson Notes, page 46

 © 2004 Sara Berman, Cara Flanagan and Adrian Frost

26

Examples of 6-mark and 3-mark versions

Original text

Craik and Lockhart (1972) proposed a different kind of model to explain lasting memories. They suggested that enduring memories are created by the *processing* that you do rather than through rehearsal. Experiences are processed in different ways when information is encoded. Some information is processed more deeply than others. Craik and Lockhart suggested that things that are processed more *deeply* are more memorable just because of the way they are processed. Memory is an automatic *by-product* of processing.

This model does not propose that the idea of separate stores (the multi-store model) should be scrapped, but that one should focus on the effect of different *encoding operations*. In the levels of processing model, there are two ways that information can be retained: (1) through deep encoding processes enduring memories are formed, (2) information can be *'recirculated'* (or rehearsed) at a lower level of processing in primary memory (i.e. like STM) (Craik and Lockhart, 1972, p.676). The difference between this *primary memory* and STM is that primary memory is a *flexible processing activity* rather than a limited store.

The key is the 'meaningfulness extracted from the stimulus' (Craik, 1973). In all of the experiments used to support this model information is being processed in a way that makes it *automatically* more memorable. No rehearsal is needed. The more you 'work over' or process the information, the more it becomes memorable. This is the core of the levels of processing model.

[239 words]

6-MARK/POINT VERSION (key words are in bold)

- **Craik and Lockhart (1972)**
- The key to enduring memories is **processing not rehearsal**.
- Memory is an **automatic by-product** of processing.
- Effect of different **encoding operations**, e.g. organisation, distinctiveness, elaboration.
- In primary memory information is **recirculated.**
- If **meaning is extracted** from stimulus it becomes memorable.

3-MARK/POINT VERSION

- **Craik and Lockhart (1972)**
- In primary memory information is **recirculated.**
- If **meaning is extracted** from stimulus it becomes memorable (through e.g. organisation, distinctiveness, elaboration).

Practice producing your own bullet versions and using these to construct exam answers.

See Lesson Notes, page 47

AS PSYCHOLOGY: THE TEACHER'S COMPANION Published by Nelson Thornes Ltd. © 2004 Sara Berman, Cara Flanagan and Adrian Frost

Experimental design

Use the following statements to complete the grid. You can use statements in more than one box.

Design	Advantages	Disadvantages	Solution
Independent groups			
Repeated measures			
Matched participants			

1 Gets rid of participant variables

2 Don't have any order effects

3 Don't have any order effects

4 There are order effects

5 Can't control participant variables

6 Randomly assign participants to each group

7 If one person in the pair drops out you lose the whole pair

8 You will need different tests, word lists, etc.

9 Don't need so many participants

10 Randomly assign each person in the pair to each condition

11 Can use the same tests, word lists, etc.

12 Can use the same tests, word lists, etc.

13 Wait a long time between the two parts of the experiment

14 Use counterbalancing

15 Participants are unlikely to be able to guess your aim

16 Takes a very long time to find participants who are perfectly matched

17 To a certain extent participant variables are controlled

18 Might not be able to perform the second part of the experiment straight away

19 need quite a lot of participants

20 Participants will know what to expect the second time and might try to guess what your hypothesis is

21 You don't need to wait between the two conditions

See Lesson Notes, page 48

AS PSYCHOLOGY: THE TEACHER'S COMPANION Published by Nelson Thornes Ltd. © 2004 Sara Berman, Cara Flanagan and Adrian Frost

28

Research activity – Waugh and Norman (1965)

Practice

	79	84	13	27	47	44	(38)	80	56	48	37	93	89	75	4	40	**38**

List *(circled number is the probe)*																	**Probe**	**Answer correct**
1	19	32	(45)	31	27	46	35	38	12	4	54	32	38	48	40	20	**45**	
2	23	46	43	37	68	62	71	34	20	19	2	81	(97)	13	90	24	**97**	
3	61	49	71	26	6	69	48	23	39	82	32	(40)	68	47	80	38	**40**	
4	12	96	59	91	(70)	5	58	83	25	46	20	84	93	31	27	40	**70**	
5	72	15	45	21	50	28	89	35	(11)	31	3	12	67	91	30	79	**11**	
6	85	18	13	60	84	57	40	24	92	36	56	28	32	(12)	77	37	**12**	
7	29	44	73	30	22	8	(59)	83	51	32	62	19	86	94	23	14	**59**	
8	33	95	4	41	64	74	19	69	10	87	(66)	23	36	55	40	29	**66**	
9	43	85	34	25	10	75	(65)	31	86	38	5	24	76	19	52	87	**65**	
10	62	73	37	51	18	41	32	66	52	35	24	(46)	88	71	9	60	**46**	
11	78	42	89	63	(67)	53	28	6	86	59	98	14	94	54	78	17	**67**	
12	81	90	(62)	72	47	88	25	26	53	50	1	45	27	16	84	58	**62**	
13	36	79	91	20	63	13	28	87	33	19	(68)	8	93	57	3	39	**68**	
14	29	11	96	42	80	49	2	64	50	21	98	56	(74)	69	85	76	**74**	
15	48	35	82	26	74	54	22	95	4	40	56	34	15	(99)	43	65	**99**	
16	12	97	61	77	7	92	75	55	(30)	83	70	44	86	23	16	29	**30**	

See Lesson Notes, page 49

AS PSYCHOLOGY: THE TEACHER'S COMPANION Published by Nelson Thornes Ltd. © 2004 Sara Berman, Cara Flanagan and Adrian Frost

Research activity – proactive and retroactive interference

List A	List B	List C	List D (for control group)
Cat	tree	stone	tack–hot
box	pick	toe	fat–lose
pen	dip	time	eye–board
meat	table	soil	cow–melon
Tile	rat	spare	track–cry
Car	small	north	star–fly
clock	true	land	hum–sank
Sea	music	blue	long–fall
stick	new	free	wood–band
nest	sun	duck	white–last
state	tea	beer	phone–sky
love	drive	home	risk–odd
park	oil	case	wet–light
shade	dog	grass	tow–half
tower	form	high	disc–wild

See Lesson Notes, page 51

AS PSYCHOLOGY: THE TEACHER'S COMPANION Published by Nelson Thornes Ltd. © 2004 Sara Berman, Cara Flanagan and Adrian Frost

30

Word lists for Tulving and Psotka research activity

List 1	List 2	List 3	List 4	List 5	List 6
Oak	Snake	North	Owl	Lasagna	Leopard
Elm	Lizard	South	Buzzard	Spaghetti	Lion
Maple	Alligator	East	Eagle	Ravioli	Panther
Ash	Newt	West	falcon		Lynx
Cup	Inch	Daffodil	Nun	Labrador	Gold
Mug	Foot	Rose	Priest	Beagle	Silver
Glass	Yard	Pansy	Vicar	Boxer	Iron
Beaker	Mile	Tulip	Monk	spaniel	Copper
Snow	Nose	Hammer	Beetle	Apple	Onion
Rain	Mouth	Screwdriver	Mosquito	Pear	Potato
Sleet	Eye	Spanner	Fly	Plum	Turnip
Hail	Ear	Wrench	Moth	Orange	Parsnip
Stone	Emerald	Robin	Foot	Trout	Happy
Rock	Diamond	Bluetit	Toe	Carp	Cheerful
Pebble	Ruby	Swallow	Heel	Grayling	Sad
Boulder	Sapphire	sparrow	Sole	Pike	Depressed
Run	Fork	Harp	Peas	Hot	Lobster
Jump	Knife	Piano	Spinach	Cold	Crab
Hop	Spoon	Flute	Broccoli	Warm	Crayfish
Skip	Teaspoon	Clarinet	Runner beans	Tepid	Shrimp
Water	Brother	Truck	Cotton	Doll	Plumber
Milk	Niece	Car	Silk	Rattle	Builder
Squash	Mother	Train	Satin	Teddy	Joiner
Coke	Uncle	Plane	Nylon	Blocks	Bricklayer

See Lesson Notes, page 52

AS PSYCHOLOGY: THE TEACHER'S COMPANION Published by Nelson Thornes Ltd. © 2004 Sara Berman, Cara Flanagan and Adrian Frost

Writing a questionnaire or interview

Research the topic

This should provide you with relevant ideas on which to base your questions, and also give breadth to your study. Read about these topics so that you gain ideas about the possible questions to ask. Your literature search will also suggest related areas of study. For example, Brown and Kulik asked participants about personal memories as well as events of national significance (last category in the table is 'a personal unexpected shock').

Organise the data

Here are details of how Brown and Kulik organised and analysed their data.

They created the list of ten events on the right. For each event the participants were asked 'Do you recall the circumstances in which you first heard that ...?' If the answer was 'no' they were asked to move on to the next event. If the answer was 'yes', the participant was asked to free recall the circumstances in any form or order.

Assassinations, attempted assassinations or other important events		Number reporting FBs Whites	Blacks
Medgar Evers	Black	0	5
John F. Kennedy	White	39	40
Malcolm X	Black	1	14
Martin Luther King	Black	13	30
Robert F. Kennedy	White	25	20
Ted Kennedy	White	13	10
George Wallace	White	11	20
Gerald Ford	White	23	16
General Franco	White	17	13
A personal, unexpected shock		37	3

1 Brown read through these free recall reports and concluded that there were only 6 classes of information reported in most of the accounts. These classes were: place (where event first heard), ongoing event (e.g. 'I was washing the dishes'), informant (person who brought the news), affect on others, affect on self, and immediate aftermath. Not all participants gave information in all six categories but these offered a basis for scoring the recall. One mark was given for content provided in each category, so a participant who provided content in all 6 categories scored 6. This reflected the extent to which it was a flashbulb memory.

2 Participants were also asked to rate consequentiality on a scale of 1 to 5 where 5 was very high consequentiality. Consequentialty was defined to participants: 'In order to rate the consequentialty in your life of the death of someone, let us say President John F. Kennedy, you must imagine the things that would have gone differently had President Kennedy lived. Probably the best single question to ask yourself when rating consequentialty is, 'What consequences for my life, both direct and indirect, has this event had?" Consequentialty should be positively correlated with the flashbulb score (the higher the personal consequence, the stronger the flashbulb memory.

3 Participants were also asked how many times they had told this account to others (to assess how much they may have rehearsed the flashbulb memory – an alternative explanation for such memories). They were offered a choice of answers:

'Never told anyone'

'Gave the same account about 1-5 times'

'Gave the same account about 6-10 times'

'Gave the same account more than 10 times'

See Lesson Notes, page 53

AS PSYCHOLOGY: THE TEACHER'S COMPANION Published by Nelson Thornes Ltd. © 2004 Sara Berman, Cara Flanagan and Adrian Frost

32

Other considerations for writing and conducting a questionnaire

Devising and testing the questionnaire

- *If necessary, develop sub-topics to investigate.* A 'top down' approach should be used in generating questions – start with broad questions and break each down into a number of different specific behaviours. Each group member should put forward ideas which are received uncritically by the group. Later, the group can select the best questions.
- *Decide on a sequence for the questions.* It is best to start with easy ones, saving difficult questions or ones which raise defences until the respondent has relaxed. Also, respondents may resist answering 'yes' or 'no' too many times in a row (response set).
- *Write standardised instructions, and also debriefing instructions.*
- *A pilot run.* The questionnaire should now be tested on a small sample, their feedback will be useful. It may also help to have critical comments from any experts available.
- *Redraft the questionnaire.* You should identify and reject questions that have failed to produce any useful answers. If you have included some open-ended questions, look at these and see if you could categorise them and make them into a set of multiple choice answers.
- *Use the questionnaire with a full sample.* A sampling technique needs to be decided on; most probably it will be opportunity sampling.

Writing the questions

- Avoid: complex, ambiguous and or leading questions which use technical or emotive language and negative terms.
- Open versus closed questions? For maximum information open questions are best, however this makes the scoring and analysis of the data difficult. Closed questions can be binary forced-choice (yes/no, agree/disagree) or have a number of possible answers (do not be afraid to give lots of choices). The inclusion of 'don't know' allows an escape for respondents especially because forced 'yes' answers may bias your results, however it may produce poor overall results when too many people opt for the 'don't know' category. If this is the case, your question is probably not a good one.
- Try to include some open (qualitative) and some closed questions to be able to compare different kinds of data collection.
- How many questions? Not too many or the respondent may become bored, too few and the information you collect will be rather thin.
- Filler questions: it may help to include some irrelevant questions to mislead the respondent as to the main purpose of the survey.

See Lesson Notes, page 53

 © 2004 Sara Berman, Cara Flanagan and Adrian Frost

Spot the mistakes

Can you find the three deliberate mistakes in each section of the following study?

Star Study on the role of repression (Williams, 1994)

Aims

In the last two hundred years the issue of *recovered memories* has caused considerable concern, mainly because it is unclear to what extent such memories are for events that actually did occur (they were repressed and are now recovered) or whether the events never happened, i.e. are failed memories. This study seeks to find out if memories are rehearsed. If there is no evidence of repressed memory then it would be difficult to explain recovered memories – because there is nothing to recover.

Procedures

The study used the records kept at a city hospital emergency room detailing all cases of sexual assaults on children in the period April 1973 to June 1975. In this period 206 girls had been admitted. Details of the assault were recorded at the time.

About 20 years later, 129 of these girls (now women) were experimented upon. They were aged 18 to 31. The women were asked to participate in a pilot study of the lives and health of women who had received medical care from the city hospital during childhood. The interviews lasted for about 3 hours, and included questions about childhood experiences with sex. The interviewers did not know the purpose of the study (in other words this was a double bluff design). The interviewees were not directly asked about child abuse as this might have unfairly triggered the recall for such events.

Findings

Over one third (78 per cent) did not show any recall for the earlier sexual abuse. Of those who did recall the abuse, 60 per cent reported that they had, at one time, not been able to recall these incidents but had 'relived' the memory.

Williams found an inverse relationship between age at the time of abuse and recall – abuse that occurred at an earlier age was more likely to be forgotten.

Conclusions

The findings suggest that having no memory of child sexual abuse is relatively common, which supports the idea that recovery of memories is impossible – because some individuals have forgotten imaginary incidents. Further the fact that some individuals said they had recovered their early memories shows that recovery occurs. Both findings dispute the notion of repression in relation to painful memories.

The finding about age and recall may be due to the fact that those children who were younger at the time of the abuse, were younger at the time of the interviews. Therefore it may be the age of re-interview rather than the age of abuse which is significant.

See Lesson Notes, page 54

AS PSYCHOLOGY: THE TEACHER'S COMPANION Published by Nelson Thornes Ltd. © 2004 Sara Berman, Cara Flanagan and Adrian Frost

34

Research activity – Loftus and Palmer (1974)

The text below should help you familiarise yourself with the original research.

Forty-five students were shown seven films of different traffic accidents. After each film the participants were given a questionnaire, which asked them to describe the accident and then answer a series of specific questions about the accident. There was one critical question. This question was 'About how fast were the cars going when they hit each other?'. One group of participants were given this question. The other five groups were given the verbs smashed, collided, bumped or contacted in place of the word hit. The mean speed estimate was calculated for each group. The group given the word 'smashed' estimated a higher speed than the other groups (about 41 m.p.h.). The group given the word 'contacted' estimated the lowest speed (about 30 m.p.h.). This shows that the form of question can have a significant effect on a witness's answer to the question. In other words, leading questions can affect the accuracy of memory (Loftus and Palmer 1974).

Or

Loftus and Zanni (1975) used a film of a car accident, and then asked a series of questions including the critical question 'Did you see a broken headlight?' Other participants were asked if they saw the broken headlight. These are leading questions which imply that there might have been a broken headlight or there definitely was a broken headlight (the *headlight) – in fact there was no broken headlight. As expected participants were more likely to answer 'yes' if they were asked the question with 'the headlight'.*

Your task is to design and execute a similar study, where a single word is changed in a questionnaire, to see if this affects subject recall. After watching a video, participants are given one of the two versions of a memory recall questionnaire about the video – half get a questionnaire where the word is changed, half get a 'control' questionnaire. Their responses are compared to see if the word change made a difference.

As with any experimental design, you will have to make a large number of decisions before you start. This can be achieved by considering the issues on **Handout 36**.

See Lesson Notes, page 55

AS PSYCHOLOGY: THE TEACHER'S COMPANION Published by Nelson Thornes Ltd. © 2004 Sara Berman, Cara Flanagan and Adrian Frost

Research activity – Loftus and Palmer (1974)

1 Write a very brief review of the study by Loftus and Palmer that you are going to replicate.

2 Describe your research aims (i.e. what particular aspects of this study will you investigate? Try to make this as simple as possible).

3 What is your independent variable? Or independent variables?

4 What is your dependent variable (hint: this is what you are going to measure).

5 Write a suitable directional hypothesis for this study.

6 Why is it appropriate to use a directional hypothesis in this study rather than a non-directional hypothesis?

7 Write a null hypothesis for this study.

8 Will you use repeated measures or independent groups design?

9 Give one reason for your choice of experimental design.

10 Decide how many participants you will need and who you will use.

11 Now write down your standardised procedures, i.e. what you will do with each participant. This should include your standardised instructions and what you will say to participants afterwards (debriefing).

NB All participants should be informed that they can choose not to take part if they wish and they will be told about the aims of the study afterwards (telling them beforehand might affect their performance).

12 Try these out with one participant and see if you should change anything.

13 Once you have collected your data, how will you analyse this so that you can draw some conclusions?

14 What measure of central tendency would be suitable to use with this data?

Your caption might read:

[Condition 1]

The gold-coloured car on the right hit the green car on the left at a road junction in a built-up area.

What speed would you estimate that the green car was travelling at?

OR

[Condition 2]

The gold-coloured car on the right bumped into the green car on the left at a road junction in a built-up area.

What speed would you estimate that the green car was travelling at?

See Lesson Notes, page 55

AS PSYCHOLOGY: THE TEACHER'S COMPANION Published by Nelson Thornes Ltd. © 2004 Sara Berman, Cara Flanagan and Adrian Frost

36

Research activity – Schema and recall

Stimulus materials

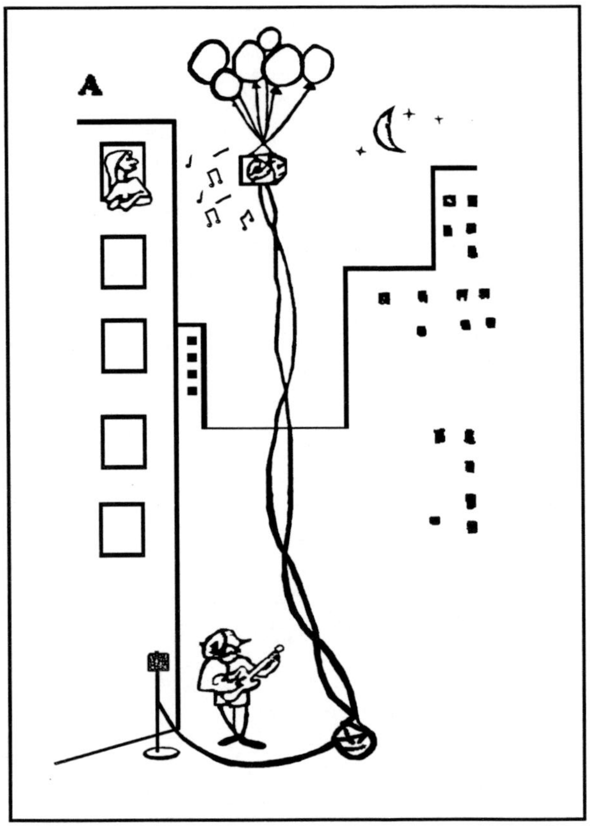

If the balloons popped the sound wouldn't be able to carry since everything would be too far away from the correct floor. A closed window would also prevent the sound from carrying, since most buildings tend to be well insulated. Since the whole operation depends upon a steady flow of electricity, a break in the middle of the wire would also cause problems. Of course, the fellow could shout, but the human voice is not loud enough to carry that far. An additional problem is that a string could break on the instrument. Then there could be no accompaniment to the message. It is clear that the best situation would involve less distance. Then there would be fewer potential problems. With face-to-face contact, the least number of things could go wrong.

See Lesson Notes, page 57

AS PSYCHOLOGY: THE TEACHER'S COMPANION Published by Nelson Thornes Ltd. © 2004 Sara Berman, Cara Flanagan and Adrian Frost

Research activity – Schema and recall

Findings

	No context	*Context after*	*Context before*	*Partial context*	*Repetition*	*Maximum score*
Comprehension	2.3	3.3	6.1	3.7	3.6	7
Recall	3.6	3.6	8.0	4.0	3.8	14

Some questions

1 What conclusions can you draw from this study?

2 Identify the independent variable and the dependent variable?

3 How is 'schema' operationalised in this study?

4 What would be a suitable directional experimental hypothesis?

5 Why would a non-directional hypothesis be preferable?

6 What would the null hypothesis be?

7 Is this repeated measures or independent measures design?

8 Suggest one advantage of this design.

9 Suggest one disadvantage of this design and describe how this might be overcome.

10 How could you randomly allocate participants to conditions?

11 Describe one way that demand characteristics might have affected this study, and describe how you would overcome this problem.

Findings from Bransford and Johnson

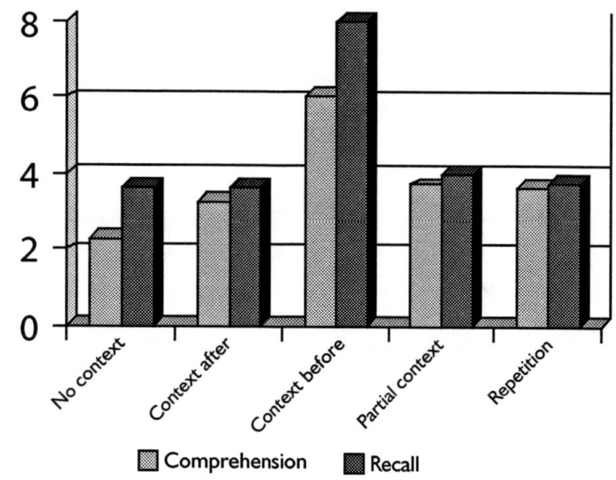

- Draw conclusions from your own study.
- How might your findings be presented in a graph?
- How else might you **describe** your data?

See Lesson Notes, page 57

AS PSYCHOLOGY: THE TEACHER'S COMPANION Published by Nelson Thornes Ltd. © 2004 Sara Berman, Cara Flanagan and Adrian Frost

38

Research activity – Bartlett's stories

The War of the Ghosts

One night two young men from Egulac went down the river to hunt seals, and while they were there it became foggy and calm. Then they heard war-cries, and they thought, 'Maybe this is a war-party'. They escaped to the shore, and hid behind a log. Now canoes came up, and they heard the noise of paddles, and saw one canoe coming up to them. There were five men in the canoe, and they said:

'What do you think? We wish to take you along. We are going up the river to make war on the people'.

One of the young men said, 'I have no arrows'.

'Arrows are in the canoe', they said.

'I will not go along. I might get killed. My relatives do not know where I have gone. But you', he said turning to the other, 'may go with them'.

So one of the young men went, but the other returned home.

And the warriors went up on the river to a town on the other side of Kalama. The people came down to the water, and they began to fight, and many were killed. But presently the young man heard one of the warriors say, 'Quick, let us go home: that Indian has been hit'. Now he thought, 'Oh, they are ghosts'. He did not feel sick, but they said he had been shot.

So the canoes went back to Egulac, and the young men went ashore to his house, and made a fire. And he told everybody and said, 'Behold I accompanied the ghosts, and we went to fight, many of our fellows were killed, and many of those who attacked us were killed. They said I was hit and I did not feel sick'.

He told it all and then became quiet. When the sun rose he fell down. Something black came out of his mouth. His face became contorted. The people jumped up and cried.

He was dead.

The Son who Tried to Outwit his Father

A son said to his father one day, 'I will hide, and you will not be able to find me'. The father replied, 'Hide wherever you like', and he went into his house to rest.

The son saw a three-kernel peanut, and changed himself into one of the kernels; a fowl coming along picked up the peanut and swallowed it; and a wild bush-cat caught and ate the fowl; and a dog met and caught and ate the bush-cat. After a little time the dog was swallowed by a python that, having eaten its meal, went to the river and was snared in a fish-trap.

The father searched for his son and, not seeing him, went to look at the fish-trap. On pulling it to the river-side, he found a large python in it. He opened it, and saw a dog inside, in which he found a bush-cat, and on opening that he discovered a fowl, from which he took the peanut, and breaking the shell, he then revealed his son. The son was so dumbfounded that he never again tried to outwit his father.

See Lesson Notes, page 58

AS PSYCHOLOGY: THE TEACHER'S COMPANION Published by Nelson Thornes Ltd. © 2004 Sara Berman, Cara Flanagan and Adrian Frost

Research activity – Bartlett's story and pictures

The Art of Lawn Tennis

'Tennis is a mutual cocktail of very high kick.' We might suppose this to refer to the effects of the temperaments of players on each other. With anyone but Mr Tilden we might sacrifice the aroma of the apothegm, and emend 'mutual' by 'mental'. But to Mr Tilden tennis is a matter of psychology. It is a question, he says, of understanding the working of one's opponent's mind, of gauging the effect on his mind of one's own play and of the effect of one's own mind of external circumstances. The chapter in which he develops this theme is one of the most interesting in the book, and it includes also a classification of players according to his theory. As we should expect he makes Mr Brookes appear of the first class, he can propound an answer to every query you put him. Next to him come players like Captain Wilding. They are too much concerned with their plan of action to consider their opponents' minds. Your hard-hitting, net-rushing player is a creature of impulse. The steady base-line player is no more scientific really; if he were he would not adhere to his base-line.

Original drawing

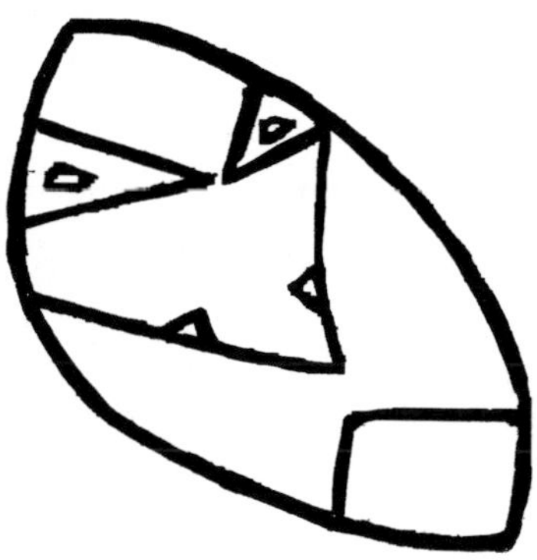

Reproduction 1

Reproduction 2

Reproduction 3

Reproduction 4

Reproduction 5

See Lesson Notes, page 58

AS PSYCHOLOGY: THE TEACHER'S COMPANION Published by Nelson Thornes Ltd. © 2004 Sara Berman, Cara Flanagan and Adrian Frost

40

Cognitive Psychology

Crossword

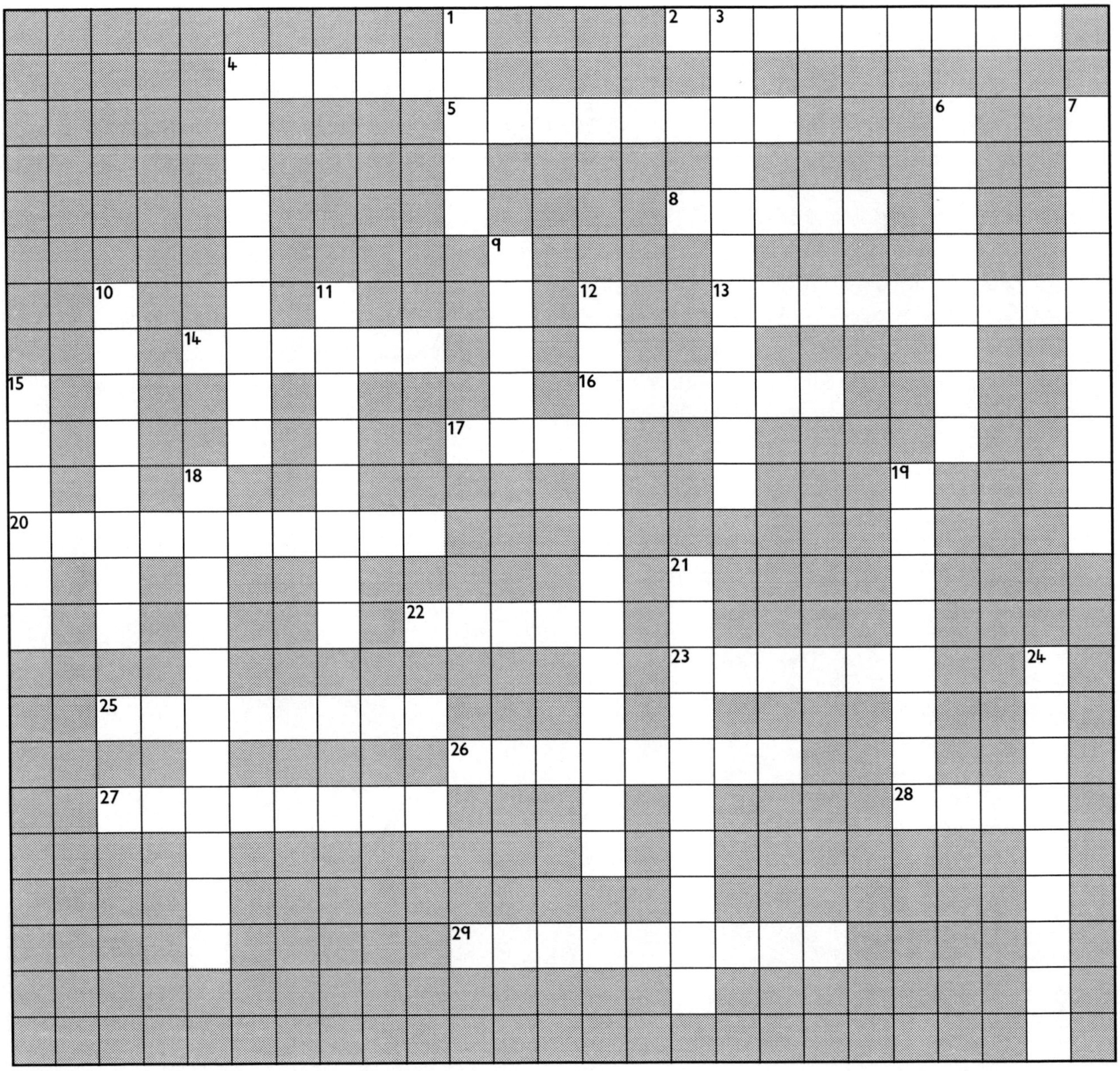

AS PSYCHOLOGY: THE TEACHER'S COMPANION Published by Nelson Thornes Ltd. © 2004 Sara Berman, Cara Flanagan and Adrian Frost

Cognitive Psychology

Crossword clues

Across

2 A type of interference where past learning interferes with current learning. (9)

4 __________ blind – technique where participants do not know the true aim of the experiment. (6)

5 A measure of the amount that can be held in memory. (8)

8 Weapon __________ The presence of a weapon may distract eyewitnesses' attention. (5)

13 The kind of psychology concerned with mental processes. (9)

14 __________ characteristics – features of an experiment that suggest a particular response to participants. (6)

16 __________ position survey – describes how memory for first and last items is better than those in the middle. (6)

17 The kind of processing (according to the levels of processing approach) that creates enduring memories. (4)

20 Person who watches a crime being comitted and reports about it later. (10)

22 Describes the physical form used to store memories. (5)

23 Key reseacher into eyewitness testimony. (6)

25 The way information is changed so it can be stored in memory. (8)

26 Method of improving the amount that can be held in short-term memory.(8)

27 Code generally used for words in long-term memory. (8)

28 Used to aid recall from long-term memory. (4)

29 According to the multi-store model, how information is transferred from short-term to long-term memory. (9)

Down

1 Explanation for fogetting that memory trace simply fades away. (5)

3 A type of interference where current learning interferes with past learning. (11)

4 Memories that disappear unless they are rehearsed. (4,5)

6 How long a memory lasts before it is no longer available. (8)

7 A way of dealing with traumatic events so that associated anxiety is not experienced. (10)

9 Serial __________ technique – a method for testing memory/forgetting. (5)

10 A memory store which has potentially unlimited capacity and duration. (4,4)

11 Psychologist who first described reconstructive memory. (8)

12 An explanation for forgetting where existing information is pushed out or overwritten by newer information. (12)

15 A cluster of related facts based on previous experience. (6)

18 Area of the brain associated with long-term memory. (11)

19 Code generally used in short-term memory. (8)

21 A model of how memory processes work based on the idea that there are three separate stores. (4,5)

24 A memory for the context in which a person first heard about an event. (9)

AS PSYCHOLOGY: THE TEACHER'S COMPANION Published by Nelson Thornes Ltd. © 2004 Sara Berman, Cara Flanagan and Adrian Frost

42

Cognitive Psychology

Crossword solutions

										[1] D					[2] P	[3] R	O	A	C	T	I	V	E	
					[4] S	I	N	G	L	E						E								
					H					[5] C	A	P	A	C	I	T	Y				[6] D			[7] R
					O					A						R					U			E
					R					Y					[8] F	O	C	U	S		R			P
					T						[9] P					A					A			R
		[10] L			T		[11] B				R		[12] D			[13] C	O	G	N	I	T	I	V	E
		O		[14] D	E	M	A	N	D		O		I			T					I			S
[15] S		N			R		R				B		[16] S	E	R	I	A	L			O			S
C		G			M		T			[17] D	E	E	P			V					N			I
H		T		[18] H			L						L			E				[19] A				O
[20] E	Y	E	W	I	T	N	E	S	S				A							C				N
M		R		P			S						C		[21] M					O				
A		M		P			S		[22] T	R	A	C	E		U					U				
				O									M		[23] L	O	F	T	U	S			[24] F	
		[25] E	N	C	O	D	I	N	G				E		T					T			L	
				A						[26] C	H	U	N	K	I	N	G			I			A	
		[27] S	E	M	A	N	T	I	C				T		S					[28] C	U	E	S	
				P											T								H	
				U											O								B	
				S						[29] R	E	H	E	A	R	S	A	L					U	
															E								L	
																							B	

AS PSYCHOLOGY: THE TEACHER'S COMPANION Published by Nelson Thornes Ltd. © 2004 Sara Berman, Cara Flanagan and Adrian Frost

Stages in development

Re-assemble the sentences below to describe the sequence of attachments in development.

- Phase 1 Pre-attachment (approximately 0–2 months)
- Phase 2 Attachment-in-the-making (approximately 2–7 months)
- Phase 3 Specific attachments (from approximately 7 months)
- Phase 4 Multiple attachments (from approximately 8 months)
- Phase 5 Reciprocal relationships (from about 8–24 months)

Sentences

Infants also show especial joy at reunion with that person and are most comforted by him/her.

The infant displays **separation protest** – the distress when an infant is separated from his/her caregiver.

Newborn infants are said to show **indiscriminate social responsiveness.**

They are equally happy being picked up by familiar or unfamiliar people, and can be comforted as easily by stranger as by their parents.

The second new behaviour is **stranger anxiety** – distress when picked up or approached by someone who is unfamiliar.

This is the beginning of real relationships.

Infants soon begin to recognise familiar smells, voices and faces (there is even evidence that at birth they recognise voices they heard when in the womb).

This phase is characterised by the increasing ability to **recognise familiar people**.

An infant is more easily comforted by someone familiar but still does not show anxiety with strangers or less familiar people.

There is some debate about whether these different attachments are equally intense, or whether the infant always has one special attachment figure at the top of a hierarchy of different attachments.

This may happen when the caregiver puts the infant down or when the caregiver leaves the room.

'Attachment-proper' is signaled by the appearance of two new behaviours.

The number of other attachments that are formed depends on how many consistent relationships the infant has.

The idea of one special attachment is called **monotropy** (which means 'focused on one person').

The infant learns to predict the responses of others and this means that it is possible consciously to influence the behaviour of others.

Initially infants show attachments to one **primary caregiver** (as demonstrated by separation protest).

But very soon after a first attachment is formed most infants also show attachments to other people.

See Lesson Notes, page 59

AS PSYCHOLOGY: THE TEACHER'S COMPANION Published by Nelson Thornes Ltd. © 2004 Sara Berman, Cara Flanagan and Adrian Frost

44

Individual differences in attachment

Profile 1

During play the baby showed little or no tendency to interact with the mother. When picked up she neither clung to her mother nor resisted. Treats the stranger very much like the mother, perhaps with a little less avoidance. Not distressed when alone with stranger but distressed when totally alone. Avoidance of mother during reunion. May greet mother casually or not at all. Averts mother's gaze.

Profile 2

When picked up baby does not especially seek to maintain contact. May mix some avoiding behaviour (such as looking away or turning away) with attempts to interact with mother. Shows little or no resistant behaviour in general. Likely to show little or no distress in the separation episodes. Greets mother with a smile and shows strong initiative to interact with her from a distance, but does not seek physical contact or closeness.

Profile 3

When picked up by mother baby shows little contact-maintaining behaviour. Doesn't cuddle in but looks away and may squirm to get down. Distressed when left alone but distress alleviated by stranger's return. Happy with stranger. Avoids mother at reunion, turns away or moves away. May just look at mother when she comes in but that's all.

Profile 4

Fairly passive baby. Rather limited exploratory behaviour throughout and lacking initiative in interactive episodes. During reunion actively seeks contact and proximity with mother, though tends to use signaling behaviour rather than a direct approach. Protests about being put down rather that resisting release. Not angry but a bit strident.

Profile 5

The baby is not frightened of the stranger but more interested in mother. When left alone is distressed which is not especially relieved by presence of the stranger. Can be comforted a bit by stranger but clearly wants mother. Baby seeks contact with mother especially at reunion. When held by mother the baby tries to maintain contact and resists when put down. The baby greets mother with a smile or a cry and approaches mother.

Profile 6

If the baby is picked up she will cling for a short while but will struggle to be put down. The baby turns her head away when held. When put down the baby may protest for a short while. The baby is not distressed when with the stranger and behaves similarly with stranger as with mother. The baby shows a mixed response to her mother's return. There is some tendency to greet but this is mixed with a strong tendency to move away and/or avert gaze.

Profile 7

Strong proximity-seeking and contact-maintaining at reunion and also during pre-separation periods. Also strong resistant episodes with quite an angry quality. Angry behaviour shown towards stranger as well as towards mother. Baby very distressed during separation.

Profile 8

Starts with proximity avoidance but this gives way to proximity seeking in the final episodes. Accepts contact if she is picked up but does not cling especially and does not resist release. Tends to show little distress during separation episodes. Baby greets mother on reunion, tends to approach her and appears to want contact. There may be some delay.

Profile 9

Baby shows strong tendency to resist contact and interaction. Moderately seeks proximity and seeks to maintain contact when gained so giving impression of ambivalence to mother. Shows little or no tendency to avoid mother at reunion or to avert her gave. Tends to be more angry than other babies in the Strange Situation or may be rather passive.

See Lesson Notes, page 60

AS PSYCHOLOGY: THE TEACHER'S COMPANION Published by Nelson Thornes Ltd. © 2004 Sara Berman, Cara Flanagan and Adrian Frost

The Strange Situation and attachment types

The Strange Situation consists of 8 episodes, each one lasting about 3 minutes

Three people are involved: a caregiver, her baby and a stranger.

1 Mother and baby enter room.

2 Mother sits quietly on a chair, responding if the baby seeks attention.

3 A stranger enters, talks to the mother then gradually approaches baby with a toy. The mother leaves the room.

4 The stranger leaves the baby playing unless he is inactive and then she tries to interest him in toys. If the baby becomes distressed this episode is ended.

5 Mother enters and waits to see how the baby greets her. The stranger leaves quietly and the mother waits until the baby settles, and then she leaves again.

6 The baby is alone. This episode is curtailed if the baby appears to be distressed.

7 The stranger comes back and repeats episode 3.

8 The mother returns and the stranger goes. Reunion behaviour recorded and then the situation is ended.

Secure attachment

An infant who is securely attached shows some protest when his/her caregiver departs but is fairly easily soothed. The infant greets the caregiver's return with enthusiasm. These children play independently, using their caregiver as a safe base for exploration and returning regularly for reassurance. Secure attachment is associated with sensitive caregiver. This teaches them to expect the same in other relationships. They learn to be trusting and realistic in relationships. Secure attachment is generally related to healthy cognitive and emotional development: independence, self-confidence and trusting relationships.

Insecure–avoidant attachment

In the Strange Situation, an infant shows apparent indifference when the caregiver leaves, and does not display stranger anxiety. At reunion the infant actively *avoids* contact with the caregiver. The caregiver tends to be insensitive and may ignore the infant during play. These children play independently.

Summary of attachment behaviours

Classification of behaviour in the Strange Situation	Secure attachment (Type B)	Insecure attachment Avoidant (Type A)	 Resistant (Type C)
Willingness to explore	High	High	Low
Stranger anxiety	Moderate	Low	High
Separation anxiety	Some, easy to soothe	Indifferent	Distressed
Behaviour at reunion with caregiver	Enthusiastic	Avoid contact	Seeks and rejects
Caregiver's behaviour	Sensitive	May ignore infant	Ambivalent
Percentage of infants in this category	66%	22%	12%

Insecure–resistant (or ambivalent) attachment

The infant is very distressed when the caregiver goes and, although they rush to the caregiver on his/her return they are not easily consoled on his/her return. The infant may actually *resist* contact with the caregiver, or may seek comfort and reject it at the same time. These children explore less than other children.

See Lesson Notes, pages 60 and 61

AS PSYCHOLOGY: THE TEACHER'S COMPANION Published by Nelson Thornes Ltd. © 2004 Sara Berman, Cara Flanagan and Adrian Frost

46

How to make culture your friend

The following are 'generic' AO2 points, that you should be able to adapt to fit a wide range of material. Take the area of the Specification that you are currently studying and see if it can be fitted into the following paragraphs.

Note that in some places there are no right or wrong answers. Any intelligent suggestion should attract credit.

1 Researchers such as Rosenzweig (1992) have pointed out how rooted Psychology is in Western, specifically American, culture and indeed it may be the case that work on *[insert area under consideration]* is subject to cultural bias.

2 On a methodological level, it may be that research techniques such as *[insert a relevant research technique]* represent what Berry (1969) might term an imposed etic, in that participants may not respond to the technique in the same way, for example *[think about why someone in a different culture might respond differently. Make an intelligent guess or suggestion]*.

3 On a more theoretical level, using a distinction suggested by Smith and Bond (1998), it may be that concepts like *[mention concepts used earlier on in the essay – try to mention ones that fit the point that you are about to make at the end of the paragraph)]* developed in a Western, individualist setting, may be difficult to apply to a more collectivist culture, where more emphasis is placed upon ties to other members of society. For example, in a collectivist culture people might *[think about why someone in a different culture might respond differently. Make an intelligent guess or suggestion]*.

See Lesson Notes, page 62

AS PSYCHOLOGY: THE TEACHER'S COMPANION Published by Nelson Thornes Ltd. © 2004 Sara Berman, Cara Flanagan and Adrian Frost

Revision task – Bowlby's theory of attachment

Please read the following summary of Bowlby's theory of attachment and select words from the list that follows it to fill the gaps.

The ________ approach: Bowlby's theory

Infants are born with a drive to become________.

Bowlby proposed that infants become attached to a caregiver because attachment is ________, in other words it is good for reproduction. Infants who do not become attached are less likely to survive and reproduce. Thus the attachment 'gene' is perpetuated and infants are born with an innate drive to become attached.

There are two reasons why attachment is good for survival and reproduction:

1 It means the infant is more likely to be well cared for when young and defenceless.

2 Attachments form the basis for later ________relationships, they provide a template for how to have relationships with other people and this promotes survival and reproduction.

Social releasers

What specific ________ promote attachment in infants? Infants are born with **social releasers.** The obvious example of a social releaser is when a baby smiles or when it cries. Such behaviours elicit ________ from others nearby. If a baby didn't have these ________ social releasers, potential caregivers would happily go about their business, ignoring the baby.

Adults respond to social releasers

But social releasers alone don't explain why the infant becomes attached to certain people rather than others. As we have seen such attachments don't simply form because individuals spend a lot of time together. Attachments form because infants and caregivers ________.

Infants form one special relationship

Infants become most strongly attached to the person who interacts best – the person who responds most sensitively to the infant's social releasers. This person becomes the infant's **primary caregiver** and plays a special role in the infant's emotional development. This concept is called ________– focused on one person.

This leads to an internal working model

The infant's relationship with his/her primary caregiver has a special significance. It is important for ________ and social development because it has emotional intensity. Bowlby suggested that the infant develops an internal working ________ of relationships based on this special emotional relationship with his/her ________ caregiver. The internal working model is like a ________ . It is a cluster of concepts about relationships – expectations about whether relationships involve consistent or ________ love, whether others make you feel good or ________, and so on. The primary caregiver's behaviour is a model for what the infant will expect from others. The infant ________ this model.

adaptive	caregiving	innate	monotropy
anxious	emotional	interact	primary
attached	evolutionary	internalises	schema
behaviours	inconsistent	model	social

Further questions

1 Can you summarise Bowlby's theory in exactly 150 words and then again in 20 words?

2 Please outline **three** negative criticisms of Bowlby's theory.

3 Please outline **two** positive criticisms of Bowlby's theory.

4 Outline, in approximately 100 words, an alternative theory of attachment to that proposed by Bowlby.

5 Briefly outline **two** differences between Bowlby's approach and the alternative approach that you have just described.

AS PSYCHOLOGY: THE TEACHER'S COMPANION Published by Nelson Thornes Ltd. © 2004 Sara Berman, Cara Flanagan and Adrian Frost

48

A short version of the love quiz

Question 1: Which of the following best describes your parents' relationships with each other?

(a) My parents had a caring relationship and are affectionate with each other.

(b) My parents appear to have a good enough relationship with each other but are not especially affectionate.

(c) My parents have a reasonable relationship and are sometimes affectionate towards each other.

Question 2: Which of the following best describes your relationship with your mother?

(a) My mother treats me with respect and is accepting and not demanding. She is confident about herself

(b) My mother is humourous, likable and respected by others. She treats me with respect.

(c) My mother treats me with respect but is sometimes cold and rejecting.

Question 3: Which of the following best describes your relationship with your father?

(a) My father is sometimes affectionate but can be unfair.

(b) My father is caring, affectionate and humourous.

(c) My father is reasonably caring.

Question 4: Select the statement that best describes your experiences of intimacy.

(a) I find that others are reluctant to get as close as I would like.

(b) I find it relatively easy to get close to others and am comfortable depending on them and having them depend on me.

(c) I am somewhat uncomfortable being close to others; I find it difficult to trust them completely, difficult to allow myself to depend on them.

Question 5: Select the statement that best describes your experiences of intimacy.

(a) I don't often worry about being abandoned or about someone getting too close to me.

(b) I often worry that my partner doesn't really love me or won't want to stay with me.

(c) I am nervous when anyone gets too close, and often romantic partners want me to be more intimate than I feel comfortable being.

Question 6: Select the statement that best describes your experiences of intimacy.

(a) I enjoy relationships but am generally quite self-sufficient.

(b) I have been lucky in love and most of my relationships are rewarding. I still like the people I was involved with.

(c) At times I wish I could just melt into someone so we could get beyond our separateness.

Question 7: Select the statement that best describes your attitudes towards love.

(a) The kind of head-over-heels love that is depicted in novels and in the movies does not exist in real life.

(b) It is easy to fall in love and I frequently find myself beginning to fall in love, though I am not sure that it really is love.

(c) Love is a positive and real experience.

Question 8: Select the statement that best describes your attitudes towards love.

(a) It is rare to find a person one can really fall in love with.

(b) In some relationships romantic love never fades.

(c) Most of us could love many people equally well, there is no 'one true love'.

Question 9: Select the statement that best describes your attitudes towards love.

(a) I think that romantic feelings do wax and wane.

(b) Romantic feelings wax and wane but at times they reach the intensity experienced at the start of a relationship.

(c) Intense romantic love is common at the start of a relationship but rarely lasts.

See Lesson Notes, page 65

AS PSYCHOLOGY: THE TEACHER'S COMPANION Published by Nelson Thornes Ltd. © 2004 Sara Berman, Cara Flanagan and Adrian Frost

The difference between Bowlby's Maternal Deprivation Hypothesis and Bowlby's Attachment Theory

It is easy to be confused between Bowlby's two theories: the Maternal Deprivation Hypothesis and his Attachment Theory. This is not surprising since one developed out of the other. This exercise may help you become more aware of the differences.

Write two headings on your paper: 'Maternal Deprivation Hypothesis' and 'Attachment Theory'.

Divide the sentences written below into these two theories. Write down the numbers of applicable sentences under each of your headings.

1 First published in 1951.

2 First published in 1969.

3 Emphasises the consequence of deprivation on the emotional development of a child.

4 Emphasises the consequences of attachment on the emotional development of a child.

5 Suggested that children form a hierarchy of attachments.

6 Suggested that infants form multiple attachments, with one primary caregiver.

7 Suggested that prolonged separations before the age of two and a half will be significant.

8 Suggested that there was a continuing risk of emotional damage if a child experienced prolonged separations up to the age of five.

9 Proposed that frequent and prolonged separations might lead to affectionless psychopathy.

10 Suggested that the special relationship formed in infancy will influence later adult relationships.

11 Incorporated the idea of the internal working model.

12 Likened the effect of emotional deprivation on mental health to the importance of vitamins and proteins for physical health.

13 Was in part based on research by Spitz and Wolf (1946).

14 Suggested that attachment was an adaptive behaviour.

15 Was influenced by research done by ethologists such as Lorenz (1952).

References

Spitz, R.A. and Wolf, K.M. (1946) Anaclitic depression. *Psychoanalytic Study of the Child*, **2**, 313–42.

Lorenz, K.Z. (1952) *King Solomon's Ring: New Light on Animal Ways*. New York: Thomas Y. Crowell

See Lesson Notes, page 66

AS PSYCHOLOGY: THE TEACHER'S COMPANION Published by Nelson Thornes Ltd. © 2004 Sara Berman, Cara Flanagan and Adrian Frost

50

Star Study by Hodges and Tizard – effects of privation

Place the following paragraphs (using the numbers) under the correct headings, as listed below.
It may help to cut out each statement and re-arrange them.

Aims	Procedures	Findings	Conclusions	Criticisms

1 The study focused on a group of 65 children who had been placed in one institution when they were less than four months old. At this age children have not yet formed attachments.

2 Sample bias: It is possible that the adopted and restored groups were different because the children first selected for adoption might have been the less troubled children.

3 An early study of the children found that 70 per cent were described as not able 'to care deeply about anyone'.

4 Thus we can conclude that most if not all of these children had experienced early emotional privation (a lack of attachment rather than a loss of attachment).

5 By the age of four, 24 of the institutionalised children had been adopted, 15 had returned to their natural homes and the rest remained in the institution.

6 Attrition: The original sample was reduced in subsequent follow-ups. This is called **attrition** and is a problem in longitudinal studies because particular kinds of participants are likely to be the ones who 'drop out'.

7 It is possible that more troubled children dropped out – though this should have affected both the adopted and restored children equally and therefore not have biased the findings.

8 *At age eight:* Most of the ex-institutional (restored or adopted) children had formed close attachments with their parents or adopted parents. The children's teachers reported that the ex-institutional children still tended to be more attention-seeking and also more 'over-friendly' than 'normal' peers. They also tended to be unpopular but did not lag cognitively when compared to 'normal' peers.

9 Parents select which child to adopt and they are likely to select those easier to get on with.

10 This could explain why the adopted children got on better at home (because they were 'easier' children) but doesn't explain why they found had more difficulties with peers.

11 According to the **Temperament Hypothesis** 'easier' children should have easier relationships with everyone.

12 This meant that the children had little opportunity to form a close, continuous relationship with an adult.

13 The children were assessed at this time and again when they were eight years old, at which time the sample was reduced to 51 children.

14 There was an explicit policy in the institution against the 'caretakers' forming attachments with the children and there was also a high turnover of staff.

15 The children were assessed again at age 16 – by then the researchers were only able to locate 23 of the adopted children (some of whom had been adopted after the age of four), 11 'restored' children and five children who had remained in institutional care.

16 At each assessment the children, their parents, and teachers were interviewed and asked to fill in questionnaires. The data collected concerned attitudes and behaviour.

Cont'd on Handout 51

See Lesson Notes, page 67

 © 2004 Sara Berman, Cara Flanagan and Adrian Frost

Star Study by Hodges and Tizard – effects of privation *(cont'd)*

17 At all ages there was also a **control group** of children raised in a 'normal' home environment.

18 *At age four:* The institutional caretakers reported that the children did not have any deep relationships. The children, in general, were more attention-seeking and more indiscriminately affectionate that non-institutional children.

19 Alternative explanations for the findings: Hodges and Tizard suggest that the findings, at age 16, might be explained in other ways.

20 At age 16 two important findings emerged:

21 The adopted children were doing fine at home but not in peer relationships. This suggests that they hadn't fully recovered from their early privation because they were less able to form relationships.

22 Relationships within the family: In general the adopted children were about as closely attached to their parents as the control group, whereas the 'restored' group where much less likely to be closely attached.

23 Bowlby's **Maternal Deprivation Hypothesis** suggested that a discontinuous relationship between a mother-figure and infant would result in emotional maladjustment. But some of the research evidence indicates that children can and do recover from early deprivation – this might not be the case with privation.

24 Peer relationships: All the ex-institutional adolescents were less likely to have a special friend, to be part of a crowd, or to be liked by other children. They were also more quarrelsome and more likely to be bullies.

25 The findings at age four and eight suggest that the children did show signs of permanent damage as a result of their early institutional life.

26 To test whether early privation did have long-term effects Jill Hodges and Barbara Tizard undertook on long-term study (a **longitudinal study**), following a group of children from early life to adolescence.

27 This means that the Hodges and Tizard findings do support the view that privation has negative long-term effects.

28 For example, it could be that the adopted children suffered from poor self-esteem stemming from being adopted, which would explain their problems outside the home.

29 Another explanation could be that the ex-institutional children lag beyond their peers in emotional development and this would explain their poor peer relationships – they are simply not yet ready to cope.

30 The findings at age 16 suggest that early privation had a negative effect on the ability to form relationships when the relationship involved someone who wasn't going to work hard at it, i.e. in peer relationships.

See Lesson Notes, page 67

AS PSYCHOLOGY: THE TEACHER'S COMPANION Published by Nelson Thornes Ltd. © 2004 Sara Berman, Cara Flanagan and Adrian Frost

Constructing a Thurstone attitude scale

1 **Select topics.** Working in a small group identify various statements (beliefs, attitudes, etc.) about day care.

2 **Write the statements.** Write a pool of about 50 attitude statements (depending on how many groups there are, each group might aim to produce ten statements, presuming there will be some overlap). Positive and negative items should be roughly in balance, plus some extreme statements. Each student might be asked to produce one positive and one negative example for each sub-area. Students could work individually or in small groups.

3 **Collate all statements.** Type, duplicate and cut up the statements into slips.

4 **Rate the statements.** Students now individually rate each statement on an 11-point scale, where 11 is highly unfavourable. The judgement is based on the contents of each item and not the student's own agreement or disagreement with the statement. The question each student should ask themselves is 'if a person agrees with this statement, where does that person stand on the continuum: in a favourable/very favourable/very unfavourable or neutral position?'

A good way to do this is to have 11 piles in front of each student, and then the student places each statement in whatever they judge to be the appropriate pile. At the end each student should finish with 11 piles, not all the same size and some may be empty. Finally, the student should record the rating on each statement slip.

5 **Select the statements**. For each statement:

- enter all ratings for that statement into a mathematical/statistical calculator;
- press the mean and standard deviation buttons;
- decide on a minimum standard deviation and exclude all items with scores above this (i.e. those where there was little agreement about where it should be placed);
- assign an integer rating to all items, rounding to the nearest whole number.

For all statements.

Using 11 overhead projector transparencies, numbered 1 to 11, write the selected statements with their standard deviation score and original (not rounded) mean rating on the appropriate sheet. For example, a statement rated as four should be written on sheet number four.

As a group, view each transparency and select the best statement(s) for each rating category. The best are the ones with the greatest agreement (lowest standard deviation). You should end up with either 11 or 22 statements.

If you have less than one statement in each category, it may be necessary to repeat the whole process again to fill in any gaps.

6 **Using the scale.** Randomise the order of the statements and present them on a sheet, with two columns 'agree' and 'disagree'. Ask participants to tick the appropriate column for each statement. The questionnaire should include other questions relevant to your hypothesis, such as age, sex, smoking habits, and so on.

7 **Scoring the scale.** For all statements which the respondent has ticked 'agree', add up the original mean values for these statements. This indicates the extent to which they favour day care. You could use this data for further analysis, such as comparing male and female attitudes, or those of school children, parents and grandparents.

See Lesson Notes, page 69

AS PSYCHOLOGY: THE TEACHER'S COMPANION Published by Nelson Thornes Ltd. © 2004 Sara Berman, Cara Flanagan and Adrian Frost

Day care and GCSE results (a correlational study)

In order to collect suitable data you need the following.

ONE A means of **operationalising** 'educational achievement' so that we can measure it. One way to do this would be to give each participant a GCSE score (10 points for a grade A, 8 points for a grade B and so on) and then divide by the number of GCSEs taken. This gives an 'educational attainment score'.

TWO A means of assessing how much time the participant's mother had worked before her child attained the age of five. For this you need to design a **questionnaire survey**. In order to collect the data it is best to use as few questions as possible and make the answers easy to record.

You might use closed questions such as shown in the box opposite. Using **closed questions** makes it easier to use the data because there are only a few possible answers. On the other hand, **open questions** allow for people to give a more exact answer to suit their circumstances. An example of an open question would be 'Did your work follow the same pattern for each child? If not, then describe your different work patterns'.

> How many hours a week did you work when your son/daughter was under one year old?
>
> - 0 hours
> - less than 10 hours
> - between 10 and 20 hours
> - between 20 and 30 hours
> - more than 30 hours

Analysing the data

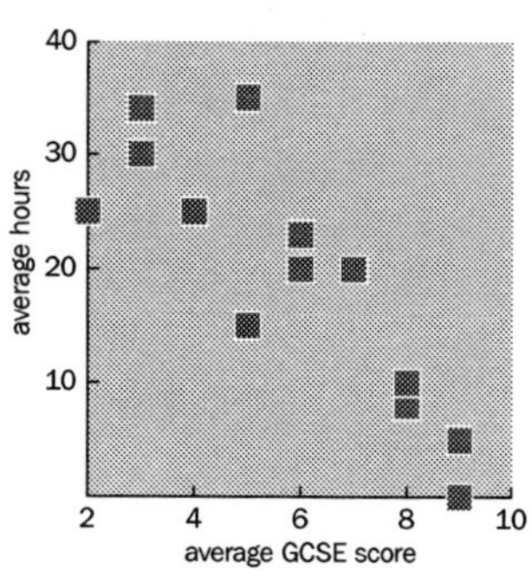

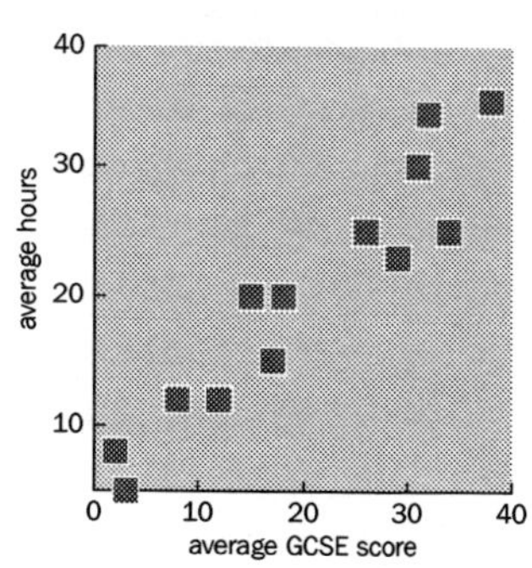

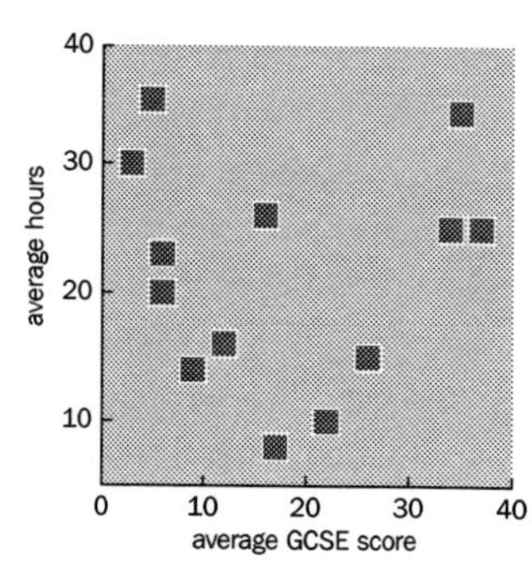

When you have collected the data you can calculate two scores for each participant: one for educational attainment and one for average number of hours mother worked. Now plot these on a scattergraph, like the one above. Is there a negative correlation, as predicted?

See Lesson Notes, page 69

AS PSYCHOLOGY: THE TEACHER'S COMPANION Published by Nelson Thornes Ltd. © 2004 Sara Berman, Cara Flanagan and Adrian Frost

54

Reviewing day care evidence

Having studied day care you will know that there are arguments both for and against the possible effects of day care on a child's development. This exercise is to help you sort out the main arguments and/or evidence in order to write an essay, and to sort out the effects on cognitive and social development.

Essay 1

Step 1 The following studies can be used to provide evidence either 'for' or 'against'. Of course there are many others you can also use but you won't need more than three for either side of the debate. Complete the table below using these or other studies:

- Andersson (1992) – Swedish study
- Baydar and Brooks-Gunn (1991) – working mothers
- Bowlby's (1953) Maternal Deprivation Hypothesis
- Brown and Harris (1978) – depressed mothers
- Bryant *et al.* (1980) – childminding
- Campbell *et al.* (2001) – quality of day care.

(see **Handout 55** for references)

For	Against
●	●
●	●
●	●

Step 2 To evaluate the arguments for and against three main factors can be considered, i.e. individual differences, number of hours in care, methodology used in the studies. Write the number of each of the following statements into the correct box below.

1 Babies who spend more than ten hours a week in day care are more aggressive when they go to school.
2 Insecurely attached children can't cope with separation very well.
3 Day care can show a correlation with the outcomes but it can't tell us about the causes.
4 Shy children find it very difficult to cope.
5 There is no difference in attachment behaviours between those children who spend lots of time in day care and those who stay at home.
6 Insecurely attached children do the best in day care.
7 There are many variables involved in the relationship between day care and the outcomes.
8 Some studies are over ten years old so their conclusions might not be very relevant today.
9 The behaviour at school of children who have attended day care before they were one year old is no different to that of other children.
10 Securely attached children become more aggressive after day care.

Individual differences	Number of hours in day care	Methodology used in studies
●	●	●
●	●	●
●	●	●
●		

Step 3 Now use the material in the two tables and write an answer to this question:
'Outline and evaluate studies into the effects of day care on children's development.'
Remember that you should aim for an essay that is about 300 words long.

See Lesson Notes, page 70

AS PSYCHOLOGY: THE TEACHER'S COMPANION Published by Nelson Thornes Ltd. © 2004 Sara Berman, Cara Flanagan and Adrian Frost

Reviewing day care evidence

Essay 2

Step 1 Now repeat the exercise given in **Handout 54** but separate your studies into social and cognitive development.

Study	Cognitive or social development?	What effects were found on cognitive/social development?
●		●
●		●
●		●
●		●
●		●
●		●

Step 2 Use the material to write an essay on:

'Outline and evaluate studies into the effects of day care on either cognitive or social development.'

References

Andersson, B.E. (1992) Effects of daycare on cognitive and socioemotional competence of thirteen-year-old Swedish schoolchildren. *Child Development*, **63**, 20–36.

Baydar, N. and Brooks-Gunn, J. (1991) Effects of maternal employment and child-care arrangements on pre-schoolers' cognitive and behavioural outcomes. *Developmental Psychology*, **27**, 932–45.

Bowlby, J. (1953) *Child Care and the Growth of Love*. Harmondsworth: Penguin

Brown, G.W. and Harris, T. (1978) *Social Origins of Depression*. London: Tavistock.

Bryant, B., Harris, M. and Newton, D. (1980) *Children and Minders*. London: Grant McIntyre.

Campbell, F.A., Pungello, E.P., Miller-Johnson, S., Burchinal, M. and Ramey, C.T. (2001) The development of cognitive and academic abilities: Growth curves from an early childhood experiment. *Developmental Psychology*, **37**(2) 231–42.

See Lesson Notes, page 70

 © 2004 Sara Berman, Cara Flanagan and Adrian Frost

56

Developmental Psychology

Crossword

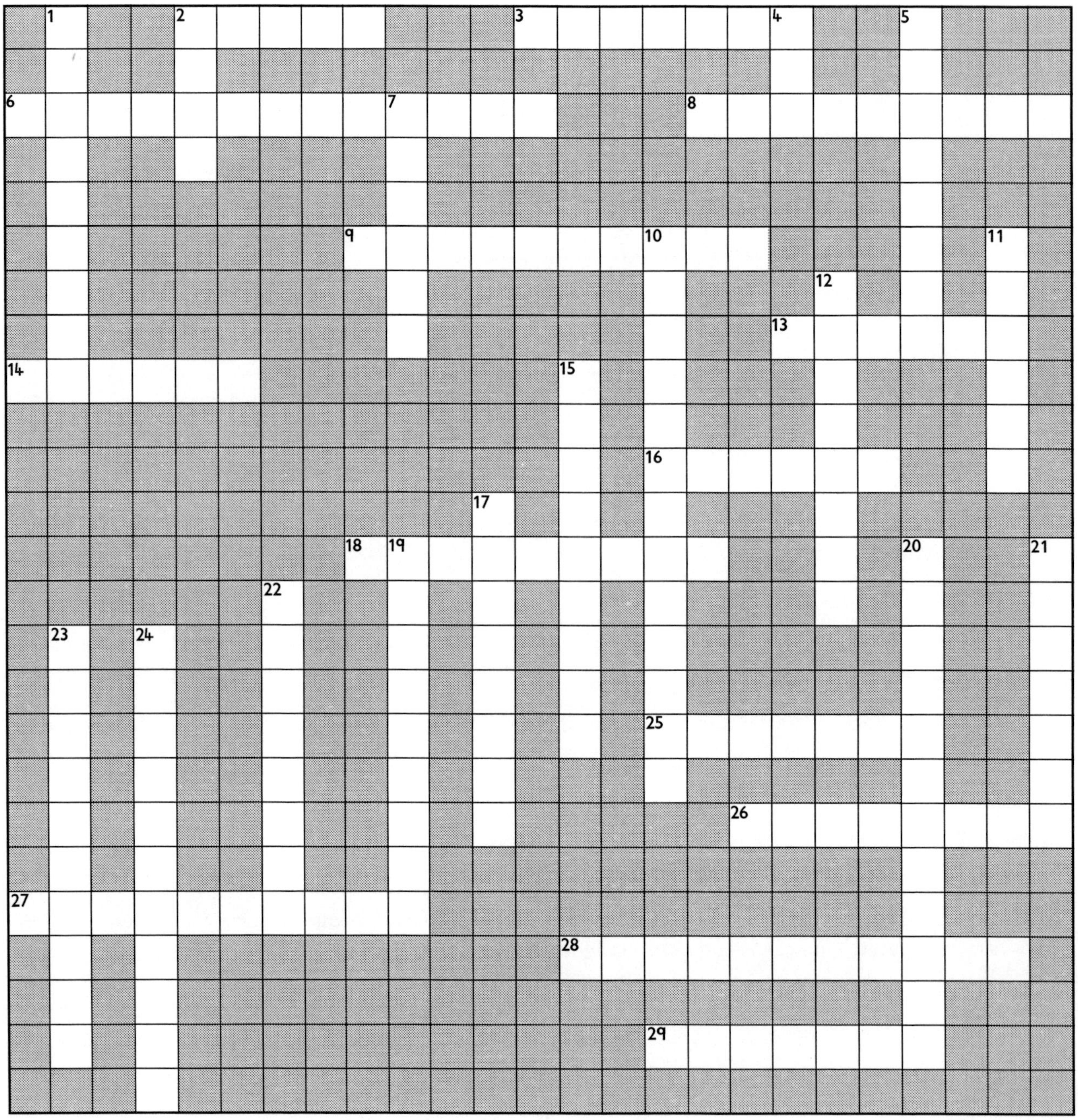

AS PSYCHOLOGY: THE TEACHER'S COMPANION Published by Nelson Thornes Ltd. © 2004 Sara Berman, Cara Flanagan and Adrian Frost

Developmental Psychology

Crossword clues

Across

2 Name of two year old studied by Robertson and Robertson while she stayed in hospital. (5)

3 The rules, customs, morals and ways of interacting that bind a group of people. (7)

6 A culture which places more value on independence that interdependence. (13)

8 Kind of conditioning where learning occurs through association.(9)

9 The emotional stability provided by a primary caregiver which helps a child feel able to explore the world. (6,4)

13 Man famous for his experiments with wire mothers and monkeys. (6)

14 Kind of attachment which develops as the result of sensitive responding from caregiver. (6)

16 Conducted a classic study with Hodges on children who were adopted or returned to their natural homes after spending time in an institution. (6)

18 The lack of care normally provided by a caregiver. (9)

25 __________ situation. A method used to investigate attachment in infants. (7)

26 A behaviour that increases an individual's survival and reproduction. (8)

27 An emotional bond between two people. (10)

28 The loss of care normally provided by a caregiver. (11)

29 Kind of conditioning where learning occurs though reinforcement. (7)

Down

1 __________ period. Window in development where a child is most responsive to certain changes. (9)

2 ________ quiz. Questionnaire used by Hazan and Shaver to investigate the continuity hypothesis. (4)

4 Abbreviation for the environment of evolutionary adaptiveness. (1,1,1)

5 __________ period. A restricted window in development. (8)

7 Man who showed that goslings became attached to the first moving thing they saw when they hatched. (6)

10 __________ psychopaths. Individuals who lack emotional sensitivity. (13)

11 Man who propsed the maternal deprivation hypothesis. (6)

12 Term used to describe mothering, as in the __________ deprivation hypothesis. (8)

15 Special emotional attachment to one person. (8)

17 Kind of insecure attachment where infant avoids contact with caregiver on reunion. (8)

19 Kind of insecure attachment where infants seeks and rejects attention on reunion with caregiver. (9)

20 A culture where members share child-rearing and other tasks as well as belongings. (12)

21 Temporary form of care for children outside their own home by non-relatives. (3,4)

22 Deprivation __________. Condition resulting from lack of care causing lack of physical development. (8)

23 The physical disruption of the infant-caregiver bond. (10)

24 Hypothesis propsed by Kagan that suggests that attachment can be explained in terms of innate personality. (11)

AS PSYCHOLOGY: THE TEACHER'S COMPANION Published by Nelson Thornes Ltd. © 2004 Sara Berman, Cara Flanagan and Adrian Frost

Developmental Psychology

Crossword solutions

	[1]S			[2]L	A	U	R	A				[3]C	U	L	T	U	R	[4]E			[5]C			
	E			O														E			R			
[6]I	N	D	I	V	I	D	U	A	[7]L	I	S	T				[8]C	L	A	S	S	I	C	A	L
	S			E					O												T			
	I								R												I			
	T							[9]S	E	C	U	R	E	B	[10]A	S	E				C		[11]B	
	I								N						F				[12]M		A		O	
	V								Z						F			[13]H	A	R	L	O	W	
[14]S	E	C	U	R	E								[15]M		E				T				L	
													O		C				E				B	
													N		[16]T	I	Z	A	R	D			Y	
											[17]A		O		I				N					
								[18]P	[19]R	I	V	A	T	I	O	N			A		[20]C			[21]D
						[22]D			E		O		R		N				L		O			A
	[23]S		[24]T			W			S		I		O		L						L			Y
	E		E			A			I		D		P		E						L			C
	P		M			R			S		A		Y		[25]S	T	R	A	N	G	E			A
	A		P			F			T		N				S						C			R
	R		E			I			A		T						[26]A	D	A	P	T	I	V	E
	A		R			S			N												I			
[27]A	T	T	A	C	H	M	E	N	T												V			
	I		M										[28]D	E	P	R	I	V	A	T	I	O	N	
	O		E																		S			
	N		N												[29]O	P	E	R	A	N	T			
			T																					

AS PSYCHOLOGY: THE TEACHER'S COMPANION Published by Nelson Thornes Ltd. © 2004 Sara Berman, Cara Flanagan and Adrian Frost

Quiz – the body's response to stressors

The stress response starts in the __________. This tiny gland has two actions. Firstly it simulates the __________ gland to secrete a hormone called __________, which in turn stimulates the __________ __________ to release hormones called corticosteroids (including cortisol). They affect the __________ to release stored glucose and they suppress the action of the __________ __________ to attack any invading antigens. Secondly, the gland stimulates the __________ nervous system, which affects the __________ __________ to release hormones, __________ and __________ into the bloodstream. These produce physiological reactions linked with the __________ or __________ response, such as increased __________ and __________.

ACTH	Flight	Noradrenaline
Adrenal cortex	Heart-rate	Pituitary
Adrenal medulla	Hypothalamus	Respiration
Adrenaline	Immune system	Sympathetic
Fight	Liver	

See Lesson Notes, page 74

AS PSYCHOLOGY: THE TEACHER'S COMPANION Published by Nelson Thornes Ltd. © 2004 Sara Berman, Cara Flanagan and Adrian Frost

60
The stressful life of Phil Mitchell

How many stressful life events can you recall that have occurred in the life of *EastEnders*' Phil Mitchell in the last 18 months? Please write a list below.

Most life event scales don't assign scores to 'Finding out that your girlfriend is an undercover policewoman' or 'getting shot by your ex', or even 'pretending to be a dangerous gangster even though you live with your mum' – so please estimate the scores of all of the life events that you list, in comparison with 'getting married', which scores 50 life change units.

- What is Phil's total life change score?
- How likely is he to develop a stress related illness?

See Lesson Notes, page 75

AS PSYCHOLOGY: THE TEACHER'S COMPANION Published by Nelson Thornes Ltd. © 2004 Sara Berman, Cara Flanagan and Adrian Frost

How well do you know your Star Study?

Details of the following study have been taken from *The Complete Companion*. Can you, without using the textbook, spot the 22 deliberate mistakes that have been built into this version of the text?

Star Study on life changes as a source of stress (Rahe *et al.* 1970)

Aim

Rahe *et al.* used the Stress Resistance Ratings Scale to test DeLongis *et al.*'s hypothesis that the number of life events a person experienced would be positively differentiated with illness. Rahe *et al.* aimed in particular to study a 'normal' population as distinct from the populations previously studied of individuals who were already ill in hospital.

Procedures

A version of the SRRS was given to air-traffic controllers, a total of over 27,000 men. The men filled the questionnaire in just before they went into hospital, noting all the life events experienced over the previous 6 days.

An illness score was calculated on the basis of the number, type and severity of all illnesses recorded during the hospital stay (about 7 months). Rahe *et al.* didn't include sick bay visits that appeared to be due to a desire to get out of work (because the men asked them not to).

Findings

An LCD score and an illness score was calculated for each man. Rahe *et al.* found a positive differentiation between these scores of +1.18. A positive differentiation is one where both cultures increase together. The number 1.18 expresses how closely the cultures increase together. 1.18 is not a very strong differentiation but given the number of participants it is stereotypical.

Conclusions

The findings support the hypothesis of a link or positive differentiation between life changes/events and physical illness. It is possible that the link is stress: life changes reduce stress and we know that stress causes illness. Therefore life changes are sources of stress. Both positive and negative events are included in the SRRS so we see that it is negativity rather than change that is important. It is the overall amount of 'psychic energy' required to deal with an event that creates stress.

See Lesson Notes, page 75

AS PSYCHOLOGY: THE TEACHER'S COMPANION Published by Nelson Thornes Ltd. © 2004 Sara Berman, Cara Flanagan and Adrian Frost

62

Assess the hassles in your life

The table below presents a scale of hassles that students commonly find irritating. You may find that some of them have no relevance to your life style. Nevertheless, try to assess yourself by indicating how often each item irritates you. Enter in the box in front of it one of 3 numbers:

0 = almost never

2 = sometimes

3 = frequently

	Traffic jams around school		Too few dates		Materials not available in the library
	Careless cyclists		Room temperatures		Not having my ironing done on time
	Library too noisy		How I look		Not enough time to talk with friends
	Sister/brother too noisy		Too little intimacy		Not enough time to exercise
	Household chores		Other students unfriendly		Physical safety after dark
	Too little time		Getting to classes on time		Conflicts with brother/sister
	Too little money		Transport problems		Constant pressures of studying
	Deciding what to wear		Quality of food I eat		Teacher difficult to understand
	Shopping		Plans for my future		Taking tests
	Not enough close friends		Relationships at work		Doing exams
	Getting up in the morning		Untidy bedroom		Tensions in love relationships
	My weight		Conflict with parent		Doing hair in morning
	Too little sleep		Crowds		
	Noisy neighbours		Other road users		
	Others' opinion of me		Sister/brother's messiness		
	Teacher absent		No emails/text messages		
	Boring teacher		Being lonely		
	Problems with a pet		Being disorganised		

See Lesson Notes, page 76

AS PSYCHOLOGY: THE TEACHER'S COMPANION Published by Nelson Thornes Ltd. © 2004 Sara Berman, Cara Flanagan and Adrian Frost

Brady's executive monkeys

Brady (1958) conducted a classic study.

In earlier research Brady found that monkeys died when they had to perform stressful tasks. They died because of stomach ulcers. The question was whether these ulcers were due to the physical restraint and electric shocks (physiological stress) or to psychological stress (the task they had to perform). After 23 days of a six hours on, six hours off schedule the executive monkey died due to a stomach ulcer.

Brady designed a new study to test his hypothesis that the physical harm (stomach ulcers) was due to psychological rather than physiological stress. To test this Brady and his colleagues used yoked controls. One monkey, called the 'executive', was strapped in a 'restraining' chair and given electric shocks unless it pressed a lever every 20 seconds. A second monkey received the shocks but had no control over the lever. Therefore only the 'executive' monkey received the psychological stress of having to press the lever but both monkeys received the shocks.

Interestingly, if the reinforcement schedule was changed to 18 hours on and 6 hours off, or 30 minutes on, 30 minutes off, no monkeys died. Brady found that stomach acidity was greatest during the rest period.

Brady concluded that it was clearly stress, not the shocks, which created the ulcers, and that the greatest danger occurred when the sympathetic arousal stopped and the stomach was flooded with digestive hormones, a parasympathetic rebound.

One limitation of this study is that the monkeys were not randomly selected. The 'executive' monkey was chosen because it was faster at learning an avoidance response. This might have parallels with the human world. These findings were supported by research with humans. For example Weiner *et al.* (1957) studied army recruits. The recruits were classified as over- or under-secretors on the basis of the amount of digestive enzymes produced in their stomachs. It was found that, after a period of stressful basic training, the recruits who were classed as over-secretors were much more likely to have developed an ulcer. This shows that even in humans stress is related to the onset of ulcers, at least in those individuals predisposed to develop them.

However, later research by Marshall *et al.* (1985) has shown that many stomach ulcers are not due to stress but to the presence of a bacterium called *Helicobacter pylori*. This showed that stress is not the only cause of ulcers. It might be that stress has some influence on the development of ulcers but the danger was that people assumed this was the only cause.

References

Brady, J.V. (1958) Ulcers in executive monkeys. *Scientific American*, **199**, 95–100.

Marshall, B.J., McGechie, D.B., Rogers, P.A. and Glancy, R.J. (1985) Pyloric Campylobacter infection and gastroduodenal disease. *The Medical Journal of Australia*, **142**(8), 439–44.

Weiner, H., Thaler, M., Reiser, M.F. and Mirsky, I.A. (1957) Etiology of duodenal ulcer: I. Relation to specific psychological characteristics to rate of gastric secretion (serum pepsinogen). *Psychosomatic Medicine*, **19**, 1–10.

See Lesson Notes, page 77

AS PSYCHOLOGY: THE TEACHER'S COMPANION Published by Nelson Thornes Ltd. © 2004 Sara Berman, Cara Flanagan and Adrian Frost

64

Make those monkeys do some work for you!

Use **Handout 63** and/or your textbook to fill in the details of the study on the left hand column. Then draw lines across to the Specification details on the right. Every time an aspect of the study can be linked to the Specification, draw an arrow linking the two areas. (The arrows don't have to go to the adjacent box, they may travel upwards or downwards across the page – for example, one of Brady's 'aims' was to examine the difference between monkeys who could 'control' the shocks and those who couldn't. This obviously links to 'The role of control in the perception of stress' on the Specification. There are many, perhaps more subtle, links though!)

For each arrow, write a sentence on the reverse of this sheet explaining why the study is relevant to that particular area of the Specification.

Brady's study

Aims

Procedures

Findings

Conclusions

'Physiological Psychology' Specification details

Stress as a bodily response

The body's response to stress, including the General adaptation Syndrome (Selye).

Research into the relationship between stress and physical illness, including cardiovascular disorders and the effects of stress upon the immune system.

Sources of stress

Research into sources of stress, including life changes (e.g. Holmes and Rahe) and workplace stressors (e.g. work overload, role ambiguity)

Individual differences in modifying the effects of stressors, including the role played by personality (e.g. Friedman and Rosenman), culture, gender.

Methods of managing the negative effects of stress

including physiological (e.g. drugs, biofeedback) and psychological approaches (e.g. the work of Meichenbaum on stress-inoculation and Kobasa on increasing hardiness.)

The role of 'control' in the perception of stress.

The strengths and weaknesses of methods of stress management.

See Lesson Notes, page 77

AS PSYCHOLOGY: THE TEACHER'S COMPANION Published by Nelson Thornes Ltd. © 2004 Sara Berman, Cara Flanagan and Adrian Frost

What type are you?

For each of the following questions circle the letter of the response that best fits you for each item.

1 How would your closest friend rate you?
- a Definitely single-minded and competitive
- b Probably single-minded and competitive
- c Probably relaxed and easy going
- d Definitely relaxed and easy going

2 How would you rate yourself?
- a Definitely single-minded and competitive
- b Probably single-minded and competitive
- c Probably relaxed and easy going
- d Definitely relaxed and easy going

3 How do you consider yourself compared to the average student?
- a More responsible
- b As responsible
- c Less responsible

4 Compared to the average student:
- a I put in much more effort
- b I put in the same amount of effort
- c I put in less effort

5 School/college has:
- a Stirred me into action
- b Not stirred me into action

6 Compared to the average student:
- a I am more precise
- b I am as precise
- c I am less precise

7 Compared to the average student:
- a I approach life more seriously
- b I approach life as seriously
- c I approach life less seriously

8 How would most people rate you?
- a Definitely single-minded and competitive
- b Probably single-minded and competitive
- c Probably relaxed and easy going
- d Definitely relaxed and easy going

9 How would you rate yourself?
- a Definitely not having less energy than most people
- b Probably not having less energy than most people
- c Probably having less energy than most people
- d Definitely having less energy than most people

10 I frequently set deadlines for myself in courses or other things.
- a Yes
- b No
- c Sometimes

11 Do you keep a regular study timetable during school holidays (e.g. half-term, summer, etc)?
- a Yes
- b No
- c Sometimes

12 I hurry even when there is plenty of time.
- a Yes
- b Once in a while
- c Sometimes

13 I have been told that I eat too fast.
- a Often
- b Once in a while
- c Sometimes

14 How would you rate yourself?
- a I eat faster than most people
- b I eat as fast as most people
- c I eat less fast than most people

15 If people are speaking I hurry them to get to their point.
- a Frequently
- b Once in a while
- c Never

16 How would most people rate you?
- a Definitely not doing most things in a hurry
- b Probably not doing most things in a hurry
- c Probably doing most things in a hurry
- d Definitely doing most things in a hurry

17 Compared to the average student:
- a I hurry much less
- b I hurry as much
- c I hurry much more

18 How often are there deadlines in your courses?
- a Frequently
- b Once in a while
- c Never

19 Everyday life is filled with challenges to be met.
- a Yes
- b No
- c Sometimes

20 I have held a position of responsibility in a club or a part-time job when in school.
- a Frequently
- b Once in a while
- c Never

21 I stay in the library while studying until school/college closes.
- a Frequently
- b Once in a while
- c Never

See Lesson Notes, page 78

AS PSYCHOLOGY: THE TEACHER'S COMPANION Published by Nelson Thornes Ltd. © 2004 Sara Berman, Cara Flanagan and Adrian Frost

66

The scoring for type A or type B questionnaire

Give yourself one point for each of the questions if your response matches the following key.

1	a or b	**12**	a
2	a or b	**13**	a
3	a	**14**	a
4	a	**15**	a
5	a	**16**	c or d
6	a	**17**	c
7	a	**18**	a
8	a or b	**19**	a
9	a or b	**20**	a
10	a	**21**	a
11	a		

Score	**13+**	**9–12**	**8**	**4–7**	**0–3**
Classification	**A+**	**A–**	**borderline**	**B–**	**B+**

See Lesson Notes, page 78

AS PSYCHOLOGY: THE TEACHER'S COMPANION Published by Nelson Thornes Ltd. © 2004 Sara Berman, Cara Flanagan and Adrian Frost

Fantasy Island

- Please write a description of an imaginary society in about 250 words.

Guidelines

Your task is to 'play God' and design a society. A whole culture in which people, live, love, grow up, work, raise families and so on. You must decide upon its structure, institutions, rituals, etc. In fact you can decide upon any aspect of the world that you are creating and make it however you want it.

The only rule is, it must be the most stressful place imaginable. It must be an absolute nightmare to live in.

BUT – be subtle. It's not stressful because there is no food, or because there's a war going on. That would be too easy. Of course that's stressful.

It must be stressful because of its culture, because of the way in which the society organises itself and because of the pressures that it places upon the people who live within it.

Here are some things to think about (but don't feel restricted to these):

1 How are people who are 'different' treated?

2 How much pressure is there on people to conform? In what way?

3 What is expected of the different genders?

4 How are family structures organised?

5 How are people expected to behave at work? Or in the home?

There are no right or wrong answers, but a good start might be to think about what aspects of our society and culture are stressful to you and to magnify those.

See Lesson Notes, page 79

AS PSYCHOLOGY: THE TEACHER'S COMPANION Published by Nelson Thornes Ltd. © 2004 Sara Berman, Cara Flanagan and Adrian Frost

Wordsearch 1

Hidden in this wordsearch are ten words.

They can be spelt upwards, downwards, forwards, backwards or diagonally.

Please circle all the words you can find.

E	T	H	K	M	N	L	I	P	O	G	Y	D	W	R
C	P	A	M	K	J	G	R	D	S	W	U	V	E	S
L	O	H	U	F	T	D	W	C	H	L	M	G	U	O
P	F	R	E	S	Z	A	V	Y	H	N	C	E	K	I
L	M	H	U	G	R	F	S	W	V	B	E	R	I	O
P	L	J	H	G	T	R	V	N	M	K	O	I	U	T
R	E	D	S	X	H	O	K	J	I	E	C	A	T	Y
N	M	L	O	H	G	R	T	V	E	H	A	L	O	P
I	E	G	U	N	B	C	R	E	W	I	J	N	G	H
Y	B	C	D	E	T	S	A	W	L	M	K	I	O	H
O	V	H	M	I	J	U	G	F	D	S	W	E	C	X
F	V	G	T	Y	H	B	N	J	G	I	O	L	M	S
A	R	E	I	O	T	G	R	V	E	C	N	H	J	U
I	B	G	D	S	E	R	W	E	L	O	P	K	I	J
U	N	M	B	G	T	R	V	C	F	D	E	R	S	E
W	C	V	T	G	B	H	Y	U	I	O	L	M	H	A

The words are:

APRIL BECAUSE CAT DECEMBER DISCOVER LION PENCIL
SPRING TOMORROW WATER

See Lesson Notes, page 80

AS PSYCHOLOGY: THE TEACHER'S COMPANION Published by Nelson Thornes Ltd. © 2004 Sara Berman, Cara Flanagan and Adrian Frost

Wordsearch 2

Hidden in this wordsearch are ten words.

They can be spelt upwards, downwards, forwards, backwards or diagonally.

Please circle all the words you can find.

E	T	H	K	M	N	L	I	P	O	R	Y	D	W	R
C	P	A	M	K	J	G	R	D	S	E	U	V	E	S
P	E	N	C	I	L	D	W	C	H	T	M	G	U	L
L	H	J	U	F	R	A	V	Y	H	A	C	E	K	I
L	M	H	U	G	R	E	S	W	V	W	E	R	I	O
P	L	J	H	G	T	R	B	N	O	K	O	I	U	N
R	E	D	S	X	H	O	K	R	I	E	C	A	T	Y
N	M	I	O	H	G	R	R	V	E	H	A	L	O	P
I	E	S	U	N	B	O	R	E	W	C	J	N	G	H
Y	B	C	D	E	M	S	A	W	L	M	E	I	O	H
G	V	O	M	O	J	U	G	F	D	S	W	D	C	X
N	V	V	T	Y	H	B	N	J	G	I	O	L	M	S
I	B	E	C	A	U	S	E	V	E	C	N	H	J	U
R	B	R	D	S	E	R	W	E	L	O	P	K	I	J
P	N	M	B	G	T	R	V	C	F	D	E	R	S	E
S	C	V	T	G	B	H	Y	U	I	L	I	R	P	A

The words are:

APRIL BECAUSE CAT DECEMBER DISCOVER LION PENCIL
SPRING TOMORROW WATER

See Lesson Notes, page 80

AS PSYCHOLOGY: THE TEACHER'S COMPANION Published by Nelson Thornes Ltd. © 2004 Sara Berman, Cara Flanagan and Adrian Frost

70

How hardy are you?

HOW HARDY ARE YOU?

Below are 12 items similar to those that appear in the hardiness questionnaire devised by Kobasa. Write down how much you agree or disagree with the following statements, using the following scale, and write in the number of your answer (0, 1, 2 or 3) beside the letter of each question on the score sheet.

0 = strongly disagree 1 = mildly disagree
2 = mildly agree 3 = strongly agree

☐ **A** Trying my best at work makes a difference.

☐ **B** Trusting to fate is sometimes all I can do in a relationship.

☐ **C** I often wake up eager to start on the day's projects.

☐ **D** Thinking of myself as a free person leads to great frustration and difficulty.

☐ **E** I would be willing to sacrifice financial security in my work if something really challenging came along.

☐ **F** It bothers me when I have to deviate from the routine or schedule I've set for myself.

☐ **G** An average citizen can have an impact on politics.

☐ **H** Without the right breaks, it is hard to be successful in my field.

☐ **I** I know why I am doing what I'm doing at work (school or office).

☐ **J** Getting close to people means I'm then obligated to them.

☐ **K** Encountering new situations is an important priority in my life.

☐ **L** I really don't mind when I have nothing to do.

TO SCORE YOURSELF: For half the questions, a high score (like 3) indicates hardiness; for the other half, a low score (like 0) does.

To get your score on 'control', add your answers to questions A and G; add your answers to B and H; and then subtract the second number from the first. [(A+G) – (B+H)]

To get your score on 'commitment', add your answers to questions C and I; add your answers to D and J; and then subtract the second number from the first. [(C+I) – (D+J)]

To get your score on 'challenge', add your answers to questions E and K; add your answers to F and L; and then subtract the second number from the first. [(E+K) – (F+L)]

Add your scores on commitment, control and challenge together to get a score for total hardiness. The highest possible score is 18.

Source: Adapted from http://www.suu.edu/ss/wellness/trauma.html

See Lesson Notes, page 83

AS PSYCHOLOGY: THE TEACHER'S COMPANION Published by Nelson Thornes Ltd. © 2004 Sara Berman, Cara Flanagan and Adrian Frost

Stress management star rating system

Which method of stress management would you recommend? How can one compare between the different methods? Lots of people use star rating systems to indicate what is best. For example, the *Radio Times* gives five stars to the best films, and one star for something fairly unwatchable. So you could use the same idea for rating stress management methods.

But before you decide on an overall rating, it might be more meaningful to break it down into different criteria which can be assessed separately and then use them to calculate a mean value.

1 Work with a small group of other students and decide on a list of criteria such as:

- ✔ expense
- ✔ ease of use
- ✔ effectiveness
- ✔ side effects.

2 Then decide on a scale for each criteria: e.g. rate each method of stress management in terms of expense on a scale of 1 to 5 where 5 is very cheap. You can use a scale of 1 to 3, or 1 to 10.

Note that the high number should also be the most desirable characteristic.

3 Calculate an average (mean) score for each method of stress management.

4 Compare your ratings with other groups in your class. Did they have some better criteria? Were their ratings very different to yours?

See Lesson Notes, page 83

AS PSYCHOLOGY: THE TEACHER'S COMPANION Published by Nelson Thornes Ltd. © 2004 Sara Berman, Cara Flanagan and Adrian Frost

See Lesson Notes, page 85

Questionnaire

	Agree *very much*	**Agree *somewhat***	**Agree *slightly***	**Disagree *slightly***	**Disagree *somewhat***	**Disagree *very much***
1 Sometimes I don't feel that I have enough control over the direction my life is taking.						
2 By taking an active part in political and social affairs people can control world events.						
3 It is impossible for me to believe that chance or luck plays an important role in my life.						
4 Many times I feel that I have little influence over the things that happen to me.						
5 Getting people to do the right things depends upon ability; luck has little or nothing to do with it.						
6 Unfortunately, an individual's worth often passes unrecognised no matter how hard he tries.						
7 Capable people who fail to become leaders have not taken advantage of their opportunities.						
8 This world is run by a few people in power, and there is not much the little guy can do.						
9 What happens to me is my own doing.						
10 Most people don't realise the extent to which their lives are controlled by accidental happenings.						
11 People's misfortunes result from the mistakes they make.						
12 There is really no such thing as 'luck'.						
13 The average citizen can have an influence on government decisions.						
14 In the long run people get the respect they deserve in the world.						
15 In my case getting what I want has little or nothing to do with luck.						
16 With enough effort we can wipe out political corruption.						
17 Who gets to be the boss often depends on who was lucky enough to be in the right place first.						
18 Many of the unhappy things in people's lives are partly due to bad luck.						
19 It is difficult for people to have much control over things politicians do in office.						
20 People are lonely because they don't try to be friendly.						

From: Mcilveen, R., Higgins, L. and Wadeley, A. (1992) *BPS Manual of Psychology practicals*. BPS Books, page 191.

AS PSYCHOLOGY: THE TEACHER'S COMPANION Published by Nelson Thornes Ltd. © 2004 Sara Berman, Cara Flanagan and Adrian Frost

Physiological Psychology

Crossword

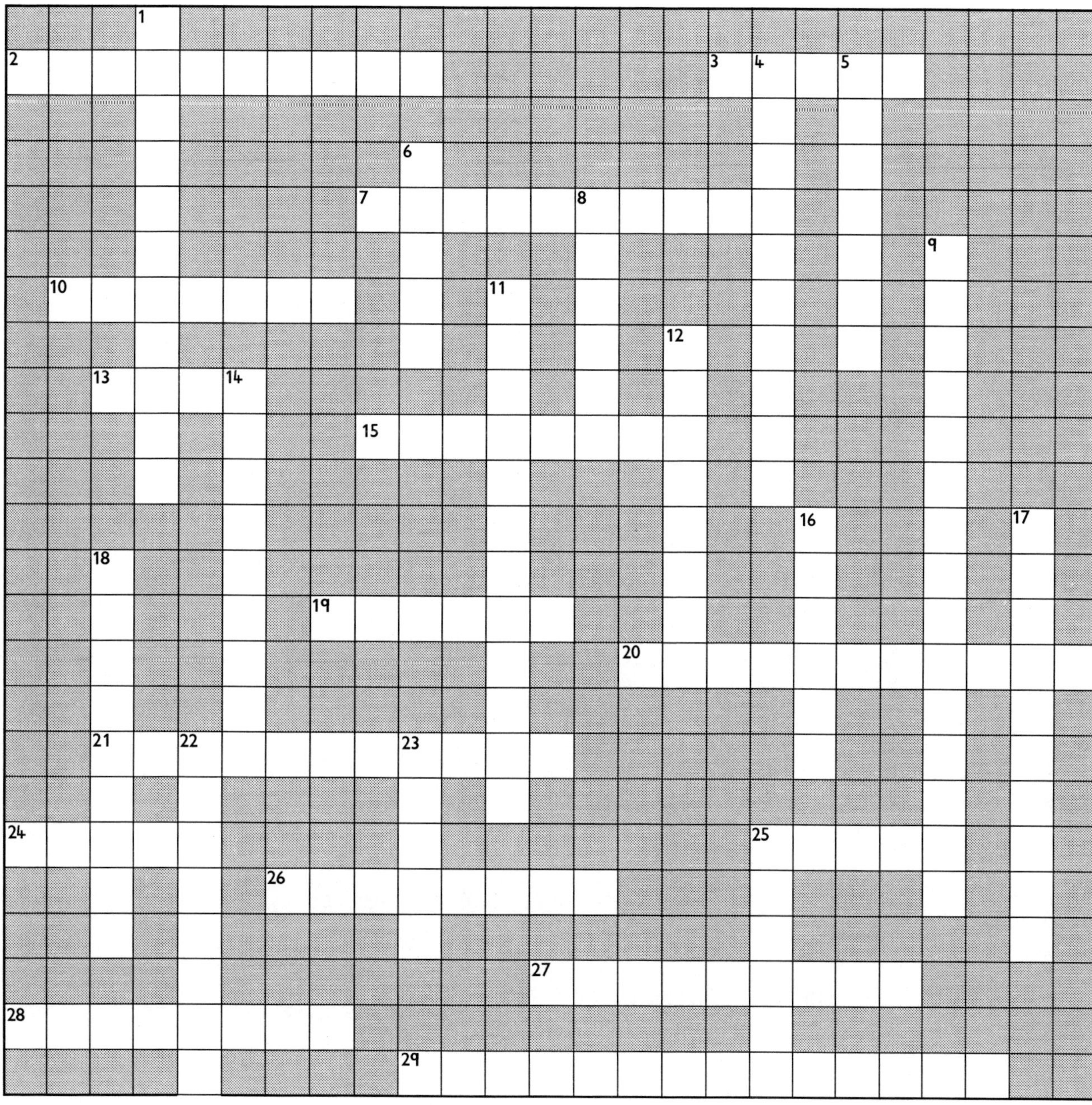

AS PSYCHOLOGY: THE TEACHER'S COMPANION Published by Nelson Thornes Ltd. © 2004 Sara Berman, Cara Flanagan and Adrian Frost

74
Physiological Psychology
Crossword clues

Across

2 The second phase of the GAS model. (10)

3 A personality type that enables individuals to cope better with stress. (5)

7 LCU stand for ______ ______ units. (4,6)

10 Adrenal ________. Region of the adrenal gland that produces adrenalin. (7)

13 Biochemical substance which is the body's natural form of anxiety relief. (4)

15 Any event that causes a stress reaction in the body. (8)

19 The system of cells within the body concerned with fighting intruders such as bacteria. (6)

20 Branch of the ANS (autonomic nervous system) concerned with arousal. (11)

21 SIT stands for stress ________ training. (11)

24 Man who conducted work with executive monkeys. (5)

25 Psychologist who suggested the General Adaptation Syndrome. (5)

26 Rotter suggested that people with this kind of control cope better with stress. (8)

27 Hardiness training involves 3 Cs which are control, commitment and ?(9)

28 Hormone associated with stress, starts with a 'C'. (8)

29 A disorder of the heart and circulatory system. (14)

Down

1 Psychological method of stress management where patient is aware of ANS activity and tries to learn to control this. (11)

4 Hormone associated with the 'flight or fight' response. (10)

5 Life event rating second on the Social Adjustment Rating Scale. (7)

6 Kind of small-scale study conducted before the real thing to check that procedures are working. (5)

8 Name of one of the doctors who developed the Social Readjustment Rating Scale. (6)

9 BZs – drug used to reduce nervous system activity. (15)

11 A term for high blood pressure. (12)

12 CHD stands for ________ heart disease. (8)

14 ________ nervous system, governs the release of hormones. (9)

16 Female psychologist associated with hardiness training. (6)

17 Class of drugs that deal with reducing anxiety. (10)

18 Master gland for the body's hormone system. (9)

22 Female hormone that may explain why women cope better with stress. (8)

23 Personality type associated with competitiveness and a sense of time urgency. (4,1)

25 Lack of fit between a person and their environment. (5)

AS PSYCHOLOGY: THE TEACHER'S COMPANION Published by Nelson Thornes Ltd. © 2004 Sara Berman, Cara Flanagan and Adrian Frost

Physiological Psychology

Crossword solutions

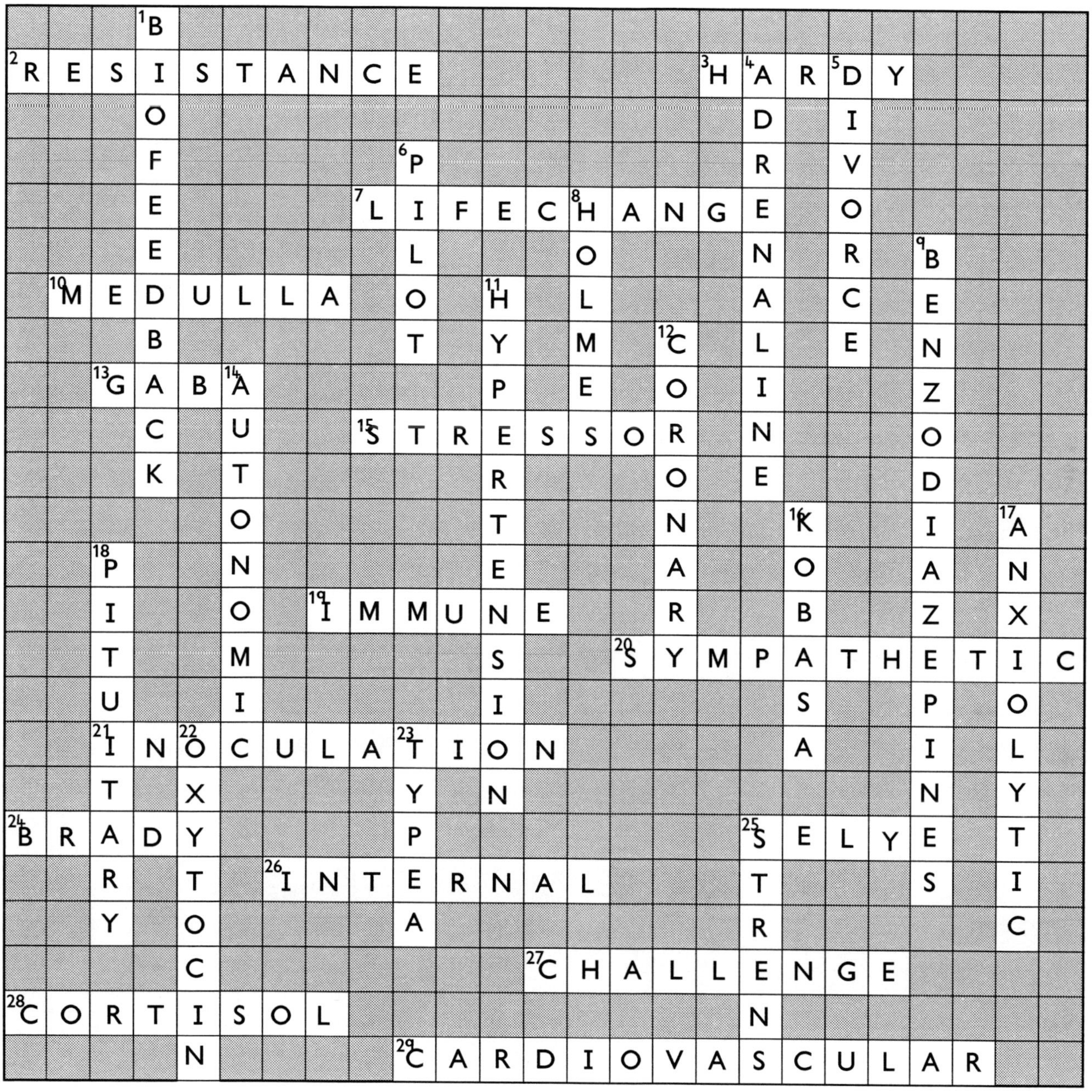

AS PSYCHOLOGY: THE TEACHER'S COMPANION Published by Nelson Thornes Ltd. © 2004 Sara Berman, Cara Flanagan and Adrian Frost

76

Recognising abnormal behaviour

Recognising abnormal behaviour is essentially a subjective judgement that each of us makes. It is influenced by many implicit values and factors. This exercise is to help you evaluate how you and your friends recognise and identify 'abnormality' in others. Please read the short vignettes below, which describe different individuals. After reading each one use the two scales at the end to rate to what extent you think the individual has a psychiatric/psychological disorder and also whether, in your opinion, they should seek treatment. Having rated each vignette, compare your ratings with your friends and discuss any agreements or disagreements in your judgements.

1 Mr Smith has always lived in an isolated cottage. He has six dogs which he looks after. He never goes out of the cottage unless absolutely necessary, and has no friends or visitors.

2 Mr Jones is intensely afraid of heights. He has left a job because it was on the fifth floor, and refuses to visit his daughter who lives in Austria because of the mountains.

3 Mrs Jarvis, who was born in Jamaica, is a follower of the Pentecostal Church and believes that on occasions she is possessed by spirits which make her 'speak in tongues'.

4 Mrs Patel was arrested for shop-lifting two weeks ago. She blamed the tablets (Valium) that she has been taking for the last five years but has recently discontinued.

5 Mr Kahn is a successful executive who has just been told by his GP that he has high blood pressure.

6 Ben is a street musician who recently dropped out of art school. He likes to 'perform' using a variety of vegetables and dead fish!

7 Mrs Lee is a housewife who spends nearly every day at home keeping the house 'spick and span'. Her husband returned home from night work early one night last week and found her dusting at 2 a.m.

8 Nadia is 22 years old and a dancer. Although she weighs only six stone she is continually dieting.

9 Bob is a loner who keeps to himself because he believes that the social-security snoopers are out to kill him. Although unemployed he refuses to seek any welfare benefits.

10 Sue is a six-year-old girl who is extremely shy and seldom speaks. She becomes very upset if her parents alter her playroom furniture.

11 Joe is nine years old and wets the bed five times a week. His parents' marriage broke up when he was five.

12 Mrs Black is married with two daughters. Last week she confided to her best friend that she had never experienced an orgasm.

	This person suffers from a psychiatric/psychological problem				
	Strongly agree	Moderately agree	Do not know	Moderately disagree	Strongly disagree
1					
2					
3					
4					
5					
6					
7					
8					
9					
10					
11					
12					

	This person needs treatment for his/her problems				
	Strongly agree	Moderately agree	Do not know	Moderately disagree	Strongly disagree
1					
2					
3					
4					
5					
6					
7					
8					
9					
10					
11					
12					

See Lesson Notes, page 86

AS PSYCHOLOGY: THE TEACHER'S COMPANION Published by Nelson Thornes Ltd. © 2004 Sara Berman, Cara Flanagan and Adrian Frost

Handout: Whose line is it anyway?

	Method of defining abnormality			
	Statistical infrequency	Deviation from social norms	Failure to function	Deviation from ideal mental health
1 Man who sits next to you on bus when plenty of other seats available				
2 Child abuser				
3 Child genius				
4 Born again Christian				
5 Person who talks to their pets				
6 Stressed executives who take time off work				
7 Person in a dead end job				
8 Person who believes that someone is watching their every move				

See Lesson Notes, page 86

AS PSYCHOLOGY: THE TEACHER'S COMPANION Published by Nelson Thornes Ltd. © 2004 Sara Berman, Cara Flanagan and Adrian Frost

78

How are definitions of abnormality limited by cultural relativism?

GENERAL DEFINITION OF CULTURAL RELATIVISM

VERY BRIEF OUTLINE OF 'DEVIATION FROM STATISTICAL NORMS' DEFINITION

EXPLANATION OF WHY STATISTICAL DEVIATION LIMITED BY CULTURAL RELATIVISM

EXAMPLE

VERY BRIEF OUTLINE OF 'DEVIATION FROM SOCIAL NORMS' DEFINITION

EXPLANATION OF WHY SOCIAL DEVIATION LIMITED BY CULTURAL RELATIVISM

EXAMPLE

VERY BRIEF OUTLINE OF 'FAILURE TO FUNCTION' DEFINITION

EXPLANATION OF WHY FAILURE TO FUNCTION LIMITED BY CULTURAL RELATIVISM

EXAMPLE

VERY BRIEF OUTLINE OF 'DEVIATION FROM IDEAL MENTAL HEALTH' DEFINITION

EXPLANATION OF WHY IDEAL MENTAL HEALTH LIMITED BY CULTURAL RELATIVISM

EXAMPLE

See Lesson Notes, page 87

AS PSYCHOLOGY: THE TEACHER'S COMPANION Published by Nelson Thornes Ltd. © 2004 Sara Berman, Cara Flanagan and Adrian Frost

Case study for a biological therapist

Read the following case study and imagine that you are a psychologist who believes in the biological model of abnormality.

- In trying to understand Adam's behaviour, what evidence would you focus on and select from this case study and why?
- What caused him to behave like this? Provide one explanation (from a biological point of view) for his behaviour.
- What assumptions underlie your explanation?
- What therapy would you offer him?

Slouching in the wide chair in the therapist's room, Adam was unconvinced. He had come for help only after his GP recommended that he see a therapist. The apparent reason was his inability to sleep at night. He did not see the point of talking about his childhood or the other problems that he had been experiencing recently, but eventually after some gentle questions from the therapist, he agreed to talk.

When Adam was only seven his mother, who he loved very much, died suddenly and over the next few years his time was spent living either with his father or his aunt. His father drank a great deal and could not get through the day without a large amount of alcohol. At the same time his father had great mood swings and had even spent a few weeks in the local psychiatric hospital where he was diagnosed as having manic-depression. As his father seldom had a job for very long, there was never enough money to pay the bills on time and they lived in a very run down part of town. There were times when his father couldn't look after Adam and so he would then go and live with his aunt.

In spite of this difficult upbringing Adam did well at school and after his A levels went to university. He got a part time job working in a pub. However, he also was aware that sometimes he felt depressed for no particular reason but at other times he felt really elated and full of energy and excitement. While at university he began to feel very self-conscious with people who he thought were in authority over him (like his boss, the lecturers and even some of his peers). He always felt slightly inferior and was very sensitive about things such as his clothes because they weren't the 'designer label' that many of the others wore. Being a member of the rugby team helped his self esteem but after a serious head injury he was advised not to play for the rest of the season.

One day at the start of his second year he started going out with an attractive girl who was on his course. To his amazement they soon fell in love although Adam could not believe that an intelligent and charming girl could fall for him. Adam became increasingly stressed as the end of year exams approached, especially as his girlfriend did not seem to find exams and revision hard. Like his father, Adam turned to drink to help him deal with the stress. Although he passed his exams, he still kept on drinking as he found that it made him feel less self-conscious and more relaxed, especially in the company of his peers.

One evening, after Adam had been in an elated mood for several days and after he had been drinking more heavily than usual, he had a violent argument with his girlfriend. He accused her of being unfaithful and almost went to hit her when he somehow managed to stop himself. He was so appalled at what he might have done that he decided to get some professional help.

See Lesson Notes, page 88

 © 2004 Sara Berman, Cara Flanagan and Adrian Frost

Behavioural therapies

Please read these two accounts of behavioural therapies and then consider the questions that follow.

Treatment for spider phobia

'One spider phobic, Beverley, heard Professor Marks on the radio describing a treatment for phobics like herself. She rang up the radio station, and made arrangements with Marks to go to his clinic for treatment. It was a considerable ordeal for Beverley, which involved progressively more intimate exposure to the symbol of her horror, the spider. She began by looking at the picture of a spider – even that made her extremely anxious and uncomfortable – and then went on to hold the picture: then she inspected, touched and eventually picked up a dummy spider. All these stages were achieved by degrees of reluctance, but with the phobic symptoms just under control.

The next step was for her to touch a dead spider, which she eventually managed notwithstanding her clear physical discomfort. And the last act in her first therapy session, directed with sympathetic firmness by Dr Raja Ghosh, was to touch a live spider in a glass dish. That took some doing, but after a number of trial efforts she succeeded. Beverley's relief at the end of the session was obvious, but so was her pride in her achievement. She viewed her next session with great apprehension, but in the event it took only a few minutes to have a middle-sized spider running over her hand.'

From: Gilling, D. and Brightwell, R. (1982) *The Human Brain*. London: Orbis Publishing Ltd. pp.135–6

Treatment for obsessive-compulsive hand washing

'Having agreed, the patient is brought into a room which contains little besides a table, two chairs, one for the psychologist and one for the patient, and a container filled with some dirt or other material that the patient is known to think 'contaminating'. The therapist then puts his hand into the dirt in the container and persuades the patient to do likewise. Now comes the crucial point: the patient is urged not to go and wash his hands (as he would normally do in order to reduce his anxiety) but rather to sit still and tolerate the very strong emotions of fear, anguish and anxiety that threaten to overwhelm him. Being 'flooded' with emotion is an unpleasant experience, but the emotion gradually subsides, and after half an hour or so the patient can tolerate the situation with a degree of composure that he would have thought impossible at the beginning.'

From: Eysenck, H. and Eysenck, M. (1981) *Mindwatching*. Book Club associates by arrangement with Michael Joseph Ltd. p.67

QUESTIONS

1 What ethical concerns do you think are raised by the treatments outlined above?
2 What are the key differences between the two approaches outlined above? How do you think these differences could affect the success of therapy?
3 How do these approaches compare with other types of treatment in terms of length of time that treatment requires?
4 How successfully do you think these patients will be in maintaining their new behaviours?
5 Can you think of any types of disorder for which the types of approach outlined above would not be appropriate?

See Lesson Notes, page 90

AS PSYCHOLOGY: THE TEACHER'S COMPANION Published by Nelson Thornes Ltd. © 2004 Sara Berman, Cara Flanagan and Adrian Frost

Abnormality is caused by faulty thinking

Ghosts are dead stories of which we refuse to let go.

This is what my ghosts were telling me:

'I told you you shouldn't listen to yourself. You should never have tried to be a writer, but you should have gone into the civil service, like I wanted you to. You've broken my heart by being a failure, despite all my sacrifices. If you'd been any kind of person at all, you'd have tried above all to make your mother happy'.

'Nothing you touch will ever go well, because you bought it at other people's cost. Now pay the price for your selfishness'.

These messages never changed, except that my ghosts became more skilful at speaking to maximum effect – whenever I had begun to hope that I might recover from the past, or when I was feeling vulnerable.

I felt possessed.

From: Lewis. G. (2002) *Sunbathing In The Rain.* London: Harper Collins, p.84

What I do feel is the scariness of being an adult, being alone in this big huge loft with so many CDs and plastic bags and magazines and pairs of dirty socks and dirty plates on the floor that I can't even see the floor. I'm sure that I have nowhere to run, that I can't even walk anywhere without tripping and falling way down, and I know I want out of this mess. I want out. No-one will ever love me, I will live and die alone, I will go nowhere fast, I will be nothing at all. Nothing will work out. The promise that on the other side of depression lies a beautiful life, one worth surviving suicide for, will have turned out wrong. It will all be a big dupe.

From: Wurtzel, E. (1995) Prozac Nation. *Quartet Books, p.3*

I try on three shirts, two pairs of pants. I smoke and put on my eyeliner. I stare at my face from all angles. It isn't right. It never is. I stand and look at my butt, my hips, my thighs, the way my upper arms look when I press them as hard as I can against my side. Are they bigger? Is the left side of my rear end bigger than it was two weeks ago? Julian comes in with coffee. Do I look like I've gained weight? I ask. He says no. This is a tired routine. I always ask, he always says no. I say, you're lying. He says, No I'm not. I look at the right side of my butt in the mirror. He sits down in my chair. I say, you always say that. He says, well Honey, I don't know what to tell you. I ask, so seriously, I don't look like I've gained weight? He says, No, you don't. I say, But I don't look like I've lost weight? He says, No, you don't.

This seems impossible to me. It seems biologically impossible to stay the same size, although I must. It seems one must always be either bigger or smaller than they were at some arbitrary point in time to which all things are compared. The panties that are possibly tighter than they were. When? You can't say when. But you are *absolutely positive no question* that it's true. It ruins your day. You get into bed that night with your husband, your lover, your friend, your boss, whoever, and roll over, facing the door, curled fetally into yourself. The hand snakes over to your side of the bed. You say: I'm tired, don't touch me, I have a headache, I feel sick, stop it, go away, leave me alone. Because you, in the course of the day, have ballooned to the size of a small hippo. You are sure of it, your skin is too tight, you wish to take it off, you're hot.

From: Hornbacher, M. (1999) *Wasted*. London: Harper Collins, pp.179–80

See Lesson Notes, page 91

AS PSYCHOLOGY: THE TEACHER'S COMPANION Published by Nelson Thornes Ltd. © 2004 Sara Berman, Cara Flanagan and Adrian Frost

Summary of approaches to abnormality

Medical/biological approach

- Behaviour may in part be influenced by genes inherited from our parents.
- Our mood, thinking and behaviour is influenced by our body chemistry.
- If there's something wrong with our mind, this is because there's something wrong with our body.

Behavioural approach

- Behaviour is learnt.
- Behaviour persists because, in the past, it has been reinforced.
- People learn to associate certain stimuli with particular bodily states.

Psychodynamic approach

- People don't always understand why they do what they do (unconscious motivations).
- Adult behaviour is influenced by events in childhood.
- Psychic energy from one conflict may be displaced onto other situations.

Cognitive approach

- People hold, and act upon, beliefs that are irrational.
- People can feel compelled by faulty beliefs ('I must do or be X at all times').
- People may interpret the world about them in line with irrational beliefs about themselves.

See Lesson Notes, page 92

AS PSYCHOLOGY: THE TEACHER'S COMPANION Published by Nelson Thornes Ltd. © 2004 Sara Berman, Cara Flanagan and Adrian Frost

Revise the models of abnormality

	Medical	Behavioural	Psychodynamic	Cognitive
Main cause(s) of abnormality				
Favoured method(s) of treatment				
Main objective(s) for treatment				
How is behaviour viewed?				
What is psychological normality?				

Task: Using the numbers for the statements, put the appropriate statement into one of the boxes above.

- Emotional disturbance (or neurosis) is caused by unresolved conflicts that come from childhood. Abnormal behaviour is a result of these conflicts. (1)
- Physical treatments such as electro-convulsive therapy, psychosurgery, drugs. (2)
- Having unrealistic or irrational beliefs and ideas about oneself and others. Not able to control or check behaviour through usual cognitive processes. (3)
- To get rid of maladaptive responses and acquire adaptive ones. (4)
- Person feels conflict because of the opposing demands made by different parts of the personality – id, ego, super-ego. Behaviour is mainly determined by the unconscious. (5)
- Cognitive behaviour therapy, Rational-emotive therapy, etc. (6)
- Behaviour therapy or behaviour modification e.g. systematic desensitisation, token economy. (7)
- Insight-oriented psychotherapy (e.g. psychoanalysis) where the unconscious is revealed using dream interpretation, free-association, etc. (8)
- The human mind is an information processor: selecting information, coding it, storing and retrieving it when necessary. (9)
- Having a reasonably large repertoire of adaptive responses. (10)
- Genetic disorders, organic disorders (e.g. brain diseases or injury), chemical imbalances. Mental illness causes symptoms that are behavioural and cognitive. (11)
- To uncover unconscious conflicts and make them conscious, to achieve a balance between the ego, id and super-ego. (12)
- To have a nervous system that is functioning properly. (13)
- Having cognitive processes that are functioning properly and the ability to use them to check and control behaviour. (14)
- Human behaviour is shaped by forces in the environment and is a collection of responses that have been learnt. The main learning processes are classical and operant conditioning. (15)
- To ease symptoms and/or actually reverse the underlying cause(s) of the illness. (16)
- Learning maladaptive responses or failing to learn adaptive ones in the first place. No distinction is made between the symptoms and the disorder. (17)
- There is an adequate balance between ego, id and super-ego but there is always some degree of conflict. (18)
- Genetic, physiological and neurobiological factors and processes determine behaviour. The central nervous system and the brain have a crucial role. (19)
- To correct irrational and unrealistic beliefs and ideas so that thinking becomes an effective way of controlling behaviour. (20)

See Lesson Notes, page 92

AS PSYCHOLOGY: THE TEACHER'S COMPANION Published by Nelson Thornes Ltd. © 2004 Sara Berman, Cara Flanagan and Adrian Frost

84

Compare and contrast the different approaches to abnormality (a discussion activity)

Use your knowledge of the four approaches demanded by the Specification to place a tick or a cross in each of the boxes below. Please note that there may be more than one tick in each row.

M=Medical/biological, B= Behavioural, P=Psychodynamic, C=Cognitive

	M	B	P	C
Treatment requires that the sufferer develop insight concerning the cause of their abnormality				
Treatment focuses upon the removal of specific, clearly-defined features of a condition				
Treatment is expensive				
Approach is scientific				
Approach is rejected by more 'client-centred' approaches				
Approach believes that cause of abnormality may be linked to parents				
Treatment takes a long time				
Successful treatment requires the active involvement of the patient				
Emphasises mental processes				
'Cure' involves identification of 'irrational' thoughts				
Approach to treatment raises ethical concerns				
Treatment places power in the hands of the therapist and not the client				
Treatment is directed at underlying causes of abnormal behaviour				

See Lesson Notes, page 92

AS PSYCHOLOGY: THE TEACHER'S COMPANION Published by Nelson Thornes Ltd. © 2004 Sara Berman, Cara Flanagan and Adrian Frost

Diet diaries – Trouble with food

Case Study 1 Bulimia Nervosa: Sarah

How should we treat any statistics about eating disorders?

____

Bulimia Nervosa is the fastest growing eating disorder: how many new cases are there each year?

____

What is the total number each year? __________

Why is Sarah disappointed with herself? ___________________________________

____

What age did her eating disorder start? __________

What was she addicted to? __________

How does she feel about the Bulimia? _____________________________________

____

Lyndel Costain, British Dietetic Association, states that a number of young women vomit, how many times a week and why?

____

Case Study 2 Anorexia nervosa: Sarah M

According to the Eating Disorder Association who is at the highest risk from AN and how many will become long term suffers?

____

Sarah states that she didn't want to grow up, how did AN help this aim?

____

____

Dr Lorenzo Pieri (Yorkshire Centre for Eating Disorders) suggests that AN is caused by:

1 per cent from __________

1 per cent from __________

About 90 per cent from __________

What does Lyndel Costain believe AN is an outward sign of?

____

Dr Pieri states that the outcome for AN is that:

One third will __________

One third will __________

One third will __________

What per cent will die prematurely? __________

See Lesson Notes, page 93

AS PSYCHOLOGY: THE TEACHER'S COMPANION Published by Nelson Thornes Ltd. © 2004 Sara Berman, Cara Flanagan and Adrian Frost

86

Do the figures support the biological explanation of anorexia?

Please read the following descriptions of research findings concerning biological explanations of anorexia nervosa and then complete the activity on **Handout 87**.

Star Study on the biological causes of anorexia nervosa (Holland et *al.*, 1988)

Procedures

Forty-five pairs of female twins were interviewed where at least one twin had had anorexia . The interviews established the clinical characteristics observed as well as the occurrence of eating disorders in any close relatives. Records were also made of body mass, length of amenorrhea and questions asked about drive to be thin and body dissatisfaction.

In order to determine whether twins were identical or not, a blood test was used. There were **25 MZ twins and 20 DZ twins** in the study.

Findings

There was significantly higher concordance in the MZ twins; 25 **(56%)** of the MZ twins were concordant for anorexia whereas only 1 **(5%)** of the DZ twins were.

There was significantly more anorexia in relatives studied than found in the normal population. The rate of anorexia in the population in general is 0.1%. The study found six cases of anorexia among first degree relatives **(4.9%)** and in second degree relatives there were two cases **(1.2%)**.

Biological explanations cannot account for the fact that anorexia has increased dramatically in the past **30** years. Nor can they explain why there is not **100%** concordance for anorexia in twins.

Park *et al.* (1995) suggest that anorexia may be the consequence of glandular-fever-like illnesses. They studied **four** cases where individuals had such an illness immediately before the onset of anorexia . Glandular fever may upset the functioning of the hypothalamus.

One possibility is that brain damage at birth causes anorexia. Cnattingius *et al.* (1999) used hospital records for about **4000** female babies born in Sweden between 1973 and 1984; 781 were subsequently hospitalised for anorexia and of this **5** had experienced birth traumas suggesting that birth trauma (brain damage) may increase risk for anorexia. Alternatively, differences in brain structure may be an effect rather than a cause of anorexia.

See Lesson Notes, page 94

AS PSYCHOLOGY: THE TEACHER'S COMPANION Published by Nelson Thornes Ltd. © 2004 Sara Berman, Cara Flanagan and Adrian Frost

Do the figures support the biological explanation of anorexia?

On **Handout 86**, several statistics were highlighted. All of these help to shed some light upon whether anorexia nervosa can be explained biologically, but it's important that we consider just *how much* support they give to the argument. The question is: Do they provide *strong* evidence for a biological explanation of anorexia?

For each of the statistics identified below, comment upon the extent to which the information supports the biological argument.

Amongst other questions, you might like to consider the following.

- How valid is the data?
- How was it obtained?
- Could it be interpreted differently?
- How does it compare to other data?

Statistics	Comment on how much this supports the biological argument
Forty-five pairs of female twins	
25 MZ twins and 20 DZ	
(56%) of the MZ twins were concordant for anorexia	
(5%) of the DZ twins were	
Six cases of anorexia among first degree relatives **(4.9%)**	
In second degree relatives there were two cases **(1.2%)**.	
Hospital records for about **4000** female babies	
Five had experienced birth traumas	
They studied four cases	
Increased dramatically in the past **30** years	
Not **100%** concordance for anorexia in twins.	

See Lesson Notes, page 94

AS PSYCHOLOGY: THE TEACHER'S COMPANION Published by Nelson Thornes Ltd. © 2004 Sara Berman, Cara Flanagan and Adrian Frost

88

Has body image changed?

A recent study (Rubenstein, S. and Caballero, B. (2000) Is Miss America an undernourished role model? JAMA, 283(12), 1569) used the height and weight figures of past Miss Americas to calculate a measure, called body mass index, and concluded that it has generally fallen over the years. BMI is weight divided by the square of height. In the 1920s, contestants had BMIs in the range now considered normal, which is 20 to 25, the researchers said. But an increasing number of winners since then have had BMIs under 18.5, which is the World Health Organisation's standard for undernutrition.

The data (from http://www.pbs.org/wgbh/amex/missamerica/sfeature/sf_list.html) is provided for you below, to make your own calculations and conclusions.

As of 2002, 75 young women have won the title of Miss America. Averaging all the winners' vital statistics, the composite winner is 20 years and 3 months old; her average weight is just over 121 pounds; her height is 5 feet 6½ inches.

The 1925 winner of the Miss America beauty pageant, Fay Lanphier

Miss America 2002 was won by Katie Harman

See Lesson Notes, page 95

AS PSYCHOLOGY: THE TEACHER'S COMPANION Published by Nelson Thornes Ltd. © 2004 Sara Berman, Cara Flanagan and Adrian Frost

Statistics for Miss America pageant winners, 1921 to 2002

Year	Finalist	Age	Height (ft/ins)	Weight (lb)	Measurements
1921	Margaret	16	5'1"	108	30-25-32
1922/3	Mary	16	5'7"	140	35-26-36
1924	Ruth	18	5'6"	137	34-25-34
1925	Fay	19	5'6"	138	34-26-37
1926	Norma	18	5'4"	118	33-25-34
1927	Lois	17	5'5"	115	33-25-34
1933	Marian B	15	5'4"	112	32-26-37
1935	Henrietta	17	5'6"	120	33-23-35
1936	Rose	22	5'6"	114	34-23-34
1937	Bette	17	5'6"	120	32-26-36
1938	Marilyn M	20	5'7"	128	34-26-36
1939	Patricia	19	5'7"	126	36-25-34
1940	Frances	19	5'9"	120	34-23-35
1941	Rosemary	18	5'5"	120	34-24-36
1942	Jo-Carroll	18	5'5"	118	34-22-34
1943	Jean	19	5'8"	130	36-23-35
1944	Venus	19	5'7"	125	36-25-37
1945	Bess	21	5'10"	135	35-25-35
1946	Marilyn B	21	5'8"	123	35-25-36
1947	Barbara Jo	21	5'7"	130	35-25-35
1948	Bebe	18	5'9"	140	37-27-36
1949	Jacque	18	5'3"	106	34-22-34
1951	Yolande	18	5'5"	119	35-24-35
1952	Colleen	25	5'10"	143	36-24-36
1953	Neva Jane	19	5'6"	118	35-23-35
1954	Evelyn	20	5'8"	132	37-24-36
1955	Lee	19	5'8"	124	34-22-35
1956	Sharon	18	5'6"	116	35-23-35
1957	Marian M	19	5'5"	120	35-23-35
1958	Marilyn v. D	20	5'8"	130	35-25-36
1959	Mary Ann	21	5'5"	114	34-22-35
1960	Lynda	20	5'7"	120	36-24-36
1961	Nancy	18	5'6"	116	35-22-35
1962	Maria	19	5'5"	118	35-24-35
1963	Jacquelyn	20	5'5"	115	36-22-26
1964	Donna	21	5'6"	124	35-23-35
1965	Vonda Kay	21	5'6"	124	36-24-36
1966	Deborah	19	5'7"	115	36-23-36
1967	Jane	19	5'6"	116	36-24-36
1968	Debra B	20	5'9"	135	26-24-36
1969	Judith	18	5'7"	125	36-24-36
1970	Pam	21	5'5"	110	34-21-34
1971	Phyllis	21	5'8"	121	36-23-36
1972	Laurel Lea	22	5'7"	118	36-24-36
1973	Terry	23	5'8"	120	36-25-36
1974	Rebecca	23	5'9"	125	36-24-36
1975	Shirley	21	5'8"	119	36-23-36
1976	Tawny	18	5'10"	128	36-24-36
1977	Dorothy	20	5'7"	120	35-23-35
1978	Susan Pe	23	5'5"	105	34-24-35
1979	Kylene	22	5'4"	108	35-24-35
1980	Cheryl	22	5'7"	114	35-23-36
1981	Susan Po	21	5'4"	110	35-24-35
1982	Elizabeth Ward	20	5'9"	129	36-24-36
1983	Debra M	25	5'7"	115	35-22-35
1984	Vanessa	20	5'6"	110	34-24-34
1984	Suzette	20	5'3"	100	33-22-33
1985	Sharlene	20	5'8"	120	35-25-36
1986	Susan A	21	5'9"	114	35-22-35
1987	Kellye	21	5'8"	116	
1988	Kaye Lani	24	5'10"	131	
1989	Gretchen	22	5'3"	108	
1990	Debbye	23	5'8"	118	Statistics no longer given
1991	Majorie	25	5'6"	110	
1998	Kate	21	5'11"	145	
1999	Nicole	24	5'9"	133	
2001	Angela	24	5'4"	118	
2002	Katie	21	5'3"	110	

Missing years: no data on height/weight

See Lesson Notes, page 95

AS PSYCHOLOGY: THE TEACHER'S COMPANION Published by Nelson Thornes Ltd. © 2004 Sara Berman, Cara Flanagan and Adrian Frost

90

Attitudes to eating disorders

Name: ____________

Age ____________ Gender M F

Home telephone ____________ Mobile Number____________

1 Most girls with eating disorders only have themselves to blame.

STRONGLY AGREE **AGREE** **DISAGREE** **STRONGLY DISAGREE**

2 It is clear that parents play a part in their daughters eating disorder and that they should be made to be accountable for it.

STRONGLY AGREE **AGREE** **DISAGREE** **STRONGLY DISAGREE**

3 Unfortunately the media is often criticised for influencing the young via vicarious reinforcement.

STRONGLY AGREE **AGREE** **DISAGREE** **STRONGLY DISAGREE**

4 People with anorexia nervosa just need to start eating and then they would get better.

STRONGLY AGREE **AGREE** **DISAGREE** **STRONGLY DISAGREE**

5 One of the best indications of anorexia nervosa is amenorrhoea.

STRONGLY AGREE **AGREE** **DISAGREE** **STRONGLY DISAGREE**

6 Everybody would agree that purging is a disgusting habit. Yes/No

7 Bingeing once or twice a month is OK, we all do it. Yes/No

8 It is generally accepted that only thin people are beautiful. Yes/No

9 Girls are more concerned with body image than boys. Yes/No

10 Very few boys are bothered by their looks. Yes/No

Please answer the following questions about yourself.

A Have you ever suffered from any of the following and if so when and for how long?

Anorexia nervosa ____________

Bulimia nervosa ____________

Pica ____________

Ruminative disorder ____________

Other (please specify) ____________

B Have you ever engaged in any of the following activities?

Restriction of calories ____________

Excessive eating ____________

Use of laxatives ____________

Describe how you feel when you see someone who is extremely thin or extremely fat, how does it make you feel and why? ____________

Thank you for your time, we will contact you if we need more information.

See Lesson Notes, page 96

AS PSYCHOLOGY: THE TEACHER'S COMPANION Published by Nelson Thornes Ltd. © 2004 Sara Berman, Cara Flanagan and Adrian Frost

A qualitative analysis of eating disorders

I have had an eating disorder since I was 15 years old and am now 28. At present I weigh 100 pounds. When I was 18 years old I got down to 65 pounds and I had 4 cardiac arrests. I've also had 3 spontaneous pneumothorax because of dehydration. When things get bad and I feel out of control, I fall back into my eating disorder. I can't stop this disease and fear I am going to die.

I am a man in recovery from anorexia. I have been in and out of hospitals over two and a half years. It started when I weighed 265 pounds and decided to diet assisted by moderate exercise. I ended up eating only 300 calories a day and exercising for 8 hours a day. This involved getting up at 4 a.m. and going to bed at 1 a.m. Then I stopped eating totally and continued exercising. I wore baggy clothing and withdrew from family and friends.

Thoughts go through my head: 'Don't eat anything all day, burn off 500 calories and then you are ahead of the game'. At night time I allow myself 300 calories at most, and if I feel I have gone too far I go off to the bathroom to get rid of it, which happens most times. I go through this cycle every day of my life, but it keeps me sane! Or at least I think it does. The fear of something going past my lips gives me nightmares. I wake up in the middle of the night with gut-wrenching pains but I won't consume more calories. I am in control, or at least I think I am.

My friend is 16. She sometimes goes without food all day at school and I can't be sure that she eats anything when she gets home. She makes excuses not to eat and always checks calories on packages. She seems obsessed with the idea that I'm thinner than she is. Any time I approach her about eating she edges around the subject or gets irritated.

I have a very low self-esteem and body-image problems. I do not have an eating disorder that I can pinpoint. I do not try and throw up and I do not stop eating. I do try diets. I do go to the gym at least 5 times a week. My problem is I was with a very abusive boyfriend who never liked the way that I looked. He told me every day that I needed to lose weight. I cannot look at myself in the mirror without clothes on. I have not been with this guy for 2 years and I can still hear what he has said in my head. Many people tell me that I am beautiful and that I look great and that I am not fat but I do not believe them. I go to the bathroom when I am at work at least 20 times just so I can punish myself by looking in the mirror and calling myself fat.

My body is very weak, my face gets paler every day, but in the back of my mind I see beauty. I see that in a couple of months I will be the model my step mom never let me be. My waist is very small but when I look in the mirror I see fat. Pain is my game. Please tell me why my dad's girlfriend hit me? I chose this route to punish myself for what I'm not sure, maybe the attention.

When year 8 started I came back to school 12kg lighter. I've stopped the dieting and all…but every time I see a picture of a beautiful girl in a magazine or Victoria Beckham (she is my idol) I start considering it and by that time I'm depressed about my looks.

I'm a 20-year-old girl. It got to the point where I'd wake up before my sister every morning in order to be able to lie to her about having breakfast. She kept asking me what I'd had for lunch every day and I felt so powerful for being able to lie to her. I find it very interesting that an anorexic's parents are more likely to get children with anorexia than others. My mother suffered from anorexia all through her life, I believe. I never got the chance to ask her because she died about 2 years ago. She'd sometimes go jogging twice a day and I was only proud of having such a healthy mother. As for me, I haven't been able to eliminate the voice in my head that keeps telling me to lose weight. Right now I'm staying with my father for a couple of days. He was watching TV in the kitchen just now and I wanted to have a snack in there. When I entered the room he turned the TV louder and that was enough to make me want to punish myself (for disturbing him). I told him I wasn't hungry after all (in reality I'm starving). I want to be perfect, I want to do well at school and in my life in general.

See Lesson Notes, page 96

92

Individual Differences

Crossword

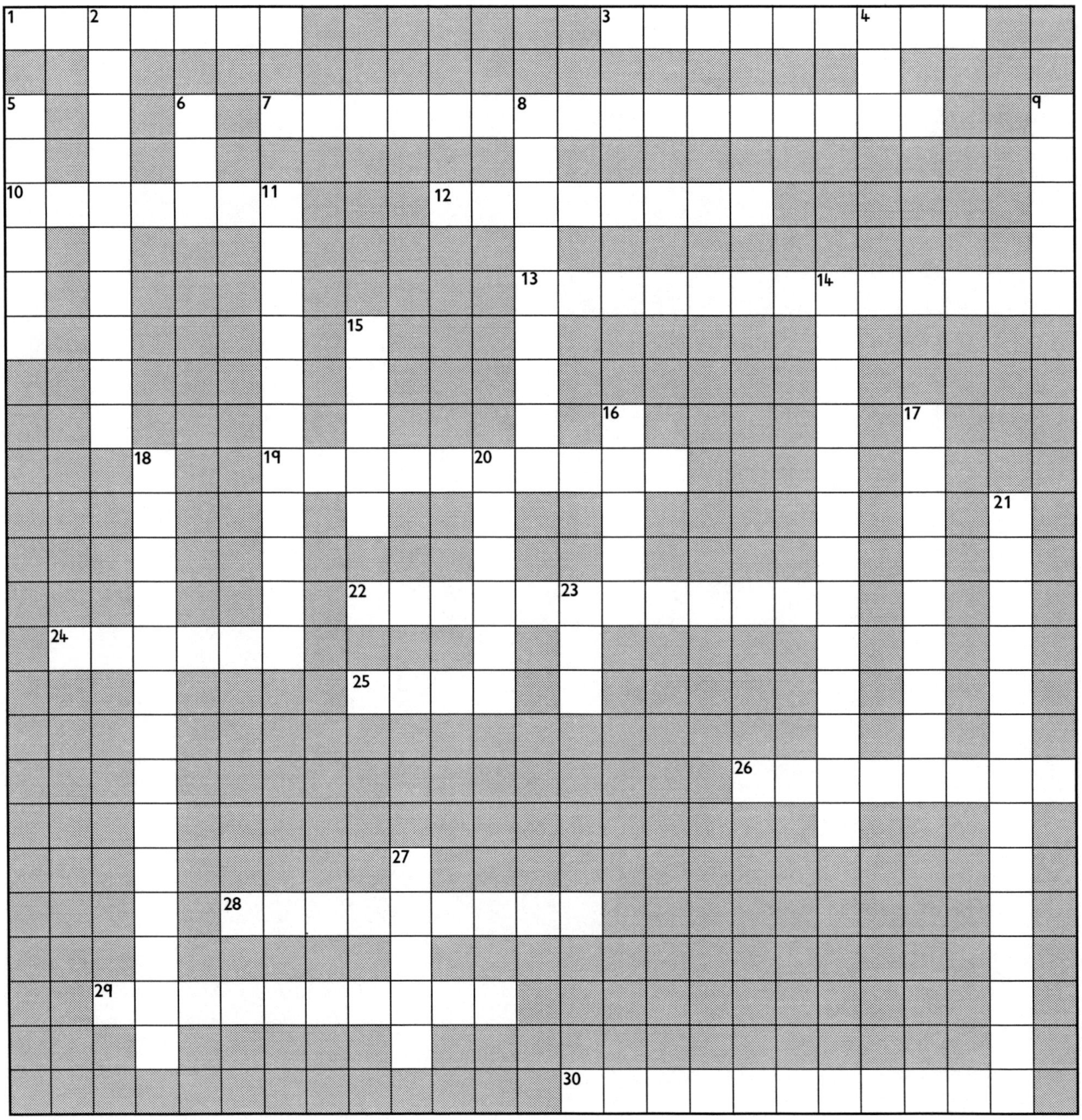

AS PSYCHOLOGY: THE TEACHER'S COMPANION Published by Nelson Thornes Ltd. © 2004 Sara Berman, Cara Flanagan and Adrian Frost

Individual Differences

Crossword clues

Across

1 The rules, customs, morals and ways of interacting that bind a group of people. (7)

3 The personality structure identified by Freud as your conscience. (8)

7 Term used to describe the degree to which two people have similar characteistics. (11,4)

10 Type of eating disorder associated with uncontrolled eating followed by purging. (7)

12 Process by which behaviours are rewarded as they progressively become closer to the desired target behaviour. (7)

13 Part of brain involved with eating behaviour. (12)

19 A form of ego defence that causes the individual to behave more like a child. (10)

22 Deviation from ________ ________, a way to define abnormality in terms of what is acceptable behaviour. (6,5)

24 Female psychologist who drew up a list of criteria for ideal mental health. (6)

25 According to Freud, the first stage of psychosexual development. (4)

26 Eating disorder associated with fear of being fat. (8)

28 Type of conditioning when an individual watches someone else receive rewards. (9)

29 Model of abnormality suggesting that genes, hormones and the nervous system cause mental disorders. (10)

30 A form of ego defence that causes anxiety-provoking thoughts to be forgotten. (10)

Down

2 Case study by Freud of a young boy. (6,4)

4 Form of treatment derived from the biological model involving the use of electric shocks (abbreviation). (3)

5 Little boys studied by Watson and Rayner to demonstrate conditioned emotional responses. (6)

6 Classification system used in the United States (initials). (3)

8 Term meaning 'constitutional disposition' or vulnerability to mental disorder. (9)

9 Kind of participants studied by Holland *et al.* to see if there was a genetic cause for anorexia. (5)

11 Means cessation of menstrual periods. (11)

14 self-________. One of the criteria for idal mental health. (13)

15 According to Freud, conflict between these two personality structures creates anxiety. (2,3)

16 ________ economy. Kind of treatment derived from operant conditioning. (5)

17 Approach that suggests mental disorders are caused by maladaptive thinking. (9)

18 Approach that suggests much of the behaviour is caused by unconscious thoughts. (13)

20 ________ learning theory explains how behaviours are acquired by observing others, as in media effects. (6)

21 A cognitive explanation for bulimia proposed by Ruderman. (13)

23 Thought that anorexia might be due to this part of the hypothalamus (abbreviation). (3)

27 Female psychoanalyst who suggested that anorexia resulted from a struggle for autonomy. (5)

AS PSYCHOLOGY: THE TEACHER'S COMPANION Published by Nelson Thornes Ltd. © 2004 Sara Berman, Cara Flanagan and Adrian Frost

94

Individual Differences

Crossword solutions

1 C	U	2 L	T	U	R	E								3 S	U	P	E	R	4 E	G	O		
		I																	C				
5 A		T		6 D		7 C	O	N	C	O	R	8 D	A	N	C	E	R	A	T	E			9 T
L		T		S								I											W
10 B	U	L	I	M	I	11 A				12 S	H	A	P	I	N	G							I
E		E				M						T											N
R		H				E						13 H	Y	P	O	T	H	14 A	L	A	M	U	S
E		A				N		15 I				E						C					
		N				O		D				S						T					
		S				R		E				I		16 T				U		17 C			
			18 P			19 R	E	G	R	E	20 S	S	I	O	N			A		O			
			S			H		O			O			K				L		G		21 D	
			Y			O					C			E				I		N		I	
			C			E		22 S	O	C	I	A	23 L	N	O	R	M	S		I		S	
	24 J	A	H	O	D	A					A		M					A		T		I	
			O					25 O	R	A	L		H					T		T		N	
			D															I		V		H	
			Y													26 A	N	O	R	E	X	I	A
			N						27 B									N				B	
			A		28 V	I	C	A	R	I	O	U	S									I	
			M						U													T	
		29 B	I	O	L	O	G	I	C	A	L											I	
			C						H													O	
													30 R	E	P	R	E	S	S	I	O	N	

AS PSYCHOLOGY: THE TEACHER'S COMPANION Published by Nelson Thornes Ltd. © 2004 Sara Berman, Cara Flanagan and Adrian Frost

General knowledge quiz

1 What is the longest river in Europe?

a. Danube

b. Rhine

c. Elba

d. Rhone

e. Volga

2 What is the capital of France?

a. Bordeaux

b. Paris

c. Rhone

d. Calais

e. Berlin

3 Henry the VIII had six wives. How many did he execute?

a. 1

b. 2

c. 3

d. 4

e. 5

4 The desert called a Pavlova is named after:

a. an Italian town

b. a Spanish folk singer

c. an Australian bush

d. a Russian ballerina

e. a kind of raspberry

5 Who was the female star of the film *Dial M for Murder*?

a. Grace Kelly

b. Elizabeth Taylor

c. Janet Leigh

d. Bette Davis

e. Rosalind Russell

6 The word Chivalry is derived from the French word for:

a. horse

b. gentleman

c. horseman

d. brandy

e. gentlewoman

7 A ptarmigan is:

a. a flower

b. a stringed instrument

c. a kind of cake

d. a 4-line poem

e. a bird

8 How many standard bottles of wine does a rehoboam contain?

a. 10

b. 8

c. 6

d. 4

e. 2

9 Sputnik I was launched by the USSR on:

a. 15th January, 1960

b. 4th October, 1957

c. 1st November, 1956

d. 4th October, 1956

e. 31st January, 1962

10 Who first showed that the earth was round?

a. The Greeks

b. Isaac Newton

c. Leonardo da Vinci

d. The Chinese

e. Copernicus

See Lesson Notes, page 97

 © 2004 Sara Berman, Cara Flanagan and Adrian Frost

96

Stimulus lines for Asch's study

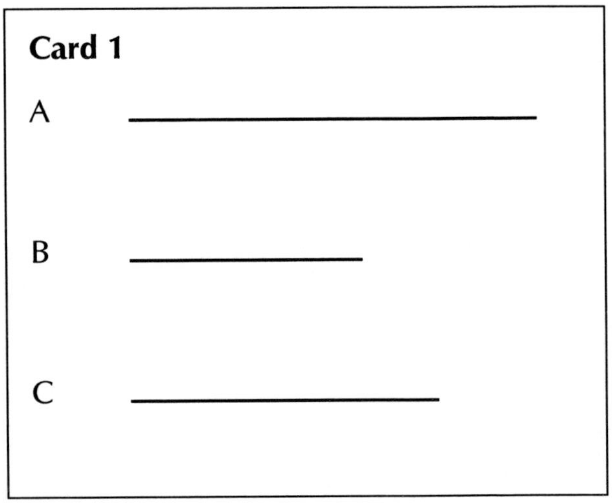

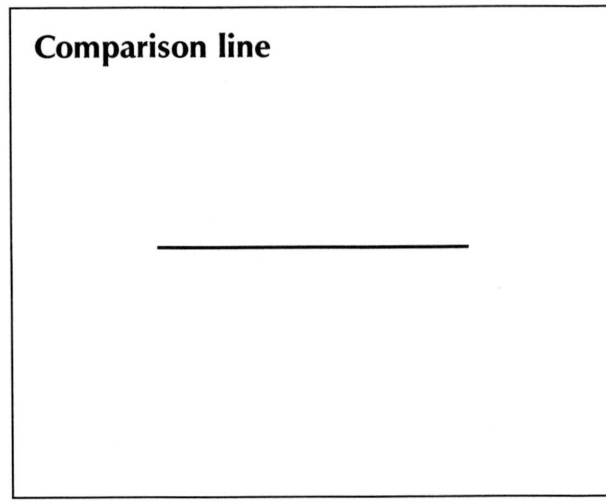

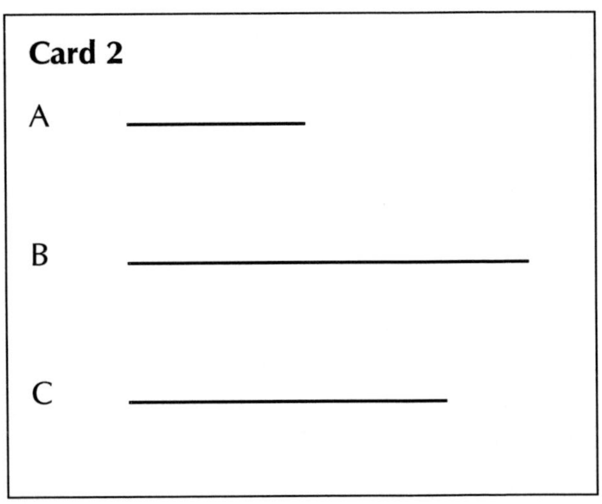

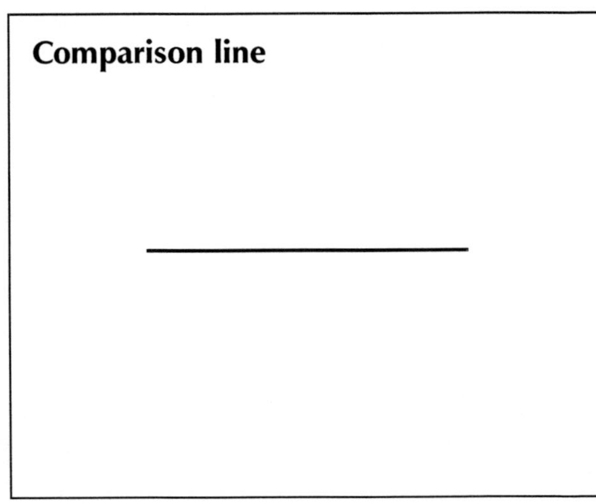

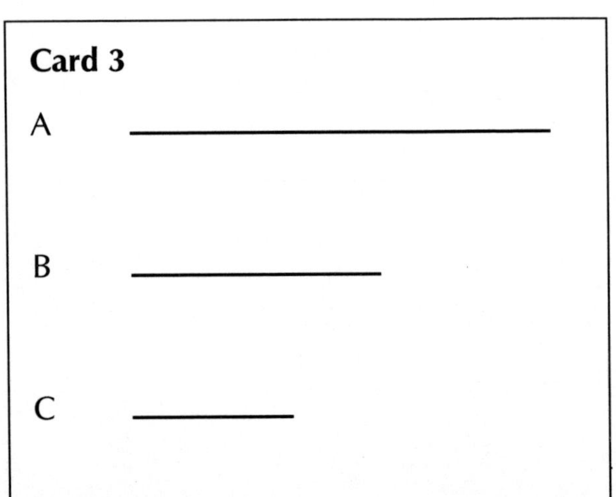

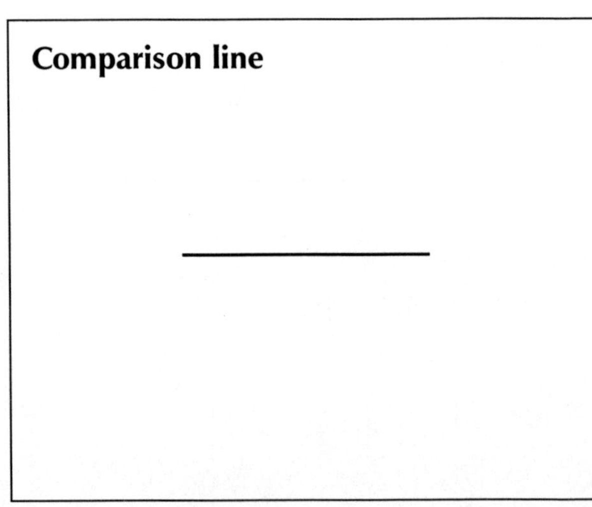

See Lesson Notes, page 99

AS PSYCHOLOGY: THE TEACHER'S COMPANION Published by Nelson Thornes Ltd. © 2004 Sara Berman, Cara Flanagan and Adrian Frost

Stimulus lines for Asch's study

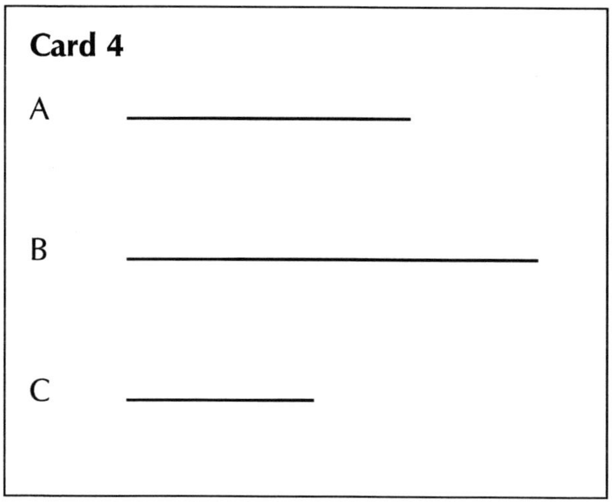

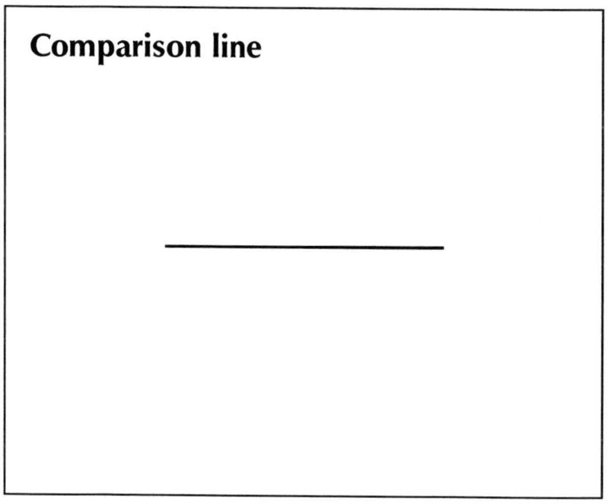

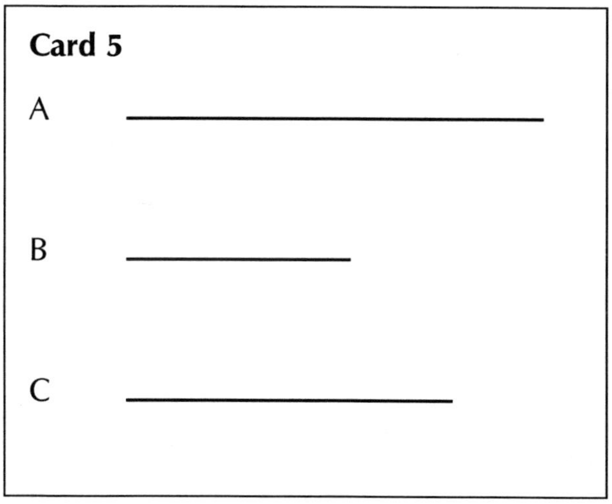

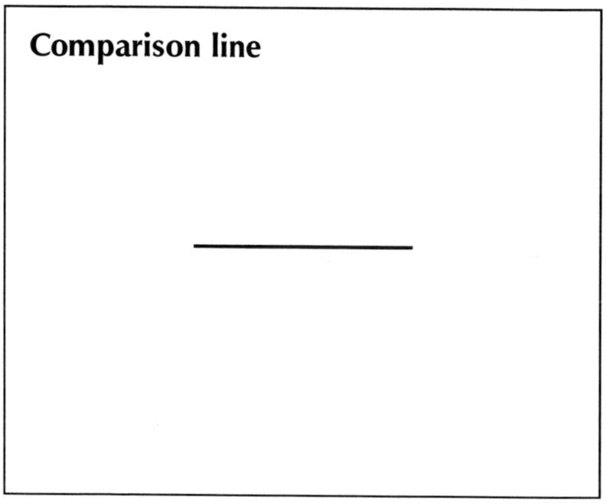

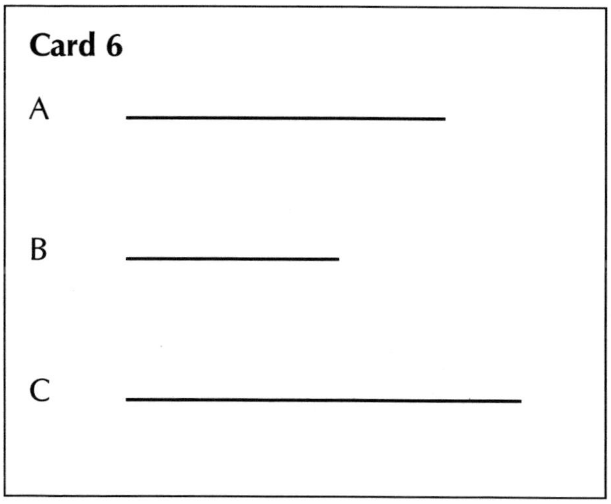

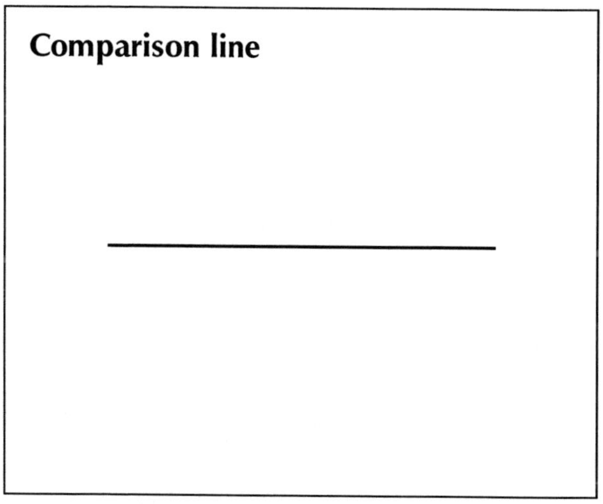

See Lesson Notes, page 99

AS PSYCHOLOGY: THE TEACHER'S COMPANION Published by Nelson Thornes Ltd. © 2004 Sara Berman, Cara Flanagan and Adrian Frost

98

Stimulus lines for Asch's study

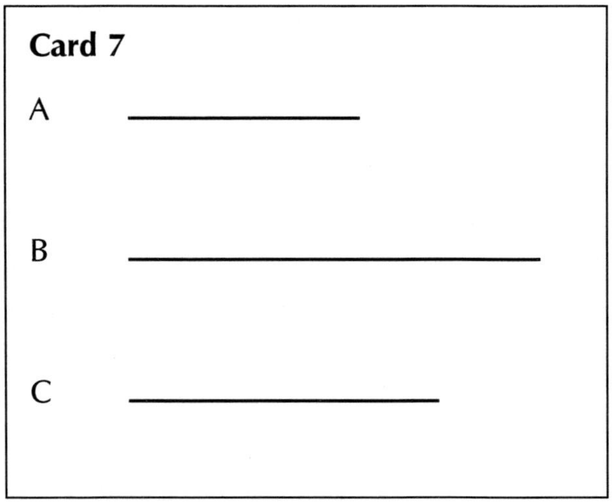

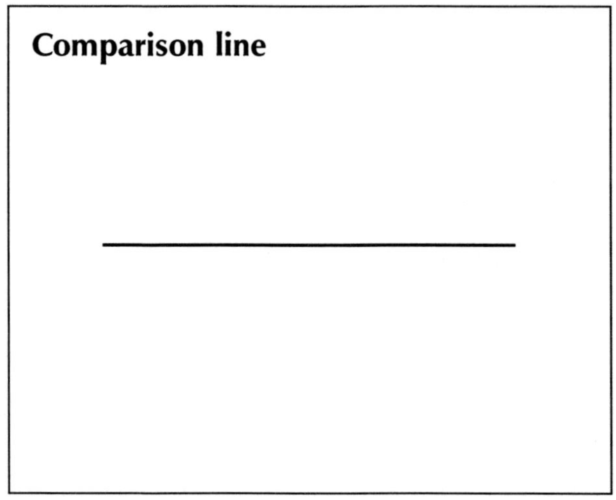

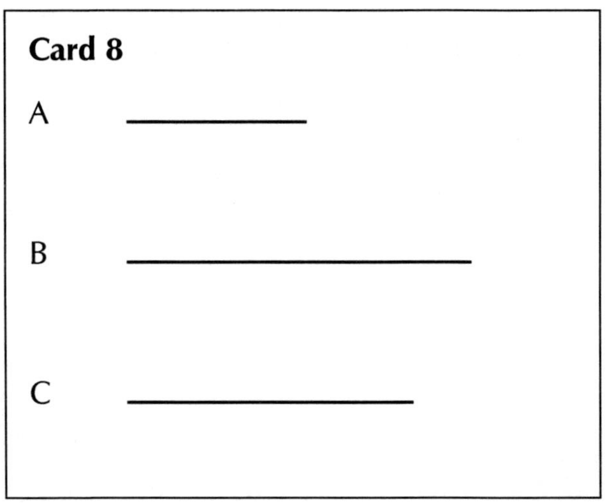

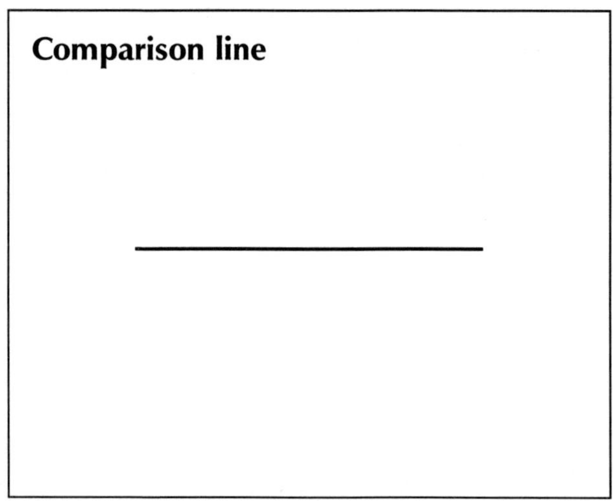

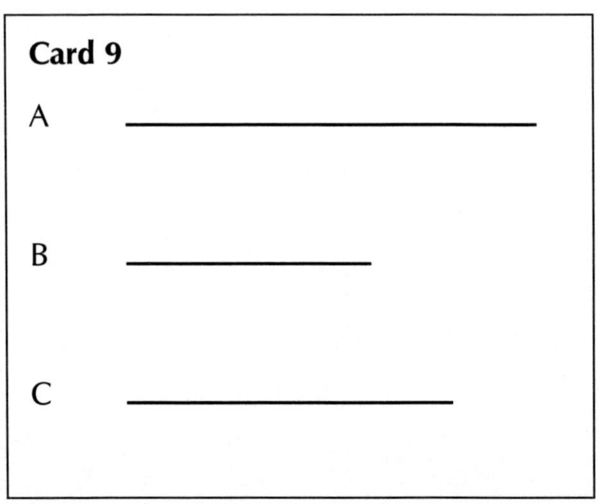

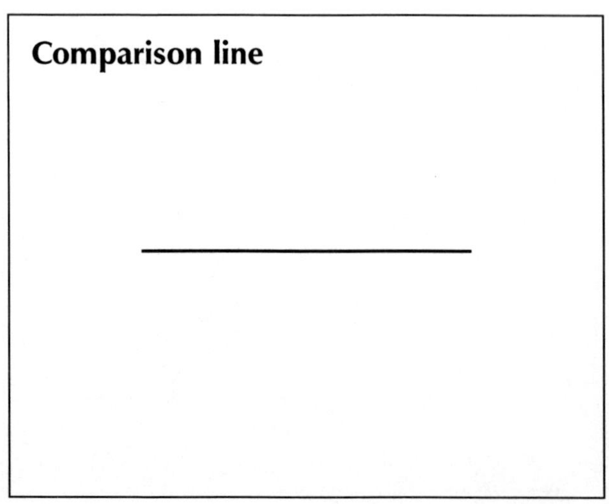

See Lesson Notes, page 99

AS PSYCHOLOGY: THE TEACHER'S COMPANION Published by Nelson Thornes Ltd. © 2004 Sara Berman, Cara Flanagan and Adrian Frost

Stimulus lines for Asch's study

Card 10

A

B

C

Comparison line

Card 11

A

B

C

Comparison line

Card 12

A

B

C

Comparison line

See Lesson Notes, page 99

AS PSYCHOLOGY: THE TEACHER'S COMPANION Published by Nelson Thornes Ltd. © 2004 Sara Berman, Cara Flanagan and Adrian Frost

100

Stimulus lines for Asch's study

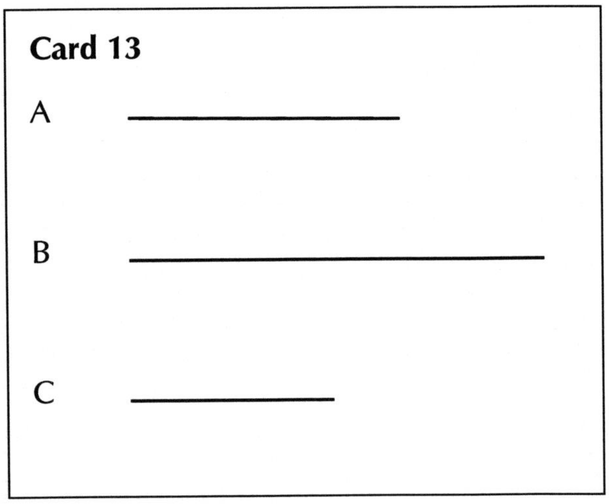

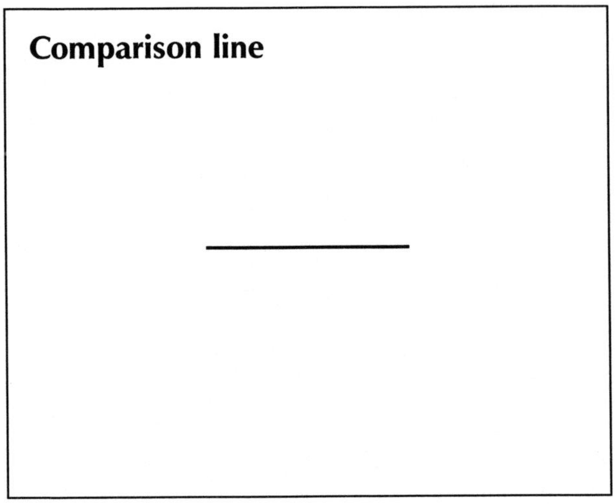

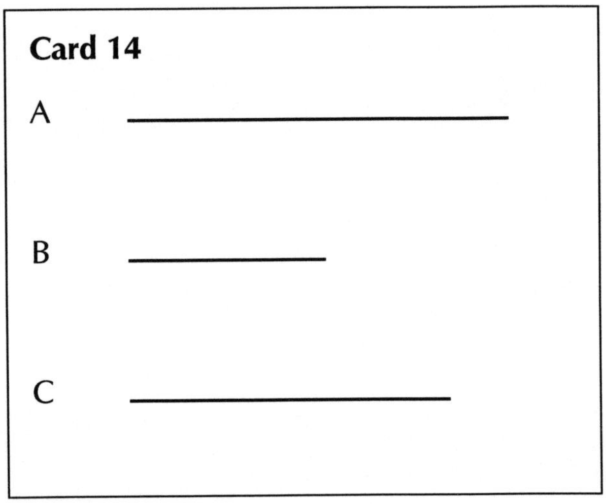

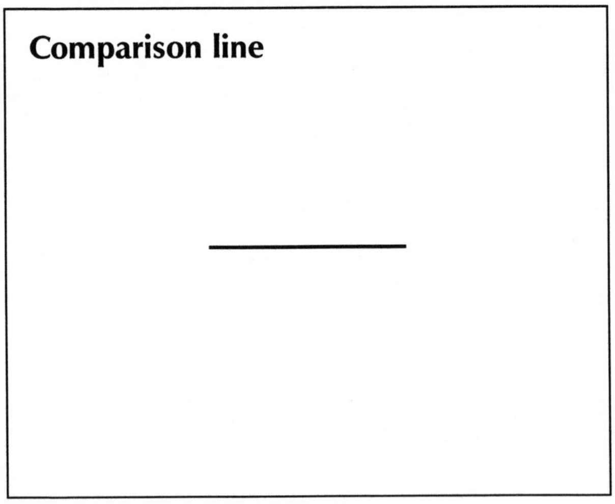

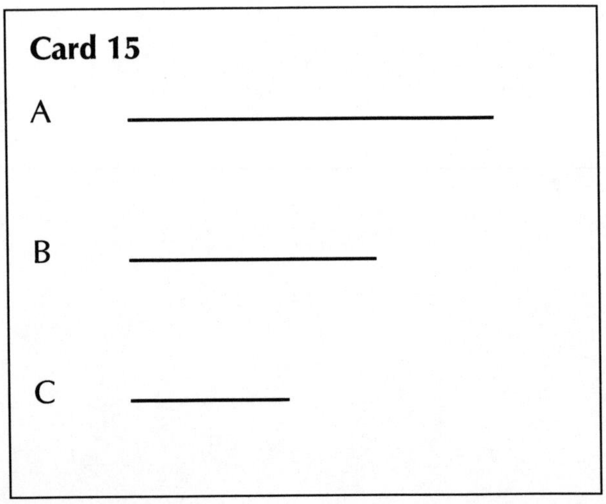

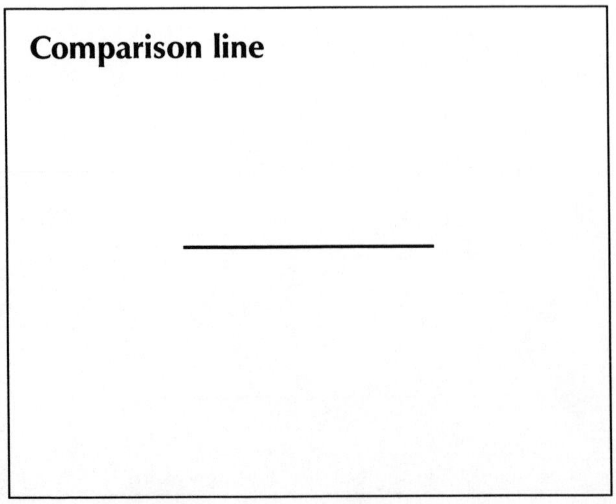

See Lesson Notes, page 99

AS PSYCHOLOGY: THE TEACHER'S COMPANION Published by Nelson Thornes Ltd. © 2004 Sara Berman, Cara Flanagan and Adrian Frost

Stimulus lines for Asch's study

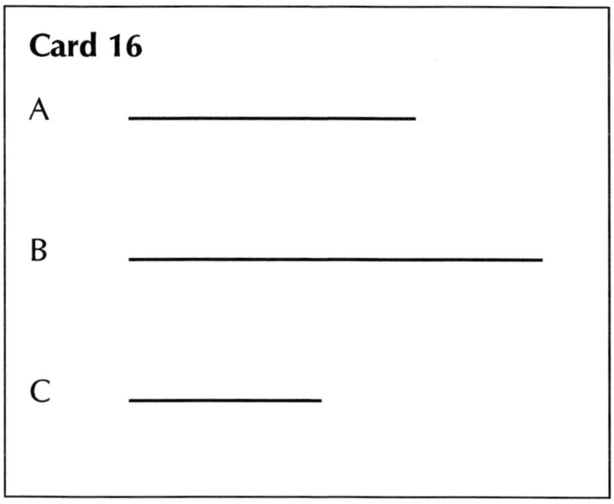

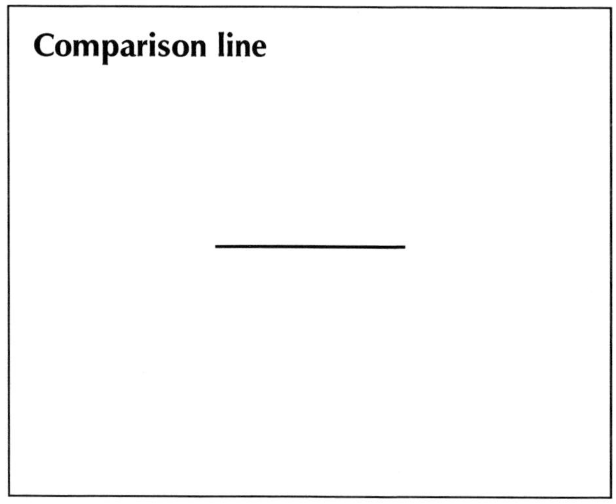

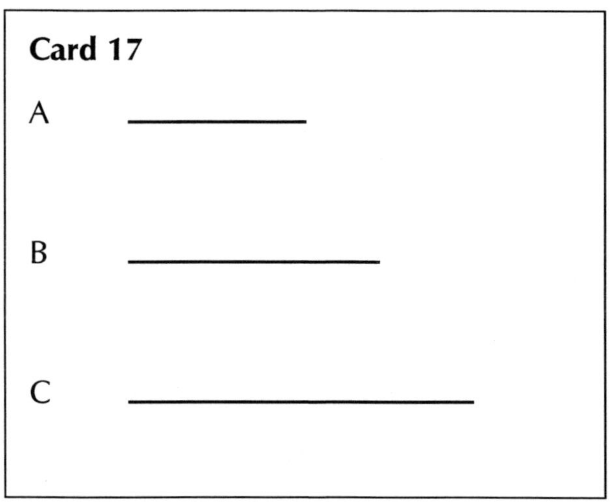

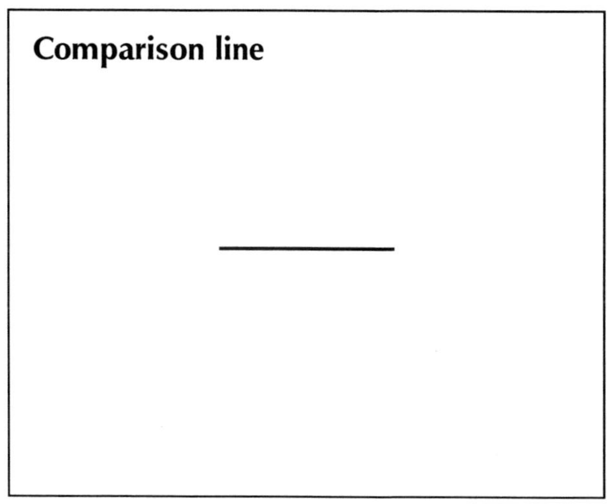

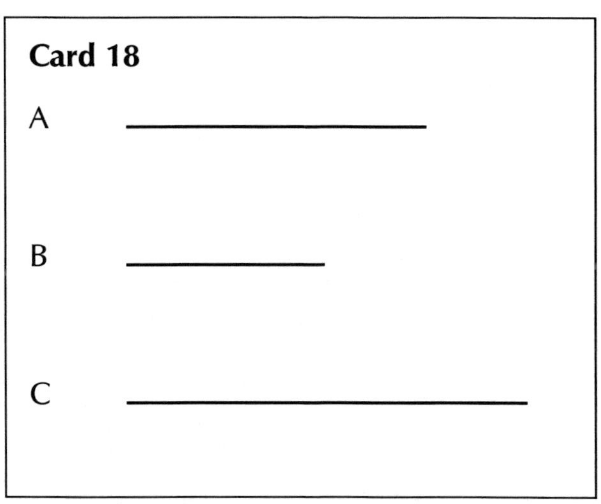

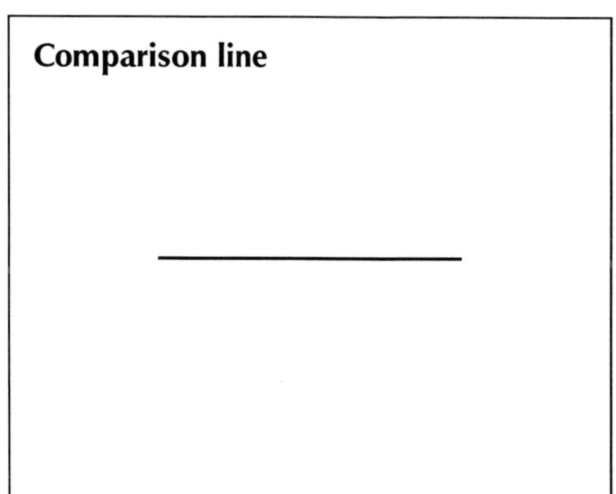

See Lesson Notes, page 99

AS PSYCHOLOGY: THE TEACHER'S COMPANION Published by Nelson Thornes Ltd. © 2004 Sara Berman, Cara Flanagan and Adrian Frost

Instructions for participants

Instructions for confederate in Group 1

When discussing the compensation in the group you are required to take an extreme position. Argue for either a very low or high figure and do not budge from this position. You may ignore the original estimate you write on this piece of paper. Read the description below and tick the compensation that you feel would be appropriate.

Rick Jackman was injured when on a skiing holiday due to faulty lift machinery at the Scottish ski resort where he was staying. This resulted in a compound fracture to his leg necessitating a week in hospital and a further three weeks off work and then another eight weeks working part-time. He is seeking compensation from the ski company to cover expenses, time off work and inconvenience. He is self-employed in the logging industry and so receives no sickness benefit and was unable to work during this period. He normally earns about £500 a week. He has put in a claim for £10,000. Previous claimants have had compensation payments ranging from £1,000 to £20,000, though personal circumstances vary considerably.

I think a reasonable compensation figure would be:

☐ £16,000 ☐ £14,000 ☐ £12,000 ☐ £10, 000 ☐ £8,000 ☐ £6,000 ☐ £4,000 ☐ £2,000

☐ Other £ ______

Instructions for other members of Group 1

Read the description below and tick the compensation that you feel would be appropriate.

Rick Jackman was injured when on a skiing holiday due to faulty lift machinery at the Scottish ski resort where he was staying. This resulted in a compound fracture to his leg necessitating a week in hospital and a further three weeks off work and then another eight weeks working part-time. He is seeking compensation from the ski company to cover expenses, time off work and inconvenience. He is self-employed in the logging industry and so receives no sickness benefit and was unable to work during this period. He normally earns about £500 a week. He has put in a claim for £10,000. Previous claimants have had compensation payments ranging from £1,000 to £20,000, though personal circumstances vary considerably.

I think a reasonable compensation figure would be:

☐ £16,000 ☐ £14,000 ☐ £12,000 ☐ £10, 000 ☐ £8,000 ☐ £6,000 ☐ £4,000 ☐ £2,000

☐ Other £ ______

Final decision

After discussion, I think a reasonable compensation figure would be:

☐ £16,000 ☐ £14,000 ☐ £12,000 ☐ £10, 000 ☐ £8,000 ☐ £6,000 ☐ £4,000 ☐ £2,000

☐ Other £ ______

See Lesson Notes, page 100

AS PSYCHOLOGY: THE TEACHER'S COMPANION Published by Nelson Thornes Ltd. © 2004 Sara Berman, Cara Flanagan and Adrian Frost

Instructions for participants

Instructions for confederate in Group 2

When discussing the compensation in the group you are required to take an extreme position at the start. Argue for either a very low or high figure but then be prepared to adjust your estimate slightly to come closer to the group norm. Maintain an extreme position but just a little less extreme. You may ignore the original estimate you write on this piece of paper. Read the description below and tick the compensation that you feel would be appropriate.

Rick Jackman was injured when on a skiing holiday due to faulty lift machinery at the Scottish ski resort where he was staying. This resulted in a compound fracture to his leg necessitating a week in hospital and a further three weeks off work and then another eight weeks working part-time. He is seeking compensation from the ski company to cover expenses, time off work and inconvenience. He is self-employed in the logging industry and so receives no sickness benefit and was unable to work during this period. He normally earns about £500 a week. He has put in a claim for £10,000. Previous claimants have had compensation payments ranging from £1,000 to £20,000, though personal circumstances vary considerably.

I think a reasonable compensation figure would be:

☐ £16,000 ☐ £14,000 ☐ £12,000 ☐ £10, 000 ☐ £8,000 ☐ £6,000 ☐ £4,000 ☐ £2,000

☐ Other £ _______

Instructions for other members of Group 2

Read the description below and tick the compensation that you feel would be appropriate.

Rick Jackman was injured when on a skiing holiday due to faulty lift machinery at the Scottish ski resort where he was staying. This resulted in a compound fracture to his leg necessitating a week in hospital and a further three weeks off work and then another eight weeks working part-time. He is seeking compensation from the ski company to cover expenses, time off work and inconvenience. He is self-employed in the logging industry and so receives no sickness benefit and was unable to work during this period. He normally earns about £500 a week. He has put in a claim for £10,000. Previous claimants have had compensation payments ranging from £1,000 to £20,000, though personal circumstances vary considerably.

I think a reasonable compensation figure would be:

☐ £16,000 ☐ £14,000 ☐ £12,000 ☐ £10, 000 ☐ £8,000 ☐ £6,000 ☐ £4,000 ☐ £2,000

☐ Other £ _______

Final decision

After discussion, I think a reasonable compensation figure would be:

☐ £16,000 ☐ £14,000 ☐ £12,000 ☐ £10, 000 ☐ £8,000 ☐ £6,000 ☐ £4,000 ☐ £2,000

☐ Other £ _______

See Lesson Notes, page 100

AS PSYCHOLOGY: THE TEACHER'S COMPANION Published by Nelson Thornes Ltd. © 2004 Sara Berman, Cara Flanagan and Adrian Frost

104

Revision activity – validity in social influence research

Insert the statements below into one of the boxes in the chart, in order to construct your revision diagram. (You will need to copy out this chart onto A3 paper to give yourself enough room in each box.)

	MILGRAM	HOFLING
EXPERIMENTAL VALIDITY (definition)	YES NO	YES NO
ECOLOGICAL VALIDITY (definition)	YES NO	YES NO

Statements

(Hint – find and insert the two definitions first, then try to construct the two sides of each argument.)

1 Does the experiment study what it sets out to study?

2 Such findings have been successfully generalised to other lab settings and other cultures.

3 Two factors ensure experimental realism here – deception and naturalistic setting.

4 Lacks mundane realism.

5 Participants weren't fooled by the set-up of the experiment.

6 Seventy per cent of his participants said they thought it was real.

7 Even though set in 'real-world' very difficult to replicate .

8 Can the results of the study be generalised to other situations?

9 Obedience has been studied in other 'real-life' settings – such as interview situations.

10 Participants were visibly distressed, shaken, sweating, etc.

11 Experiment was unique social situation with unique demand characteristics, e.g. $4, prompts, experimenter present.

12 Set in a lab – artificial, unrealistic, says nothing about 'real life'.

13 Nurses had to administer unknown drug and were not allowed to consult.

See Lesson Notes, page 105

AS PSYCHOLOGY: THE TEACHER'S COMPANION Published by Nelson Thornes Ltd. © 2004 Sara Berman, Cara Flanagan and Adrian Frost

Ethical concerns raised by obedience research

Can you defend the work of Milgram from the criticisms outlined below?

'DONNY'	'MARIE'
Criticism of Milgram's research	Defence of Milgram's research
Experiment involved **deception**, e.g. • False set of objectives. • Role of confederate in the deception. • Only one electric shock ever given (15 V to teacher as a 'test').	
• Deception was 'disrespectful to participants' (Kelman, 1972)	
• Participants couldn't give **informed consent** as they weren't told what to expect. • Newspaper ad didn't mention electrocution.	
• Milgram was suspended by the American Psychological Association.	
• Milgram's participants were not **protected from harm** (Baumrind, 1964)	
• Short-term distress and emotional arousal. • Long-term damage to self-esteem.	
• Given the range of ethical concerns, these experiments should never have been undertaken.	

See Lesson Notes, page 106–108

AS PSYCHOLOGY: THE TEACHER'S COMPANION Published by Nelson Thornes Ltd. © 2004 Sara Berman, Cara Flanagan and Adrian Frost

106

The BPS Ethical Guidelines Quiz

1 **General:** Researchers must always consider the __________ implications and the __________ consequences for the participants in their research. This should be done for all the participants taking into account ethnic, __________, age and __________ differences.

2 **Consent:** Researchers should always try to obtain __________ from the participants. Wherever possible this should be __________ __________, that is the researcher should explain in as much detail as possible the aim and procedure of the research before starting the study.

3 **Deception:** Researchers must avoid __________ participants about the type of research if at all possible. If deception is being considered the researcher must get advice from __________ or __________ __________. Sometimes deception is unavoidable but at all times researchers should consider how the deception will affect the __________.

4 **Debriefing:** Participants should be fully __________ . This must take the form of __________ __________ i.e. the researcher must be ready to discuss the procedures and findings with the participants.

5 **Right to withdraw:** Researchers must tell participants of their __________ __________ __________, without __________, at any time during the study. This might be difficult to achieve with __________ or with __________ __________, but it should still be attempted. If a participant withdraws they can ask for their own data to be __________.

6 **Confidentiality:** Participants have the right to expect that all information they provide will remain __________ unless they agree beforehand. They are protected by the 1984 __________ __________ __________.

7 **Protection of participants:** Researchers must protect their participants from __________ or __________ harm during the study. Participants shouldn't have to face __________ greater then those they would face in everyday life.

Use the words below to fill in the blanks.

active intervention
children
colleagues
confidential
consent
data protection act
debriefed
deceiving
destroyed
distress
ethical
ethical committee
informed consent
mental
observational research
participants
penalty
personality
physical
psychological
right to withdraw
risks
sex

See Lesson Notes, page 110

AS PSYCHOLOGY: THE TEACHER'S COMPANION Published by Nelson Thornes Ltd. © 2004 Sara Berman, Cara Flanagan and Adrian Frost

Social Psychology

Crossword

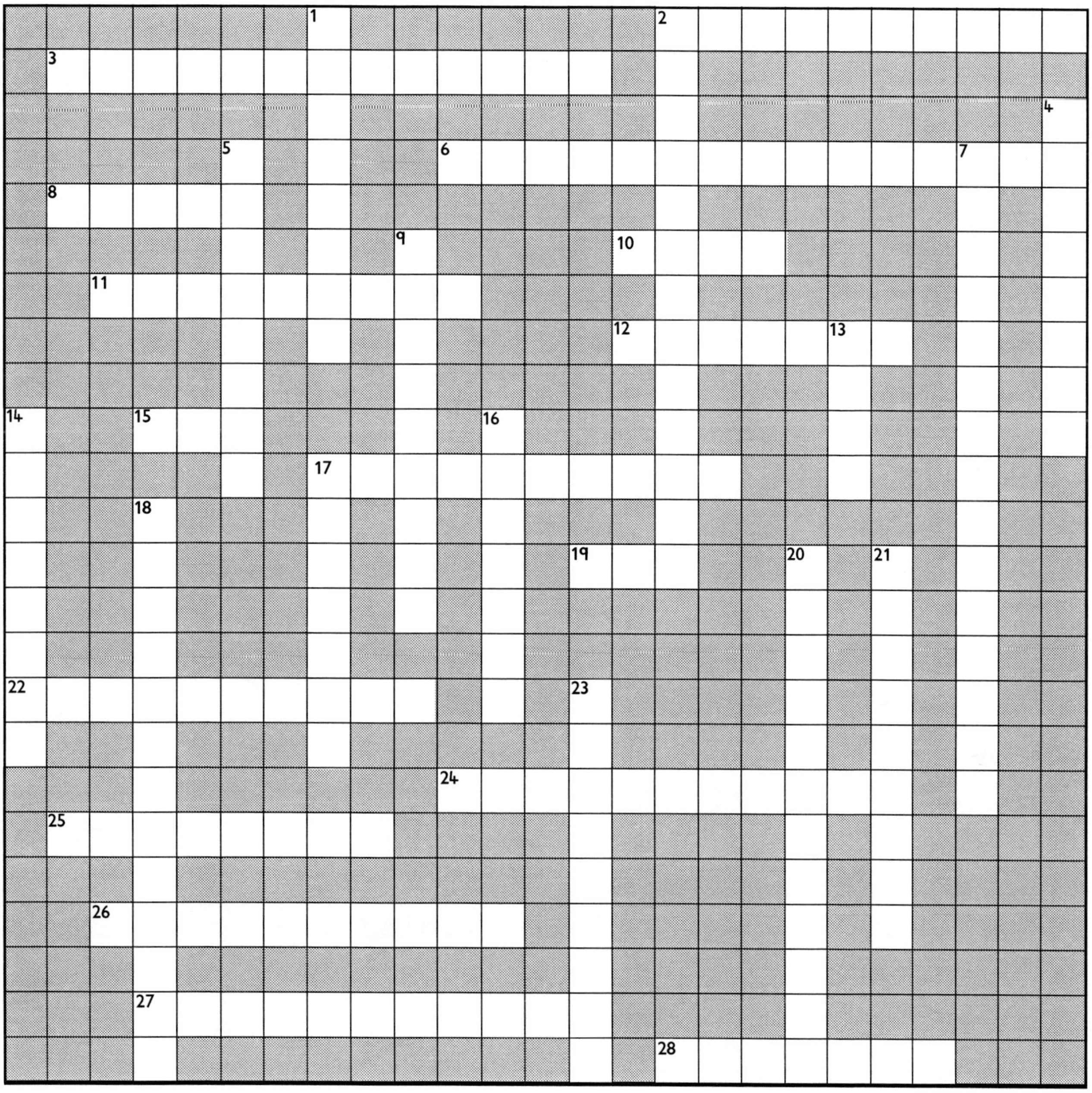

AS PSYCHOLOGY: THE TEACHER'S COMPANION Published by Nelson Thornes Ltd. © 2004 Sara Berman, Cara Flanagan and Adrian Frost

108

Social Psychology

Crossword clues

Across

2 Validity concerned with generalising from an experimental effect beyond the particular setting in which it was demonstrated (10)

3 Explanation that suggests the reason a person behaved as they did was due to their personality rather than the situation. (13)

6 Term used to describe the loss of personal identity through, for example, wearing a uniform. (15)

8 Coloured slides used to study minority influence were blue but described by confederates as __________. (5)

10 An important ethical guideline – protecting participants from psychological __________.(4)

11 Ethical issue raised in Asch's study of majority influence. (9)

12 Psychologist who conducted classic studies on obedience to unjust authority. (7)

15 Professional association for psychologists in America (abbreviation).(3)

17 __________ state. According to Milgram, a state where a person sees themselves as responsible for their own actions. (10)

19 Professional association for psychologists in Britain (abbreviation). (3)

22 After the study is completed, this is a way of overcoming a lack of informed consent. (10)

24 A form of consent that can be obtained by asking participants to agree to a range of studies one of which involves deception. (11)

25 The type of validity that concerns the extent to which findings can be generalised beyond an experiment. (8)

26 A form of social influence resulting from exposure to the majority position. (10)

27 Effect used by Sherif to investigate the development of group norms and informational influence. (11)

28 Psychologist who conducted research on obedience in nurses in a hospital setting. (7)

Down

1 __________ influence; social influence that leads to innovation and rejection of established norms. (8)

2 Arise when there is conflict between the goals of participants and researchers. (7,6)

4 Effect that describes how minority influence becomes majority influence once enough people have changed their views. (8)

5 The type of validity that concerns what goes on inside an experiment. (8)

7 When deception is used in an experiment it prevents a research seeking this. (8,7)

9 __________ influence. Going along with the majority without really accepting their views, in order to be accepted. (9)

13 Psychologist who conducted classic conformity experiment which required participants to judge the length of lines. (4)

14 Psychologist who set up a role play of prisoners and guards. (8)

16 A way to describe those people that are members of our group, the people we identify with. (7)

17 __________ state, according to Milgram an explanation for why people obey – because they see themselves as an agent of a person in authority. (7)

18 __________ influence. Going along with the majority because one is uncertain of what to do and believe the majority to be right. (13)

20 __________ validity, the kind of validity that concerns the legitimacy of experiments. (12)

21 Form of social influence where an individual responds to direct orders. (9)

23 Psychologist particularly associated with research into minority influence. (9)

AS PSYCHOLOGY: THE TEACHER'S COMPANION Published by Nelson Thornes Ltd. © 2004 Sara Berman, Cara Flanagan and Adrian Frost

Social Psychology

Crossword solutions

							1 M								2 E	C	O	L	O	G	I	C	A	L
	3 D	I	S	P	O	S	I	T	I	O	N	A	L		T									
							N								H									4 S
					5 I		O			6 D	E	I	N	D	I	V	I	D	U	A	T	7 I	O	N
	8 G	R	E	E	N		R								C							N		O
					T		I		9 N					10 H	A	R	M					F		W
		11 D	E	C	E	P	T	I	O	N					L							O		B
					R		Y		R					12 M	I	L	G	R	13 A	M		R		A
					N				M						S				S			M		L
14 Z			15 A	P	A				A		16 I				S				C			E		L
I					L		17 A	U	T	O	N	O	M	O	U	S			H			D		
M			18 I				G		I		G				E							C		
B			N				E		V		R		19 B	P	S			20 E		21 O		O		
A			F				N		E		O							X		B		N		
R			O				T				U							P		E		S		
22 D	E	B	R	I	E	F	I	N	G		P		23 M					E		D		E		
O			M				C						O					R		I		N		
			A							24 P	R	E	S	U	M	P	T	I	V	E		T		
	25 E	X	T	E	R	N	A	L					C					M		N				
			I										O					E		C				
		26 C	O	N	F	O	R	M	I	T	Y		V					N		E				
			N										I					T						
			27 A	U	T	O	K	I	N	E	T	I	C					A						
			L										I		28 H	O	F	L	I	N	G			

AS PSYCHOLOGY: THE TEACHER'S COMPANION Published by Nelson Thornes Ltd. © 2004 Sara Berman, Cara Flanagan and Adrian Frost

110

Research Methods

Crossword

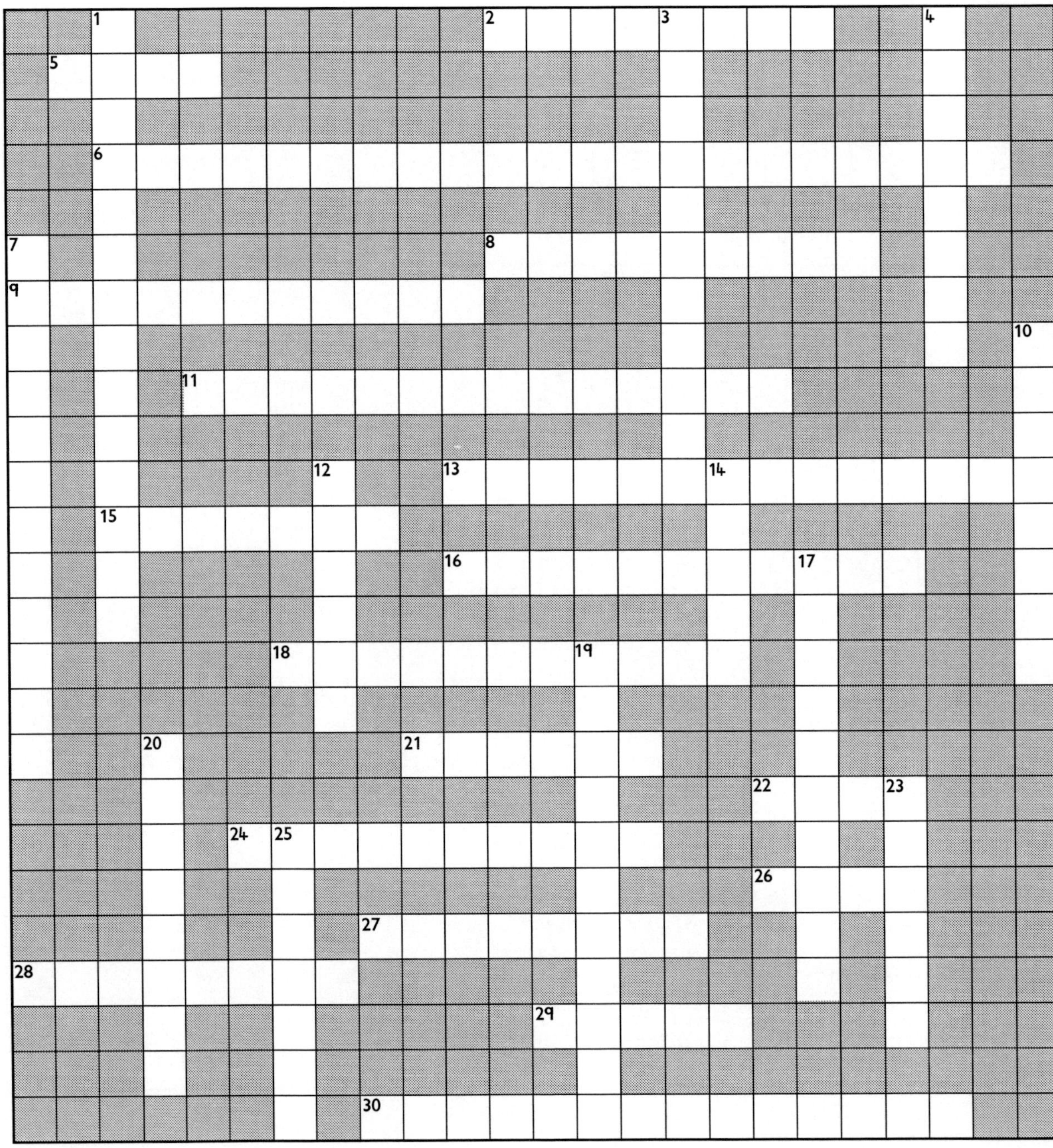

AS PSYCHOLOGY: THE TEACHER'S COMPANION Published by Nelson Thornes Ltd. © 2004 Sara Berman, Cara Flanagan and Adrian Frost

Research Methods

Crosswörd clues

Across

2 __________ measures, kind of experimental design where each participant is tested in both conditions. (8)

5 Kind of average which represents the most common value(s). (4)

6 Features of an experiment that elicit a predictable response from participants. (6,15)

8 In an experiment, the variable that is measured. (9)

9 Correlation __________ gives us a numerical value for the exent that two variables are related. (11)

11 Putting two variables in a form that is suitable for testing.(14)

13 A method of dealing with order effects. (14)

15 Kind of experiment where the independent variable is not manipulated directly; it is one that occurs naturally. (7)

16 In an experiment, the variable that is manipulated by the experimenter. (11)

18 Participant in an experiment who has been instructed how to behave by the experimenter. (11)

21 ________ blind. Deception used to prevent experimenter and participant not knowing the true aims of an experiment. (6)

22 The stated intentions of a study. (4)

24 ______________ validity, concerns whether experimental findings can be generalised from the experimental setting to other settings. (10)

26 Average calculated by adding all values together and dividing by the number of values. (4)

27 Kind of correlation where one variable increases as the other decreases. (8)

28 Concerns the legitmacy of an experiment. (8)

29 Kind of experiment conducted in more natural surroundings but where the independent variable is controlled by the experimenter. (5)

30 A statement of no difference or no relationship. (4,10)

Down

1 Kind of hypothesis which predicts there will be a difference but does not state the direction of the difference. (3,11)

3 Another word used for an experimental hypothesis is the __________ hypothesis. (11)

4 Graph used to represent frequency data where the data may not be continuous. (3,5)

7 Graph used to represent correlational data. (12)

10 __________ validity, concerns the extent to which an observed effect can be atributed to the experimental manipulation. (8)

12 Kind of sampling technique where each member of a population has an equal chance of being selected. (6)

14 Measure of dispersion that is easy to calculate. (5)

17 Research method used to investigate cause and effect relationships. (10)

19 Concerns the extent to which a measure of experiment is consistent over time. (11)

20 Kind of correlation where both variables increase together. (8)

23 __________ blind.Deception used to prevent a participant guessing the true aims of an experiment. (6)

25 __________ group, participants in a experiment who receive no treatment. Their behaviour acts as a baseline to compare the effect of the independent variable on the experimental group. (7)

AS PSYCHOLOGY: THE TEACHER'S COMPANION Published by Nelson Thornes Ltd. © 2004 Sara Berman, Cara Flanagan and Adrian Frost

Research Methods

Crossword solutions

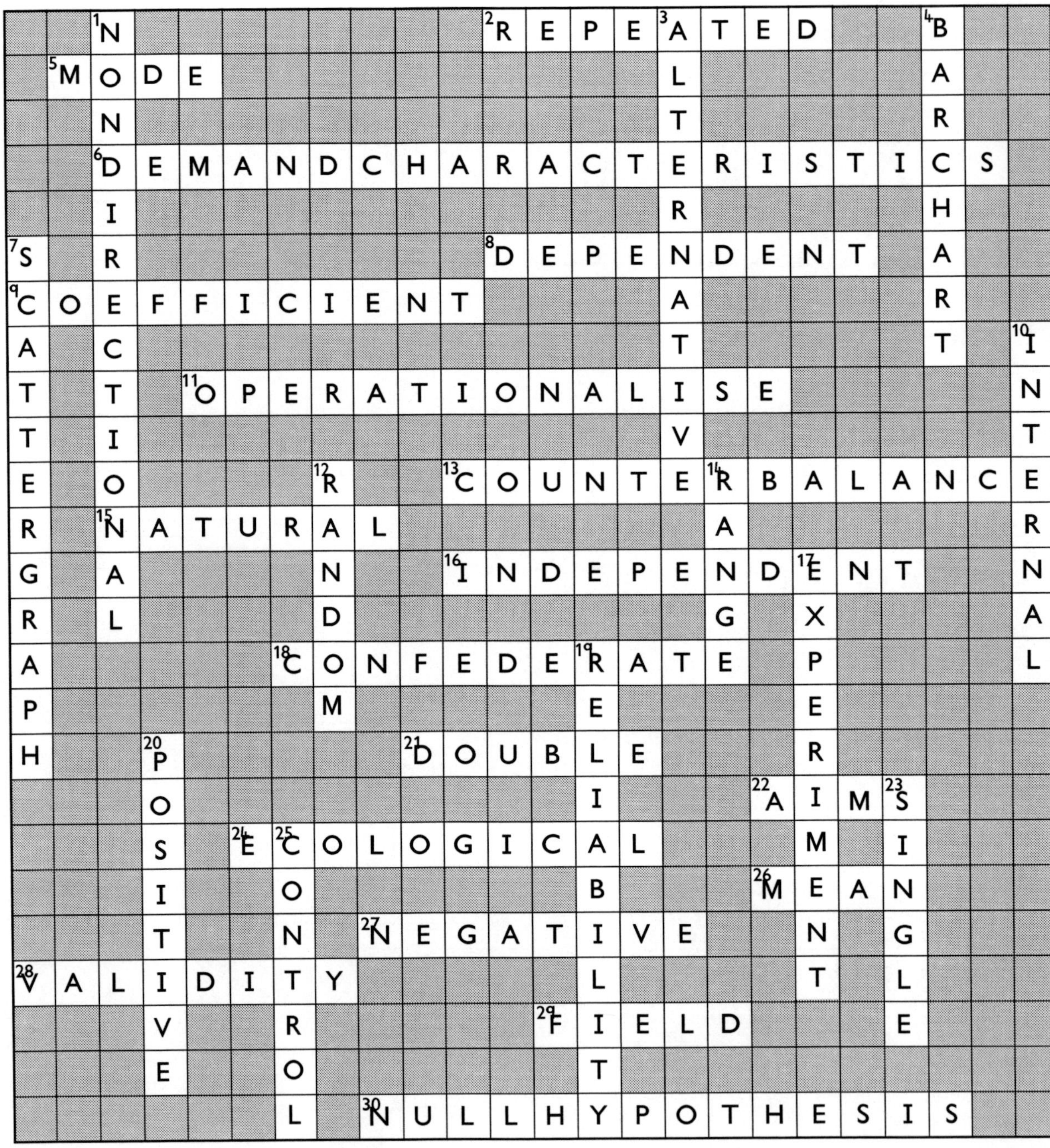

AS PSYCHOLOGY: THE TEACHER'S COMPANION Published by Nelson Thornes Ltd. © 2004 Sara Berman, Cara Flanagan and Adrian Frost

Research Methods
Student Booklet

Key concepts
These are concepts identified in the specification, which means that questions may be asked in the exam that specifically use these terms.

Other terms
Research concepts not identified in the specification, but that are likely to be useful when answering questions.

Question Bank
This is adapted from *The Complete Companion*. The Question Bank allows students (or teachers) to create their own questions to test research methods knowledge. There are descriptions of studies and graphs, and questions that can be used with these.

Key concepts

Alternative hypothesis

What is it?

An example of an alternative hypothesis:

When do you use it?

Bar chart

What is it?

How is a bar chart different from a histogram?

▶ *See histogram and frequency polygon*

AS PSYCHOLOGY: THE TEACHER'S COMPANION Published by Nelson Thornes Ltd. © 2004 Sara Berman, Cara Flanagan and Adrian Frost

Control

What is it?

Why is it necessary?

Correlational analysis

Nature and use

Advantages and weaknesses

(+)

(+)

(–)

(–)

Ethical issues

Correlational coefficient

What is it?

Demand characteristics

What is it?

Dependent variable (DV)

What is it?

AS PSYCHOLOGY: THE TEACHER'S COMPANION Published by Nelson Thornes Ltd. © 2004 Sara Berman, Cara Flanagan and Adrian Frost

Directional hypothesis

What is it?

An example of a directional hypothesis:

Why would a psychologist use a directional hypothesis instead of a non-directional hypothesis?

Ecological validity

What is it?

How is it different from experimental validity?

▶ *See validity*

Ethics

What are they?

Ethical issues

What are they?

Name three ethical issues and for each state how you would deal with them.

1

AS PSYCHOLOGY: THE TEACHER'S COMPANION Published by Nelson Thornes Ltd. © 2004 Sara Berman, Cara Flanagan and Adrian Frost

2

3

Ethical guidelines

What are they?

Experimental design

What is it?

List three kinds of experimental design.

1

2

3

Experimental hypothesis

What is it?

▶ *See alternative hypothesis*

AS PSYCHOLOGY: THE TEACHER'S COMPANION Published by Nelson Thornes Ltd. © 2004 Sara Berman, Cara Flanagan and Adrian Frost

External validity

What is it?

How is this different from internal validity?

▶ *See validity*

Field experiment

Nature and use

Advantages and weaknesses

(+)

(+)

(–)

(–)

Ethical issues

Frequency polygon

What is it?

▶ *See bar chart and histogram*

AS PSYCHOLOGY: THE TEACHER'S COMPANION Published by Nelson Thornes Ltd. © 2004 Sara Berman, Cara Flanagan and Adrian Frost

Histogram

What is it?

How is this different to a bar chart?

▶ *See bar chart and frequency polygon*

Hypothesis

What is it?

▶ *See alternative hypothesis, directional hypothesis, non-directional hypothesis, null hypothesis*

Improving reliability

Name one method of demonstrating reliability and describe how you would do this.

Improving validity

Name one method of demonstrating validity and describe how you would do this.

AS PSYCHOLOGY: THE TEACHER'S COMPANION Published by Nelson Thornes Ltd. © 2004 Sara Berman, Cara Flanagan and Adrian Frost

Independent groups

What is it?

Advantage and weakness

(+)

(–)

Independent variable (IV)

What is it?

Internal validity

What is it?

▶ *See validity*

Interview

Nature and use

Advantages and weaknesses

(+)

(+)

(–)

(–)

Ethical issues

AS PSYCHOLOGY: THE TEACHER'S COMPANION Published by Nelson Thornes Ltd. © 2004 Sara Berman, Cara Flanagan and Adrian Frost

What factors would you consider when designing an interview?

Investigator effects

What are they?

Laboratory experiments

Nature and use

Advantages and weaknesses

(+)

(+)

(–)

(–)

Ethical issues

What factors would you consider when designing an experiment?

Matched pairs

What is it?

Advantage and weakness

(+)

(–)

AS PSYCHOLOGY: THE TEACHER'S COMPANION Published by Nelson Thornes Ltd. © 2004 Sara Berman, Cara Flanagan and Adrian Frost

Measures of central tendency

Measure 1:

Explain how to calculate:

Advantage and weakness

(+)

(–)

Measure 2:

Explain how to calculate:

Advantage and weakness

(+)

(–)

Measure 3:

Explain how to calculate:

Advantage and weakness

(+)

(–)

Measures of dispersion

Measure 1:

Explain how to calculate:

Advantage and weakness

(+)

(–)

AS PSYCHOLOGY: THE TEACHER'S COMPANION Published by Nelson Thornes Ltd. © 2004 Sara Berman, Cara Flanagan and Adrian Frost

Measure 2:

Explain how to calculate:

Advantage and weakness

(+)

(–)

Natural experiment

Nature and use

Advantages and weaknesses

(+)

(+)

(–)

(–)

Ethical issues

Naturalistic observation

Nature and use

Advantages and weaknesses

(+)

(+)

(–)

(–)

AS PSYCHOLOGY: THE TEACHER'S COMPANION Published by Nelson Thornes Ltd. © 2004 Sara Berman, Cara Flanagan and Adrian Frost

Ethical issues

What factors would you consider when designing an observational study?

Negative correlation

What is it?

Non-directional hypothesis

What is it?

An example of a non-directional hypothesis:

Why do psychologists use a non-directional hypothesis rather than a directional hypothesis?

Null hypothesis

What is it?

An example of a null hypothesis:

AS PSYCHOLOGY: THE TEACHER'S COMPANION Published by Nelson Thornes Ltd. © 2004 Sara Berman, Cara Flanagan and Adrian Frost

When do you use it?

Operationalisation of variables

What is it?

Pilot study

What is it?

Why do psychologists use them?

Positive correlation

What is it?

Qualitative data

What is it?

Qualitative research method

Definition:

Advantage and weakness

(+)

(–)

AS PSYCHOLOGY: THE TEACHER'S COMPANION Published by Nelson Thornes Ltd. © 2004 Sara Berman, Cara Flanagan and Adrian Frost

Quantitative research method

Definition:

Advantage and weakness

(+)

(–)

Questionnaire survey

Nature and use

Advantages and weaknesses

(+)

(+)

(–)

(–)

Ethical issues

What factors would you consider when designing a questionnaire survey?

Random sampling

What is it?

How do you do it?

AS PSYCHOLOGY: THE TEACHER'S COMPANION Published by Nelson Thornes Ltd. © 2004 Sara Berman, Cara Flanagan and Adrian Frost

Reliability

What is it?

▶ *See improving reliability*

Repeated measures design

What is it?

Advantage and weakness

(+)

(–)

Research aims

What are they?

Research design

What is it?

Research method

What is it?

Scatter graph

What is it?

AS PSYCHOLOGY: THE TEACHER'S COMPANION Published by Nelson Thornes Ltd. © 2004 Sara Berman, Cara Flanagan and Adrian Frost

Selection of participants

Why do psychologists need a method of selecting participants?

▶ *See random sampling*

Name one method other than random sampling.

How do you do it?

Validity

What is it?

▶ *See improving validity, internal validity, external validity, ecological validity*

AS PSYCHOLOGY: THE TEACHER'S COMPANION Published by Nelson Thornes Ltd. © 2004 Sara Berman, Cara Flanagan and Adrian Frost

Other terms

Confederate	
Control condition	
Control group	
Counterbalancing	
Cross-sectional design	
Debriefing	
Double blind	
Experimental condition	
Experimental group	
Experimenter bias	
Opportunity sampling	
Order effect	
Placebo conditions	
Random allocation	
Significance	
Single blind	
Social desirability bias	
Standardised instructions	
Standardised procedures	
Volunteer sampling	

AS PSYCHOLOGY: THE TEACHER'S COMPANION Published by Nelson Thornes Ltd. © 2004 Sara Berman, Cara Flanagan and Adrian Frost

Question Bank 1

Specification content	Comment

Specification content

The nature and usage of the following research methods, their advantages and weaknesses, and how they relate to the scientific nature of psychology. The nature and usage of ethical guidelines in psychology.

- Experiments (including laboratory, field and natural experiments)
- Investigations using correlational analysis
- Naturalistic observations
- Questionnaire surveys
- Interviews

Comment

You are expected to be familiar with the main **research methods** used in psychology. This includes being able to describe the essence of each method, and knowing how it differs from the other methods.

It also includes familiarity with how to **conduct studies** using each method.

Further, you should have an awareness of at least **two advantages** and **two weaknesses** of each method.

An appreciation of how research methods 'relate to the scientific nature of psychology' refers to the need for **objectivity** in research. This is what distinguishes psychological knowledge from **common sense**. You should base all knowledge on scientific research rather than common sense.

Finally, an understanding of **ethical guidelines** is relevant to each method studied.

Sample questions

To be answered with the stimulus examples below.

1. What is the research method that has been used in this study?
2. Explain **one** advantage and **one** weakness of this method in the context of this study.
3. Identify **one** ethical issue that might arise in this study and suggest how you would deal with it.
4. How else could you investigate this behaviour? Describe the aims and procedures of another study.

1 A study was conducted to investigate the effects of anxiety on performance. Participants were given a task to complete in a set time. One set of the participants were mildly stressed during the task. This was achieved by arranging for the researcher to watch their performance closely. The other set of participants were watched but in a friendly manner.

2 Another study was conducted to investigate the effects of anxiety on performance. In this study, participants were given a set of questions to answer about anxiety.

3 A group of psychology students were studying social influence. As part of their studies they decided to investigate the extent to which drivers complied to the rules of the road. To do this they stood near to a pedestrian crossing and noted how often drivers stopped when a pedestrian stood by the crossing, waiting to cross.

4 After the initial study on conformity the students decided to conduct a further investigation and look at gender differences. They wanted to see whether male or female drivers were more compliant. They had noted, in the first study that women seemed to be more compliant than men.

5 The students decided to conduct a further investigation to see if the gender of the pedestrian had any effect on drivers' behaviour. In this third study the students took turns to stand at the pedestrian crossing. Sometimes it was a girl who stood at the crossing and sometimes it was a boy. They noted the behaviour of male and female drivers.

6 For their final research project, the students decided to investigate gender bias further. They were interested in the idea that female participants in an experiment may be treated differently than male participants by male experimenters. As a starting point they conducted a simple memory experiment with a male experimenter and male and female participants. After the experiment, they asked the participants various questions about how the experimenter had treated them. They had a few predetermined questions but tried to elicit as much information as possible from the participants.

AS PSYCHOLOGY: THE TEACHER'S COMPANION Published by Nelson Thornes Ltd. © 2004 Sara Berman, Cara Flanagan and Adrian Frost

Question Bank 2

Specification content	Sample questions
In the research methods part of the examination you may be expected to *define* terms, but are most likely to be required to *use* the terms.	*To be answered with the stimulus examples on the next page.*
Aims and hypotheses (including the generation of appropriate aims; the formulation of different types of experimental/alternative hypotheses (directional/non-directional) and the null hypothesis).	**1 a** Describe the aims of this study. **b** Suggest a suitable experimental (alternative) hypothesis. **c** Identify whether your hypothesis is directional or non-directional. **d** Explain why you used a directional (or a non-directional) hypothesis. **e** Suggest a suitable non-directional hypothesis for this study. **f** Suggest a suitable directional hypothesis for this study. **g** Suggest a suitable null hypothesis for this study. **h** Identify the independent variable in this study. **i** Identify the dependent variable in this study. **j** Describe how you might measure the dependent variable. **k** Identify the variables in this study.
Research designs: experimental (including independent groups, repeated measures and matched participants) and the design of naturalistic observations, questionnaire surveys and interviews.	**2 a** What kind of research design has been used in this study? **b** What kind of experimental design has been used in this study? **c** Give one advantage and one disadvantage of the research/experimental design in the context of this study. **d** In an observational study, how would you sample behaviour?
Factors associated with research design, including the operationalisation of the IV/DV; conducting pilot studies; control of variables; techniques for assessing and improving reliability and validity (including internal and external (ecological) validity); ethics.	**3 a** Identify ways that you might operationalise a named variable. **b** Suggest two reasons for using a pilot study in this investigation. **c** Identify two variables that might need to be controlled in this study. Explain how you would control these variables. **d** Describe one way you could minimise the intrusive nature of your observations. **e** Describe two factors in good questionnaire design. **f** Describe one way you could minimise the effects the interviewer's behaviour might have on an interviewee. **g** Identify one way to ensure reliability among observers, and explain how you would do this. **h** Describe two features of the study that might affect the validity of the data being collected. **i** Describe two features of the study that might affect the internal validity of the investigation. **j** Describe two features of the study that might affect the external (ecological) validity of the investigation. **k** Describe two features of the study that might affect the reliability of the data being collected. **l** Describe one ethical issue that might arise in this study and suggest one way of dealing with it.
The selection of participants (including random sampling).	**4 a** Explain how the investigator might have selected a 'random sample' of participants. **b** How would you select participants to take part in your study? **c** Give one advantage and one disadvantage of your chosen sampling technique.
The relationship between researchers and participants (including demand characteristics and investigator effects).	**5 a** Explain one way in which the relationship between researcher and participant (e.g. an investigator effect) might have influenced the results obtained in this study. **b** How might you overcome this problem? **c** Name one possible investigator effect. **d** Suggest how demand characteristics might have been a problem in this study.

AS PSYCHOLOGY: THE TEACHER'S COMPANION Published by Nelson Thornes Ltd. © 2004 Sara Berman, Cara Flanagan and Adrian Frost

Question Bank 3

For each of the studies below, state the research method used and explain why it is an example of that method. Then try to answer as many questions on the left as are relevant to the study.

1 A psychologist chose to investigate the kinds of tasks that created stress for teachers. He asked for teachers from several schools to volunteer to take part in the study, and selected 20 male teachers. Each volunteer was asked to perform two tasks. One task involved presenting a prepared speech to a group of 200 students. The second task involved marking a set of books that were full of mistakes. At the end of each task the experimenter recorded the participants' blood pressure.

2 A group of psychology students conducted a study of obedience. They selected a random sample of pupils from the school register and asked them to come to a certain classroom in the lunch hour. Some pupils were assigned to a condition where they were greeted by an 'experimenter' wearing a white coat. Others were greeted by the same person dressed in her ordinary clothes. The 'experimenter' told each pupil to sit down and spend 30 minutes writing the word 'psychology' on a piece of paper.

3 In order to investigate the effects of early privation on popularity at school, a team of psychologists used the records of a local children's home. They identified babies who were placed in care under the age of 3 months and who were not adopted until after their first birthday. They were then able to locate 20 of these children, now of school age, and compared them with a control group of 20 children raised entirely at home. Both groups were assessed in terms of their ability to get on with peers.

4 A study involved the investigation of a link between age and conformity by giving participants a set of questions to answer. Some answers were already written on the questionnaire by previous participants. Some questions were ambiguous and others were not ambiguous. Each participant was given a conformity score at the end of the test and a scattergraph was drawn to show the relationship between age and conformity. The study found a positive correlation.

5 As part of their AS studies, a group of students conducted a project to look at the differences between children in day care and those at home. Students worked in pairs and either observed a child in day care or a child at home. They spent 1 hour observing their target child and repeated this 5 times. Before beginning the study the class decided on a set of behavioural categories.

6 A research project into eating problems sought to find out about adolescent and pre-adolescent dieting practices. The study involved the use of a questionnaire, including both quantitative and qualitative questions. The questionnaire was piloted with a small group of university students.

7 A research project on memory aimed to find out about individuals' earliest memories. In order to do this the research team conducted unstructured interviews with people aged 10 to 50. The interviewers started with a set of standard questions but then adapted their questions in response to the answers given by the interviewees.

Revision notes: Aims and hypotheses

	Definition	Reasons for using
Research	The process of gaining knowledge through the examination of data derived empirically or theoretically.	To produce objective facts.
Aims	The stated intentions of a study.	To be clear about the purpose of a study.
Hypothesis (or **research hypothesis**)	A clear statement, made at the beginning of an investigation, that aims to predict or explain events.	To make sense of the findings.
Experimental (alternative) hypothesis	A statement of the relationship between the IV and DV.	An alternative to the null hypothesis.
Directional hypothesis	States which set of scores will be better/faster, positively/negatively correlated.	Previous research suggests the direction.
Non-directional hypothesis	Proposes that there will be a difference or relationship but does not state the direction.	Allows for a difference/relationship occurring in either direction, or previous research has been inconclusive.
Null hypothesis	A statement of no difference or no relationship.	To have a baseline conclusion in a research study.

AS PSYCHOLOGY: THE TEACHER'S COMPANION Published by Nelson Thornes Ltd. © 2004 Sara Berman, Cara Flanagan and Adrian Frost